ALSO BY DAVID LEHMAN

An Alternative to Speech
The Perfect Murder
Operation Memory

POSEIDON

PRESS

||||||||||||||||||||||||||||||||||

NEW YORK

LONDON

TORONTO

SYDNEY

TOKYO

SINGAPORE

SIGNS OF THE TIMES

DECONSTRUCTION AND THE FALL OF PAUL DE MAN

DAVID LEHMAN

POSEIDON PRESS

Simon & Schuster Building
Rockefeller Center
1230 Avenue of the Americas
New York, New York 10020

POSEIDON PRESS is a registered trademark
of Simon & Schuster

POSEIDON PRESS colophon is a trademark
of Simon & Schuster

Designed by Liney Li
Manufactured in the United States of America

1   3   5   7   9   10   8   6   4   2

Library of Congress Cataloging-in-Publication Data
Lehman, David, date.
Signs of the times : deconstruction and the fall of Paul de Man / David Lehman.
p.   cm.
Includes bibliographical references and index.
1. Deconstruction.   2. De Man, Paul.   I. Title.
B809.6.L44   1991   90-25825
149—dc20   CIP
ISBN 0-671-68239-3

ACKNOWLEDGMENTS

Deconstruction, the first time you hear the word, sounds like what happens when your four-year-old has a temper tantrum with his erector set. Or maybe it reminds you of the mayhem in the museum scene in *Batman*, in which the Joker and his henchmen deface paintings and knock over sculptures with manic delight and much giddy laughter. Deconstruction doesn't altogether shed such fanciful connotations as these when you get to know it better and start gauging its impact on the study of the humanities in America. As an academic phenomenon, deconstruction is unquestionably so divisive and arguably so pernicious that it would (I told myself as I embarked on this book) surely be a worthy goal to render it intelligible to the common reader. I was convinced as well that the case of Paul de Man may come to be considered the most significant academic controversy of our period. But I would be lying if I didn't admit that I sometimes felt about writing this book as Jonah felt about going to Nineveh; there were times when I'd have much rather stayed inside the whale. At such times in particular I benefited from the counsel and the support of numerous friends and well-wishers, including my agent, Glen Hartley, and my editor, Elaine Pfefferblit. I am grateful as well to John Ackerman, Lynn Chu, Wolfgang Holdheim, Ron Horning, Robert Polito, and John H. Weiss, all of whom made valuable suggestions for improving the manuscript. Lauren Oppenheim copyedited it skillfully. Others were liberal with their time, thoughts, and recollections; a partial list includes M. H. Abrams, Ian Balfour, Joel Black, Linda Brooks, Stephen G. Crane, Roger Gilbert, John Gordon, Nathanael Greene, David Grossvogel, Donald Hall, John Hollander, Lawrence Joseph, Roger Kimball, Richard Klein, Charlotte Levrard, Alison Lurie, Steven Marcus, Michael R. Marrus, Edward Said, and Renee and Theodore Weiss. The views of the people with whom I spoke or corresponded sometimes conflicted with my own but were appreciated no less for that. Finally, my collective thanks go to the professors, students, writers, and critics who allowed me to interview them, in some cases on condition of anonymity to protect them from the wrath of their academic adversaries.

FOR MY MOTHER

CONTENTS

We were wise indeed, could we discern truly the signs of our own time; and by knowledge of its wants and advantages, wisely adjust our own position in it. Let us, instead of gazing wildly into the obscure distance, look calmly around us, for a little, on the perplexed scene where we stand. Perhaps, on a more serious inspection, something of its perplexity will disappear, some of its distinctive characters and deeper tendencies more clearly reveal themselves; whereby our own relations to it, our own true aims and endeavours in it, may also become clearer.

—*Thomas Carlyle, "Signs of the Times"*
(1829)

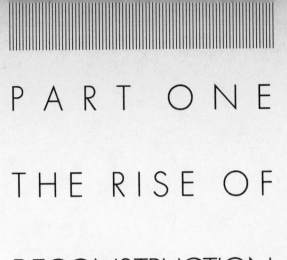

PART ONE

THE RISE OF

DECONSTRUCTION

CHAPTER 1

THE END OF

THE WORD

Deconstruction: the very word has an austere
sound to it which makes it some sort of sign
of our timid and disabused times.

—*Michael Wood, "Deconstructing Derrida"*

Signs of the times: A bookstore in the university town of Ithaca, New
York, has a sign on the wall advising patrons that "Shoplifters Will
Be Deconstructed." A professor in the English department at Columbia tells a telephone caller that she has had to move her campus
office because "Philosophy Hall is in a state of deconstruction." In the
New York Times Book Review, Allan Bloom complains about the way
literature professors are treating books: "A classic's content is no longer
of interest; the only concern is how it made it. This is called deconstruction." And in the recondite pages of *Critical Inquiry,* one critic
tells off another. It's not that he doesn't "trust" her, he explains. It's
that he "distrusts trust": "One need not deconstruct the penny to see
that even God must finally pay cash."

A new multipurpose word has entered the American vernacular.
Deconstruction—the word, though not necessarily the concepts for
which it stands—has made itself irresistible to speakers across a wide
spectrum of experience. It provokes a profusion of metaphors; it seems

to have as many figurative applications as there are sentences you can freshen up just by substituting the term for a more familiar locution. This is how the anthropologist Clifford Geertz describes the impact that Claude Lévi-Strauss's book *Tristes Tropiques* had on his field: "Whatever anthropologists may think of *Tristes Tropiques*—that it is a pretty tale, a revealing vision, or another example of what's gone wrong with the French—few come away from it without being at least a little bit deconstructed." The statement appears in Geertz's *Works and Lives,* which won the National Book Critics Circle Award for criticism in 1989. The winning book in biography that year was the late Richard Ellmann's magisterial life of Oscar Wilde. In his discussion of *The Picture of Dorian Gray,* Ellmann notes that Wilde's preface "flaunted the aestheticism that the book would indict." The result: "Wilde the preface-writer and Wilde the novelist deconstruct each other."

Turn to the sports pages and you find *deconstruction* put to other uses. In his annual postseason report, the *New Yorker's* Roger Angell declines to offer a full-fledged "deconstruction" of Kirk Gibson's climactic home run in the first game of the 1988 World Series ("it was whacked against an Eckersley slider—supposedly, but not quite, a slider *away,* etc.") on the grounds that such an analysis can only diminish the grandeur of the mythic moment. The 1989 baseball season begins and the *Village Voice* headlines its profile of the Mets' strong, silent Kevin McReynolds with the promise that it will "deconstruct" the estimable left fielder. In April, the sports section of the Sunday *New York Times* runs an essay by baseball commissioner A. Bartlett Giamatti, the one-time president of Yale University, a scholar of Renaissance literature. Two weeks later a letter from an irate fan blasts the essay: Giamatti "should forget about his narrative cliché of the fan as audience reinventing the text of baseball every season and return to deconstructing *The Faerie Queene* or unions."

Poets, too, have appropriated the word. When Walt Whitman heard the learned astronomer lecture, he couldn't wait to go outdoors and drink in the sight of the stars. A poet today, wanting to produce a similar effect, might weigh in with a two-line poem: in the first line we hear the fragment of an oration on deconstruction, and in the second line, the buzz of an insect sipping a flower's nectar. The space between the lines has been the poet's way of exiting the lecture hall, trading in one kind of buzzing noise for another. Deconstruction: the very word performs the rhetorical gesture known as the *metonymy*—it's the single example that can communicate the whole flavor of contemporary academic discourse.

Popping up in poems and conversations, spicing up book reviews and sports reports, *deconstruction* is used in the American vernacular with the cheerfully airy abandon that once marked *existentialism,* that midcentury salute to death-of-god theorizing in the Gallic manner. Part of the charm of this linguistic situation is that few people, in or out of academe, have a very firm grip on what deconstruction means. Evidently, you don't need a grounding in the major deconstructionist texts to add the word to your vocabulary. Speakers have little fear of being corrected—and much apparent justification for taking liberties with the term. Whether by design or by a general slackening of the standards of academic prose, the purveyors of deconstruction don't exactly sweat to make themselves understood in their tomes on the subject. The prose they perpetrate functions as a "no trespassing" sign, warning outsiders to keep on their side of the fence. The mystification surrounding their practice has helped turn *deconstruction* into a totemic word, and the general confusion has licensed speakers to appropriate the term for their own ends. It is a pleasant irony that the rambunctious career of the word itself should illustrate a basic tenet of the deconstructive world-view: the idea of linguistic free-play. Words can have no single fixed meaning. Like wayward electrons, they can spin away from their initial orbit and enter a wider magnetic field. No one owns them or has a proprietary right to dictate how they will be used. Just so, *deconstruction* has been used in all sorts of ways never intended or foreseen by the coiner of that neologism and the members of his academic sect.

Entering the public vocabulary, *deconstruction* has acquired a range of figurative meanings—many of which, it may be argued, are implied by the word's own properties as an oxymoron, its fusion of *destruction* and *construction.* In the examples given, Roger Angell uses *deconstruction* as a deliberately starchy substitute for *analysis;* in the *Voice* headline, it's slang for character dissection, a substitute for the old-fashioned "what makes him tick?" For Richard Ellmann, *deconstruct* embraces the senses of *contradict, negate,* and *cancel out;* for Clifford Geertz, to be *deconstructed* is to be *challenged, perplexed, disconcerted,* perhaps *undone.* Often the word carries a menacing edge, thanks to the force of the *de-* prefix. *Deconstruction* embodies some vague threat, a fit fate for bookstore shoplifters, an unhappy fate for *"The Faerie Queene* or unions."* Allan Bloom discerns a specific and concrete threat, something resembling an academic cabal's conspiracy against "classic literature" and the "canon" of great books. To the Columbia professor, *deconstruction* identifies the stage of architectural decay that precedes a complete overhaul of the premises. It can be used with strict accuracy as a term of literary analysis (Ellmann) but also wryly as a rhetorical fillip (Angell, Geertz), with jocular or mordant wit (the Ithaca bookstore, the letter to the *Times*), as a metaphor suggesting a wrecking ball and crane (the Columbia professor), as an aspect of an academic state of affairs to be loudly lamented (Bloom), or as a name for any brand of criticism that promises or threatens to debunk cherished assumptions and devastate its objects of study: "One need not deconstruct the penny to see that even God must finally pay cash."

In the aftermath of the Ayatollah's Valentine's Day death sentence on novelist Salman Rushdie in 1989, journalism's herd of independent minds converged on a marvelous new application for a term already on everyone's glamour list. Given its connotations, *deconstruction* seemed made to order for cases in which literary criticism equals war by other means. With his eye trained on the global Zeitgeist, columnist Charles Peter Freund took stock in the *New Republic* of an attempt by Muslim fundamentalists to censor Dante. (True believers revile the author of the *Divine Comedy* for placing the prophet Mahomet in the eighth circle of hell, where he endures a particularly nasty ordeal; he is cloven from chin to crotch, with his entrails dragging between his legs.) The self-described "Guardians of the Revolution," demanding that Dante be publicly denounced, threatened to blow up the poet's tomb in Ravenna—an effort Freund characterized, with suitable irony, as "a new line of deconstructionist criticism, at this post–de Man stage in its development." *National Review,* a rival magazine, ran an ad in the same March 1989 issue of the *New Republic*—a quote box with the quip: "We had no idea the Ayatollah was into literary criticism. Now we find out he's a deconstructionist."

It is not difficult to multiply the examples, and easy enough to come across two usages of *deconstruction* that seem to be in fundamental contradiction. Frances McCullough, who edited Sylvia Plath's journals, illustrates one common meaning of the term. Writing about her marriage to fellow poet Ted Hughes, Plath claimed that she bit Hughes on the cheek and drew blood on the occasion of their first meeting—

but her account of the incident, McCullough notes, "is deconstructed by Hughes's friends" in Anne Stevenson's recent biography of Plath. You can deconstruct something, it would appear, simply by exposing it as a falsehood or an exaggeration. The implication is that the object of the deconstructive exercise is spurious. For other writers, the contrary is the case. To deconstruct is to devalue, to retain the shell of a thing while dispensing with its core, to replace the genuine article with a counterfeit, a parody or a simulation. Thus Jacques Barzun, surveying the field of crime fiction, deplores two popular developments: BBC television adaptations of the classics, and murder mystery weekends, holidays, and tours. These are symptoms, Barzun declares, of "the disease of the age: theory and make-believe preferred to the thing itself, the professor and the tourist guide busy deconstructing every true Study in Scarlet."

As a rule, the immediate context will allow us to frame an approximate idea of what an author means by *deconstruction*. In academic discourse, however, context is often of little help. The American Sociological Association holds its annual convention in Atlanta, and this is how a speaker assesses the social implications of women's sexual habits: "In the emphasis on diversity, the notion of a hegemonic sexual discourse is deconstructed, even among those who claim to have one." Even among those who speak that way, it's not clear what's being said. What *is* clear is that *deconstruction* is the magic word—to be spoken with either the eulogist's reverence or the anathematist's snarl. The *Wall Street Journal* thinks it knows whom to blame for the assault on "Western culture" courses at major universities. The villain, the editorial tells us, is "an intellectual fashion known as 'deconstruction'— reading texts not as inherently worthy but to serve some professor's private agenda." That is a caricature rather than a definition, but it is possible that the word itself inspires the caricaturist. Certainly it stimulates a writer's powers of metaphoric invention. A book reviewer striving to convey the spirit of Thomas Pynchon's latest novel, *Vineland,* tells us that the book "is an intentional subversion of orderliness. You'd deconstruct it by pulling its pin and heaving it." The act of deconstruction seems to entail the lobbing of a hand grenade. On the other hand, a survey of American intellectual life in the *Chronicle of Higher Education* identifies deconstruction as a modern theory that is "as Balkanizing as social history." What *is* deconstruction? Well, it's like this: "For deconstructionists, the world is made up of empty rooms, with impenetrable walls and no doors, in which individual minds are bent upon rending texts with a slight smile." It sounds pretty claustrophobic, the stuff of a locked-room murder. You wonder why the characters wear that "slight smile" and how the room can be empty with them inside. And what does "rending texts" entail—or was that a printer's error for "reading" them? Yet whatever is being done has "Balkanizing" consequences, just as "social history" does. Very mysterious.

How to explain the cachet of *deconstruction,* the way it has infiltrated public discourse? At the crudest level of its appeal, the word announces the writer's knowingness: *I'm hip to what's hip. I know what's happening in the world of big ideas.* A Los Angeles-based screenwriter named Mark Horowitz, trying to explain the current French enthusiasm for movies starring Mickey Rourke, places the deconstruction craze in the perspective of "a constant war between the U.S. and France." In Horowitz's words, "We sent them Jerry Lewis, so they retaliated by sending us deconstruction and Jacques Derrida." There is some truth to this jape: deconstruction in America owes much to our starry-eyed reverence for French culture, based perhaps on a misguided notion of French culture. Deconstruction conforms to an American preconception of the cerebral French in the same way that Jerry Lewis in *The Nutty Professor* represents a Frenchman's impression of an American type. Something is gained and something lost in translation. In the early 1980s, Paris taxi drivers, those sophisticates of invective, could be heard barking, *"Hé, va donc, structuraliste!"*—"Get lost, structuralist!" The Broadway equivalent today, presuming that job-hunting Ph.D.s do drive cabs, might be "Go deconstruct yourself!" It is only a matter of time before *deconstruction* is routinely used—as its older cousin *existentialism* has steadily been used—as the squiggle of fancy French mustard on the hot dog of a banal observation. You'll be reading a feature on *Miami Vice* in a Sunday newspaper supplement when suddenly your eye lights upon this sentence: "The episode where rocker Ted Nugent blows up Sonny Crockett's Testarossa in a deserted sand pit had a sort of existential Samuel-Beckett-hits-Dade-County quality." Uh huh; sort of. And when the article goes on to eulogize the episode "about the achingly vulnerable hooker who falls in love with Rico Tubbs, ties him to a bed between stabbings and then shoots herself in the head," you are positively disappointed when this isn't characterized as a deconstruction of prostitution.

But behind the journalistic appropriation of *deconstruction* there is something more complicated than one writer's desire to sound intellectually fashionable and another writer's wish to mock that impulse. The plain truth is that *deconstruction* has achieved talismanic status—and has aroused tremendous anxiety in the larger intellectual community. "The very word has an austere sound to it which makes it some sort of sign of our timid and disabused times," the critic Michael Wood wrote in 1977. The word has lost little of its shock value since. As the key word of the hottest (and most hotly contested) European cultural import since existentialism, it has become the graduate student's *porte-parole,* the humanist's *bête-noire,* and the literary theorist's *sine qua non.* It is also the supreme badge of contemporary academic jargon, reminding us that the gap has never been wider between public communication and lit-crit lingo. To people inside academe—who sometimes talk wistfully of "the real world," as if they were not participating in it—the word *deconstruction* signals a development in the history of ideas, though some professors prefer to regard it as an episode in the history of the youth culture that came of age in the 1960s and 1970s. To people outside of academe, the word seems a handy synonym for academic trendiness—for the remarkable way they do things today in the land of the discourse and the text.

Deconstruction is the brainchild of Jacques Derrida, the Algerian-born French philosopher, a resident of Paris and a frequent visitor to the United States, where he has held faculty appointments at several universities. The pervasiveness of his influence in the American academy today is beyond dispute. A prolific author and indefatigable lecturer, Derrida is a man of many neologisms, the maker of supernally complex puns, and *deconstruction* is only the most famous of these. The word has its etymological root in Martin Heidegger's concept of *Destruktion*—or, more exactly, in Heidegger's call for the destruction *(Destruktion)* of ontology, the branch of metaphysics that studies the nature of being. One may wonder how so recondite a project has managed to achieve such notoriety.

Deconstruction is elusive of definition, and Derrida means to keep it that way. "All sentences of the type 'deconstruction is X' . . . a priori miss the point," Derrida has written. Derrida and his followers ridicule the notion that deconstruction is a "theory," or a "philosophical project," or a "method"—such terms, they maintain, are inaccurate and reductive. This attempt to defy categorization may be part of the seductive appeal that deconstruction holds for its academic proponents: it is so "new" that you can't fit it into your existing frames of thought, and so "radical" that it would declare those frames of thought invalid, obsolete, exploded. Academic deconstruction blends together elements of linguistics, literary criticism, and philosophy into a method of analysis that can be used within diverse intellectual disciplines; a stated goal is to dissolve the borders that traditionally separate one discipline from another. The very appearance of a deconstructive text may announce the project's vaunted novelty. The pages of *Glas,* one of Derrida's most celebrated tomes, are divided into two columns: the one on the left deals with Hegel and the one on the right with Jean Genet, and the effect is of two monologues having an oblique dialogue with each other. From the strictly stylistic point of view, the maneuver generates tremendous excitement. But it is difficult to categorize such products and such procedures—which is, of course, Derrida's intention. The difficulty is compounded vastly by Derrida's notorious word-drunkenness and by the imprecise and sometimes conflicting accounts of his theories that his epigones proffer. One practical result is that *deconstruction,* as it is used in academic debate, signifies at least four different but overlapping things. When people talk about deconstruction they might mean a theory or a nexus of theories, a way of doing philosophy that seems to want to do *away* with philosophy; more specifically, the word stands for a type of literary criticism that aspires to being universally applicable; or the speaker might have in mind the specific manifestations of the deconstructive impulse in his or her own field; or the word may be used more generally to designate a whole climate of opinion, an academic movement, a sociological phenomenon.

Although deconstruction is now firmly entrenched in disciplines as technically remote as law and history, it first made its presence felt in literary studies, and in that domain it has achieved extraordinary prestige and institutional power. If Derrida, as deconstruction's founding father, remains its ultimate authority figure, the late Paul de Man is generally considered to be the guiding light of literary deconstruction. It was de Man who gave deconstruction its first American headquarters—the French and comparative literature departments of Yale University—and it was he who was most responsible for converting it into a full-fledged academic cult. It would be foolish to deny Derrida's originality or de Man's brilliance. If used judiciously, moreover, their methods and their ideas may help to elucidate certain riddling poems and novels, films and plays. But deconstruction in its purer forms doesn't want to be a party to anything so reactionary as the elucidation of literature. The aim is not to elucidate but to expose and unmask, to demystify and dismantle—to deconstruct—and you can deconstruct just about anything. Everything is equally "literature"—not in the sense that it is good writing, but in the sense that its meaning is a function of interpretation. And therefore "literature" itself has been devalued—or deconstructed: there is no reason, theoretically, for the "literary" critic to favor a novel by Dickens, say, over an episode of *All in the Family,* since either will serve as an appropriate object of study. Academic literary theorists have their own ponderous way of making this point. Here is Duke professor Barbara Herrnstein Smith's statement of the theme in her book *Contingencies of Value:* "Since there are no functions performed by artworks that may be specified as generically unique and also no way to distinguish the 'rewards' provided by art-related experiences or behavior from those provided by innumerable other kinds of experience and behavior, any distinctions drawn between 'aesthetic' and 'nonaesthetic' (or 'extra-aesthetic') value must be regarded as fundamentally problematic." And two centuries of aesthetic philosophy go sailing out the window. As the critic David Bromwich noted in a percipient review of Smith's book, the utilitarian philosopher Jeremy Bentham "said it faster: 'Quantity of pleasure being equal, push-pin is as good as poetry.'" It is a line of reasoning that, Bromwich observes, would reduce questions of literary value to a cost-benefit computation. The iconoclastic aim would appear to be the obliteration of the difference between aesthetics and philistinism—or, to say it faster, the deconstruction of art.

The leveling of literature to the status of a soap opera, a board game, or "innumerable other kinds of experience and behavior" must seem a perverse doctrine for a literature professor to espouse. There is certainly a place in a comic campus novel for the solemn-faced professor who declares that Shakespeare and Milton are not intrinsically superior to daytime TV. But art is only one item on the list of things that the avatars of deconstruction call into question. One of Derrida's prize explicators has gone to some length to deconstruct causality—as if the laws of cause and effect could be undone in the course of a word game. Jonathan Culler rests his case against causality on the idea that the *pain* we feel precedes our discovery of the *pin* that caused it. "The experience of pain, it is claimed, *causes* us to discover the pin and thus causes the production of a cause," Culler writes. "To deconstruct causality one must operate with the notion of cause and apply it to causation itself." To deconstruct causality is, in short, to turn the tables on it—"the deconstruction reverses the hierarchical opposition of the causal scheme." Ergo: "If the effect is what causes the cause to become a cause, then the effect, not the cause, should be treated as the origin." In the *New York Review of Books,* the philosopher John Searle writes a devastating critique of Culler's "tissue of confusions." Searle points out that Culler confuses the discovery of a cause with the production of a cause; moreover, "there isn't any logical hierarchy between cause and effect in the first place since the two are correlative terms." Exposing the logical fallacies of Culler's deconstructive reasoning, Searle performs a valuable service. But Searle knows that it isn't sufficient to refute the topsy-turvy logic that confuses effects with origins. One must also investigate the specific causality of such deconstructive displays. For it stretches belief to imagine that the blithe deconstructor of causality seriously means what he says—or intends to test out his theory in the realm of action.

[The deconstructive method appears to entail a kind of devil's advocacy taken to the point of bad faith. Deconstructionists have the knack of exempting themselves from their own strictures, expecting to be understood even as they insist that all messages are unintelligible.] Though irony is a word that some of them favor, few have any flair for it; your average deconstructionist tends to carry on in the manner of the earnest pedant rather than that of the put-on artist. For these and other reasons, a debate with a disciple of Derrida is a curious and somewhat maddening proposition. It is hard to argue with someone who resides in an alternative universe—a realm of discourse in which opposites unite, black can mean white, a green light can mean stop, and the defense attorney can be counted on to hang his own client. The immediate question is *why:* what would prompt a sane and rational professor to assert that the *pain* somehow precedes the skin-puncturing *pin* that caused it? What's in it for him? And no wink accompanies the outlandish assertion, just as there is no hint of a smile when—in an example presented by the physicist James Trefil—"a philosopher of science says that the laws of physics are merely social conventions, like traffic laws." To deconstruct *that* position you would need only to cross the street against the flow of rushing traffic. Any volunteers?

The persistent assault on our fundamental cultural assumptions—

if not on the laws of physics—is one reason for deconstruction's notoriety. There are others. You must consider its novelty (undeniable), its real or apparent difficulty (in which it takes pride), and its peculiar lingo. You must take into account, above all, the professedly "subversive" intent of the deconstructionists. Their outrageousness is calculated; they seem to relish having a disruptive impact, and they are certainly good at it—their ability to polarize whole faculties and provoke vitriolic debate is both well-documented and legendary. In the face of deconstruction, gentle scholars turn ferocious. Asked to characterize the deconstructionists he has known, an exasperated professor who specializes in modern British literature delivered this tirade: "Arrogant, smug, snotty, meretricious, addicted to straw-man arguments, horrible writers who demand to be considered of the company of Jane Austen and Chaucer, appallingly ingrown and cliquish at the same time that they talk about expansiveness and new frontiers of discourse, unbelievably wooden and mechanical at the same time that they make their wooden and mechanical obeisances to *jouissance** and free-play, like all perpetual adolescents contemptuous of the past and convinced that by great good fortune the truth happened to be discovered just as they were hitting puberty, a daisy-chain of brown-nosers declaring their high-flown independence from the normal irksome constraints of community and continuity, who without the peculiar heads-I-win-tails-you-lose rationale of their arguments—if evidence and logic bear me out, fine, if not, we can always deconstruct them—would almost none of them have written an essay that could stand up in a decent senior seminar." The fury in this professor's speech helps explain why journalists find *deconstruction* so irresistible a word to appropriate, with whatever degree of irony. It is guaranteed to inflate the diction—and raise the reader's blood pressure. The very word signals controversy, claim, counterclaim, clash: a universe of fierce cabalistic disputation, an atmosphere charged with threat and recrimination, at a time when the words *crisis* and *higher education* tend to go together naturally.

The critic Harold Bloom proposes "the School of Resentment" as an umbrella term for the critical theories that have been proliferating

---

*Jouissance—sexual ecstasy—is the term used by Roland Barthes to describe the reader's orgasmic "pleasure of the text."

dizzily in university literature departments. He names some factions: there are the "Lacanians, deconstructionists, Foucault-inspired New Historicists, semioticians, neo-Marxists, and latest-model feminists." All have their place in the School of Resentment, where literary criticism is used as a weapon on behalf of groups perceived as historical victims—it's their way to get even with their oppressors. New theories—amalgamations or conglomerations, for the most part—come and go. Each acquires its tenured partisans, its prestigious journal, and its clout within the teaching profession. But while deconstruction is, technically, just one theory among many, what is really extraordinary about it is the degree to which it has informed and affected the others. It is possible, for example, to describe a "New Historicist" as a Marxist who has read Derrida, while a "latest-model feminist" may be one who propounds the deconstruction of gender—or, to get into the spirit of the thing, what she (or he) might call a counterhegemonic inversion of the male-female paradigm. The real measure of deconstruction's influence in the academy is the prevalence of its idiosyncratic and arcane vocabulary.

Deconstructionists claim that theirs is the most rigorous method of close textual analysis ever devised. At the same time, however, they seem indifferent to the question of which texts, if any, are chosen for discussion; their primary emphasis is on theoretical propositions stripped of reference to any particular author or body of work. Deconstructionists offer relatively few examples of solid literary analysis, since they operate on a high level of generality and assume that every text operates the same way. You'll find deconstructive analyses of a handful of authors (Proust, Nietzsche, Rousseau), but you're as likely to come across a deconstruction of an abstract concept (such as the concepts of origin, continuity, and closure) or of a beer commercial's system of signs. Perhaps it is simply that deconstructive methods make better sense and produce more interesting results when applied to popular culture, to traffic signs and fashion statements, rather than to high literature. The more conventionally "literary" deconstructionist has, in any case, a permissive attitude toward textual interpretation. As one critic sympathetic to deconstruction has put it, "I cannot find it in myself to worry the question of the relation of empirical evidence to theory." Never before have literary critics indulged so much in pure speculation and made so little effort to demonstrate their claims.

Not all students are enamored of the deconstructive approach.

The director of the Tokyo American Center was a teaching assistant in comparative literature at Yale until 1977—when a surfeit of critical theory drove him to chuck academe in favor of the foreign service. Another disenchanted grad-school veteran, Elizabeth Connell Fentress, put in several years at Louisiana State University before deciding that the professional study of literature—or what it has become—was not for her. The buzzwords of critical theory rang in the corridors, Fentress reports, and one of these could be heard above the rest: "An exercise in one theory course called for students to 'deconstruct something.' Triumphantly, one student told me that he had chosen to deconstruct the game 'Trivial Pursuit' and that the professor had 'loved it.' " Fentress had, she says, a difficult decision to make. If she chose to ignore "the tidal wave of theory," she ran the risk of forfeiting "that dear document of endurance—the master's degree." But to immerse herself in "the muck" of fashionable theory would clash with her reason for attending graduate school in the first place—to study literature, not to theorize in a void. She was troubled, too, by the deconstructive assault on "meaning": everywhere she encountered the view that no real relation exists between a piece of writing and the world we live in. "If meaning was going to be demoted as another 'outdated' view, I concluded, what's the point? If I couldn't teach what I thought was good writing, if what I read was to be explained away as inaccessible, why go on? I deemed it best to leave LSU, and to learn what I wanted to learn on my own."

What makes Fentress's testimony so troubling is that hers is not at all an unusual case. One suspects that the student with an authentic literary vocation may be the one who feels least at home with the academic orthodoxies of our day. It is a disquieting fact that the number of students electing to major in literature has steadily declined over the last twenty years—the period when critical theorists were becoming the hottest properties in an increasingly fashion-conscious profession.

Years have gone by since the first wishful thinker predicted deconstruction's imminent demise. But while it is no longer au courant in France, where it originated in the 1960s, its influence in the United States has not appreciably waned. At first, deconstruction was limited to a handful of universities: Yale, Cornell, Johns Hopkins. Yale in particular was home for the trio of professors—Derrida, de Man, and J. Hillis Miller—whom their colleague Geoffrey Hartman dubbed "boa-deconstructors." By 1979 Derrida was the most frequently cited authority in papers submitted to the journal of the Modern Language Association (MLA), the professional organization to which nearly all literature professors are presumed to belong. De Man published his most influential book that year, and Miller weighed in with several aggressive briefs for the deconstructive method. At the time, wrote one contemporary observer, going from Harvard to Yale would have been like "a journey to the moon." But by the mid-1980s that was no longer true. The spread of deconstruction to campuses across America was now an accomplished fact; deconstruction had become a routine part of the curriculum. Princeton and Harvard, johnnies-come-lately, were making up for lost time with their latest hirings. In 1986, the University of California at Irvine sprang for a reported six-figure salary to lure Miller from Yale. Confident predictions of deconstruction's decline have, in the light of such ballyhooed appointments, a hollow ring.

Geoffrey Hartman, who is ardently protheory, has a punning name for deconstruction. He has called it "Derridadaism," as if it were a kind of philosophical poltergeist of dadaism, surrealism's forerunner, an art movement whose most celebrated single gesture was Marcel Duchamp's installation of a urinal in a museum. Hartman has also likened deconstructionists to "clowns or jongleurs." M. H. Abrams, the distinguished author of *The Mirror and the Lamp,* is, in contrast to Hartman, no fan of deconstruction, but he, too, stresses its antic disposition. Deconstruction, Abrams has written, is "the serious philosophy of the absurd," and Derrida "is the Zen master of Western philosophy."

The tactics of deconstruction are impish, its logic absurdist. There is, however, no denying the seriousness of its intent. Deconstruction portends, if we are to believe its proponents, an "epistemic" shift—a momentous and irrevocable change in the way we think, write, and acquire knowledge. Institutionally, it hasn't quite worked that way; it may be argued that deconstruction has, in the long run, modified rather than transformed critical practice. Many students, having spent their obligatory time with Derrida's texts and de Man's rhetorical readings, feel it is possible to deploy the strategies of deconstruction without necessarily adhering to its general principles. Still, deconstruction advertises itself as an all-or-nothing proposition, and that was part of its original appeal for aspiring assistant professors. Claiming to call everything into question, deconstruction consciously poses itself as a challenge to accepted procedures. It thus affords a perfect means for young faculty members to wage generational warfare against their elders. And conversely, those who resist deconstruction can't feel free to ignore it; where it does not set the intellectual agenda, it remains an unavoidable issue. In the realm of academic politics, deconstruction even has a compelling *ur*-myth. Adherents were embattled at first, and have ever since favored the posture of the embattled outsider—though the pose is belied by the fact that many are tenured and wield considerable institutional power; there are some things that can't be deconstructed (death) and some things that won't be (tenure). Abrams gives deconstruction its due as a force to be reckoned with: "By J. S. Mill's maxim that the opinions of bright people between twenty and thirty years of age are the best index to the intellectual tendencies of the next era, it seems probable that the heritage of deconstruction will be prominent in literary criticism for some time to come."

Very nearly as remarkable is the influence of deconstruction on other academic fields and among contemporary writers. You are likely to hear the buzzwords of deconstruction in the published thesis of the with-it art historian. When an abstract painting by Mark Rothko is described as "a palimpsest of traces" in which the painter's "image-sign enabled him to elide or dismantle such conventional binaries" as birth and death, we suspect that the student may have spent more time mastering Derrida's vocabulary than looking at Rothko's pictures. The ultimate in painterly deconstruction is the self-erasing work of art conceived by the late French author Georges Perec in his brilliant novel *Life, A User's Manual.* The character whom Perec calls Percival Bartlebooth, a wealthy English eccentric who lives in Paris, decides at the age of twenty to devote his entire life to a single project whose "perfection would be circular: a series of events which when concatenated nullify each other." Bartlebooth's plan requires him to take lessons in watercolor painting for ten years, though he has no real aptitude for it. He then spends twenty years painting five hundred seascapes in as many ports around the world. Each is sent back to Paris, where a puzzle-maker makes a 750-piece jigsaw out of it. For the next twenty years Bartlebooth plans to reconstruct each puzzle in turn. There is an elaborate procedure for detaching the picture from the puzzle, and this enables Bartlebooth to bring the original watercolors with him as he returns to the five hundred ports where he painted them in the first place. Finally, he will apply a chemical to remove the paint from the picture—and end with blank paper. Though Bartlebooth dies before the work is done (or undone), his purely conceptual triumph is as suggestive as it is enigmatic. It proposes a notion of art as gratuitous, an activity rather than an object, bound up with temporality rather than with eternity. Bartlebooth's self-erasing masterpiece implies that the artistic impulse expires in the act of being satisfied. Construction, reconstruction, and deconstruction are merely stages in the progression of a work of art from nothing to something and back to nothing again.

There is much to be said for fictional deconstruction, if that is what novelists like Perec and Italo Calvino are doing. While they furnish analogues to certain deconstructive theories, the imaginative fictions of Perec and Calvino are in no way derivative of, or secondary to, those theories. The same cannot be claimed for the more pedantic writers affiliated with the so-called "Language school," a movement in American writing that has gained considerable prominence in the past decade. Not all but some of these self-styled, university-trained experimentalists appear to spend half their time dismantling syntax and referentiality, and the other half taking dictation directly from Derrida. Derrida's essay "The Law of Genre" appeared in an English translation in 1980. It begins with these sentences: "Genres are not to be mixed. I will not mix genres. I repeat: genres are not to be mixed. I will not mix them." Turn to page four of *Vice* by Carla Harryman, a poet who gets consistently high marks from her "Language school" colleagues, and this is what you'll find:

> Genres are not to be mixed.
> I will not mix genres.
> I repeat: genres are not to be mixed.
> I will not mix them.

The writer Tom Clark, reviewing the "Language school" phenomenon, charges that its poets "are as long on critical theory as they are (relatively, and I think also absolutely) short on poems." And certainly these poets have a distinct predilection for fancy theorizing: so-and-so is said to have "subverted patriarchal assumptions" or maybe "deconstructed the Romantic image" in a poem consisting exclusively of the word *tampon* repeated twelve times in a vertical column. The poem seems rather less substantial than the critical jargon whose weight it bears. Reviewing several anthologies devoted to the works of the "Language" poets, Clark hears the sound of "an assistant professor who took a wrong turn on the way to the Derrida Cookout and ended up at the poetry reading."

The person or persona of Jacques Derrida has entered our poetry in surprising ways. He is, together with Cary Grant and Katharine Hepburn, a character in Bob Perelman's remarkable narrative poem "Movie." Perelman, a master of comic invention, is one of a number of "Language school" writers who have absorbed the lessons of contemporary critical theory without letting their work get bogged down in jargon-riddled excursions in meaninglessness. In "Movie" we follow a screwball plot in which Grant and Hepburn, seemingly on loan from *Holiday,* play out their romance with Derrida looking over their shoulders. One of the surprises Perelman has in store for us is that "Derrida's summer home is / in fact a gulag in Nicaragua." Unlike Perelman, neither Rodney Jones nor Norman Dubie seems to have any sort of affinity with poststructuralism or its projects. Yet both invoke the Napoleon of deconstruction in recent poems. Jones's "Pastoral for Derrida" concludes with a threatening image: the poet standing "under the hermeneutical circle of the vulture." The speaker in Dubie's "The Apocrypha of Jacques Derrida" disavows being Napoleon Bonaparte: "I don't really believe I am the Corsican. But then / Neither did he." It is as though Derrida (or what he stands for) has become a troubling issue that contemporary poets feel obliged to address, however obliquely. In his frequently anthologized poem "Meditation at Lagunitas," Robert Hass describes "the new thinking" with its proposition that

> because there is in this world no one thing
> to which the bramble of *blackberry* corresponds,
> a word is elegy to what it signifies.

What Hass calls "the new thinking" sounds an awful lot like deconstruction. It is similarly unnamed but described—and with unconcealed animus—by Louis Simpson in his poem "The Professor." The eponymous speaker of Simpson's poem explains that he "taught there is no truth, / that words mean what we want them / to mean, and nothing else." Simpson consigns the speaker to an infernal place next to Pilate. He pictures them up to their necks in "the substance they were increasing / continually out of themselves."

A biblical scholar is "convinced now of the necessity of an iconoclastic moment in biblical studies." He reports that his field has begun to feel tremors of a "seismic activity" and that this "upheaval is more than a methodological shift; it is rather an epistemic shift that portends to change the way we think, across a span of disciplines, about texts, about method, even about the human and material world." The biblical scholar is speaking of deconstruction. He proceeds to "illustrate its potential in the sphere of gospel studies"; like it or not, it is a challenge that biblical scholarship needs to meet. Deconstructive analyses of the parables of Jesus are still comparatively rare, though you'll find some in Stephen Moore's book *Literary Criticism and the Gospels: The Theoretical Challenge.* Moore offers abundant evidence that Derrida's doctrines have been taken to heart at the Yale Divinity School. Indeed, according to Moore, "the more-deconstructionist-than-thou game" has become quite popular in the biblical "guild." Let one example suffice. At a conference in 1986 in Atlanta, a scholar named Gary Phillips presented a paper titled "Deconstruction and the Parables of Jesus," and another professor countered with "Deconstructing 'Deconstruction and the Parables of Jesus' by Gary Phillips, or Does the Cat Perpetually Chase Its Tail?" Harold Bloom, for one, is not sanguine about the "rabblement of lemmings" who "are now converging upon the Bible, which they will find the most recalcitrant of texts, though that finding is not likely to deter them."

The profound impact of deconstruction on anthropology is more difficult to gauge, since the influence has worked both ways. From the anthropological investigations of Claude Lévi-Strauss in the 1950s and 1960s, the theorists of deconstruction derived something of their original impetus. Paul de Man sums up the anthropological parallel with literary deconstruction: "In the act of anthropological intersubjective interpretation, a fundamental discrepancy always prevents the observer from coinciding fully with the consciousness he is observing. The same discrepancy exists in everyday language, in the impossibility of making the actual expression coincide with what has to be expressed, of making the actual sign coincide with what it signifies." In dwelling on such discrepancies, deconstruction seems to call into question the fundamental project of anthropology as a discipline. Not only is the emphasis shifted away from *what* is represented and toward the means of representation but, since language is inherently a slippery medium, it follows that any attempt to represent other people and places must be held suspect.

To the deconstructively minded anthropologist, description is necessarily infused with ideology, and reports from the field of a third world country may, whatever the writer's intentions, help perpetuate a colonialist perspective. Ethnography, that branch of anthropology whose purpose is the accurate description of individual cultures, is necessarily compromised by its literary character—that is, by the fact that all ethnography involves writing. "The true historical significance of writing is that it has increased our capacity to create totalistic illusions with which to have power over things or over others as if they were things," argues Stephen Tyler, an advocate of "post-modern ethnography." Tyler goes on: "The whole ideology of representational signification is an ideology of power. To break its spell we would have to attack writing, totalistic representational signification, and authorial authority, but all this has already been accomplished for us." The attack on writing has been accomplished by Derrida, who "has made the author the creature of writing rather than its creator," and other theorists of language and literature who undermine "authorial authority" and call representation into question. "Post-modern ethnography," Tyler writes, "builds its program not so much from their principles as from the rubble of their deconstruction." It is not entirely clear what Tyler's "program" might entail. He proffers the paradox that "there is no instance of a post-modern ethnography, even though all ethnography is post-modern in effect, nor is one likely." A case can be made that some of the most intelligent and fruitful work being done today in anthropology is speculative and theoretical in nature. After all, questions about the self, about how the observer affects that which he or she observes, and about the narrative strategies for reporting these observations, are fundamental in this line of study. Nevertheless, the prospect of that metaphorical "rubble" isn't calculated to cause a universal shout for joy. And in the meantime, the profs in the faculty lounge are still chuckling over the one about the postmodern ethnographer in the field with a representative of an indigenous culture. At the end of their three-hour tape-recorded conversation, the subject of the interview says, "This has been very nice. Do we have time now to talk about me?"

In architecture, deconstruction is known as "deconstructivism" and seems to involve the deliberate perpetration of ugliness. Proponents of "deconstructivism" are inclined to shatter symmetry in favor of distorted structures, tilting columns, and skewed angles. It is a movement with some currency; the Museum of Modern Art in New York considered it important enough to warrant a show of "Deconstructivist Architecture" in 1988. "Deconstruction," writes Mark Wigley, the show's co-curator, "gains all its force by challenging the very values of harmony, unity, and stability, and proposing instead a different view of structure: the view that the flaws are intrinsic to the structure." A deconstructive architect, Wigley explains, is "not one who dismantles buildings, but one who locates the inherent dilemmas within buildings. The deconstructive architect puts the pure forms of the architectural tradition on the couch and identifies the symptoms of a repressed impurity. The impurity is drawn to the surface by a combination of gentle coaxing and violent torture: the form is interrogated." If all architecture is based on a vision of humanity, Wigley's choice of metaphors is singularly revealing. In the deconstructivist design for living, it appears that the imagined inhabitant is undergoing psychoanalysis and dwelling in a torture chamber. After all that, what of the work itself? Walking through the deconstructivist exhibition, one recalled the character in Evelyn Waugh's *Decline and Fall* who went to Greece to look at the buildings there. His assessment: "They are unspeakably ugly. But there were some nice goats."

Has deconstruction hit Wall Street? Richard Rand of the University of Alabama, a co-translator of Derrida's *Glas,* thinks so. In the spring of 1989, when Michael Milken was slapped with a ninety-eight-count indictment on charges of racketeering and securities fraud, Rand—an English professor—sent a letter to the *Wall Street Journal* defending the misunderstood junk-bond king as a "deconstructive financier." Rand stated that the two things he had studied with rapt attention over the course of twenty years were Jacques Derrida's texts and the *Journal*'s financial pages. To Rand's mind there was quite a lot of continuity between the two, and particularly between Derrida's theoretical maneuvers and Milken's leveraged buyouts. Milken, in Rand's words, "is an inventive thinker whose thoughts about capital formation happen to coincide uncannily with Mr. Derrida's thoughts about concept formation." Milken had apparently made a deconstructive move when he turned the junk bond from "a 'marginal' (and despised) 'supplement' to the overall investment machine" into "a central and dynamic feature." With his leveraged buyouts he had accomplished a "reversal" and a "rewriting"—two more terms from the Derrida lexicon—of the merger-and-acquisition strategies already in place in postwar America.

Rand's letter reads like an unconscious self-parody, but a brilliant one—you have to pinch yourself to remember that his intent is to *praise* Derrida by linking his methods to those of Wall Street's disgraced prince of leverage. Why would a diehard deconstructor like Rand want to put Derrida in the company of an indicted felon? Perhaps because the mystique of the outlaw is one to which deconstructors are particularly susceptible; deconstruction has thrived in academe because and not in spite of its capacity to outrage people and make them mad. And perhaps there *is* something in Rand's analogy. Junk bonds, the apotheosis of an age of greed, are high-risk, high-yield debt securities used to finance corporate takeovers. Isn't it possible that Derrida and his cronies have aimed at doing something comparable in the academic marketplace, palming off a debased currency of empty "signifiers" for which they nevertheless claim value and prestige? In any case, Rand is being perfectly serious in contending that "both Messrs. Milken and Derrida deserve a respectful hearing." The letter-writer's purpose, he announces, is to dispute Allan Bloom's contention that deconstruction is a fading Paris fashion, "like a late arriving miniskirt." No, deconstruction is as up to date as insider trading. The junk bond has its parallel in the trashing of literature.

There are hip professors of popular culture who maintain that deconstruction provides the theoretical rationale for MTV, and maybe it does, though the television people aren't saying. By contrast, the influence of deconstruction in the professional study of the law has been enthusiastically defended and as hotly assailed by the parties directly affected. Deconstruction is the driving intellectual force behind the movement known as "Critical Legal Studies"—"CLS" for short. The movement has polarized the faculties of several leading law schools, Harvard's most prominently, and has been fought out in the pages of major law reviews. For some of its proponents, it is a phenomenon with an unambiguously political edge. According to Gary Peller, a CLS activist who teaches at the University of Virginia School of Law, "the significance of the deconstructive practice is not simply to reveal the constructed nature of what gets taken as fact, knowledge and truth as opposed to opinion, superstition and myth. It is an important practice because, in our social world, these claims to truth have played powerful political roles in the construction of our social relations—in the ways that those in power have justified their power and those out of power have been made to feel that their powerlessness is their own fault and inadequacy." By implication and extension, the deconstruction of "our social world" and "our social relations" entails a transfer of "power" to the "powerless"—or, in deconstructive parlance, a reversal of the "binary opposition" between the rich and the poor. Law is conceived to be the instrument of ideology, the ideology of the ruling class, and it is the legal scholar's duty to demystify it, exposing rhetoric as sham and putative truths as spurious.

The notion that law is not value-free but has an ideological basis is an old and familiar one. But it has never been presented in quite this way before. The underpinning of Critical Legal Studies is a theory of indeterminacy derived from deconstruction—as if the interpretation of statutes and precedents were somehow an extension of literary criticism rather than a fundamentally different activity, involving different objectives, undertaken in a different spirit. Laws, after all, are not prose poems; the deliberate ambiguity that can enrich our experience of a literary text would be, in the sphere of law, highly irregular and quite undesirable. Yet CLS specialists approach the law as a branch of literature awaiting deconstruction. They accept as a given, and even revel in, the indeterminancy of all texts, all writing. Duncan Kennedy of the Harvard Law School, who has been described as the CLS's answer to Abbie Hoffman, speaks of a "fundamental contradiction" at the core of any normative concept, which causes it to break down into antithetical senses. The contradiction would allow a judge to choose, with impunity and without constraint, either of two diametrically opposed interpretations in any case that comes before the court. There can therefore be no criteria for determining the correctness of a judicial decision, and the rational basis for law is, at a stroke, fatally compromised.

It remains to be seen whether the final effect of legal deconstruction would tend more in the direction of pure critique than in the pursuit of a particular political agenda. So far, the absence of any proof for the theory of "fundamental contradiction" has not stood in the movement's way, despite the well-articulated fears of its opponents, such as Owen M. Fiss, professor of public law at Yale. In an article in the *Cornell Law Review,* Fiss explained why the CLS critique of law is intellectually without merit (since it is based on a misunderstanding of how the judiciary works) as well as politically irresponsible (inasmuch as the aim of the critique is critique itself, "without a vision of what might replace that which is destroyed"). The title of Fiss's piece—"The Death of the Law?"—made it clear just how much is at stake.

There is a further sense in which deconstruction—precisely because of the "epistemic shift" it portends—colors the thought and speech of scholars who may not uphold Derridean principles. On May 12, 1989, close readers of the *New York Times* encountered an excerpt from the forty-third annual Cardozo lecture at the City Bar Association in New York City. The speaker at this prestigious event was Professor Laurence H. Tribe of the Harvard Law School, an eminent scholar of constitutional law. Tribe's lecture had an unlikely title: "Law's Geometry and the Curvature of Constitutional Space." Tribe described a "paradigm shift" in the field of law as drastic as the conceptual changes in modern physics. He challenged "a conception that sees law as nothing more than a force that enters our lives on isolated instances to resolve discrete events and then moves on." What Tribe recommended was not altogether brand new, but there was something novel about his approach. He was in effect recommending judicial interventionism as a kind of corollary to Heisenberg's uncertainty principle. For judicial rulings, Tribe argued, do not merely make "observations about law and society"; they "change the fabric of the society itself." If, in the Supreme Court case Tribe cited, a parent beats a child to death, may the state—in the form of "social workers and other local officials"—be held accountable for not preventing the tragedy? By a majority ruling the court decided that it wasn't the state that deprived the unfortunate boy of his liberty in violation of the due process clause of the fourteenth amendment. But in Tribe's view, the majority rested on a "quite primitive vision" of the state—a "stilted pre-modern paradigm" showing no hint that "the hand of the observing state may have itself played a role in shaping the world it observes."

What was new in Tribe's address was not so much its substance but its rhetoric—not its judicial program but its vocabulary of "conceptual shifts" and its sweeping dismissal of a rationalist world-view. "The still-reigning paradigm of constitutional law," Tribe said, "stands in sharp contrast to most contemporary modes of social thought, which recognize the pervasive relationship between observer and observed and deny the primitive notion that subjects act upon a background of distinct, fixed objects rather than existing in a reciprocal and ever-changing subject-object tension." Deconstruct this paragraph, and you find that it relies on the same contagious theory of indeterminacy we've already encountered—a theory that owes almost as much to the postmodernist paradigms of deconstruction as to those of modern physics. If the notion "that subjects act upon a background of distinct, fixed objects" is "primitive," what happens to the concepts of individual responsibility and free will? And if people exist less as entities in themselves than "in a reciprocal and ever-changing subject-object tension," hasn't the speaker deconstructed the self as an autonomous, independent agent entitled to be judged by its actions? The effect would be to foster a drastically reduced conception of human freedom.

The protean nature of deconstruction raises a fundamental problem: the reader may wonder what it is that links these various manifestations of the deconstructive enterprise. Presuming that all these activities do proceed from some central impulse, are we any nearer to understanding what deconstruction is or was meant to be?

It is possible that the linking element is simply—or complexly—the word itself. J. Hillis Miller has this riff on the most fascinating and suggestive of Derrida's punning neologisms. "There is no deconstruction which is not at the same time constructive, affirmative," Miller writes. "The word says this in juxtaposing 'de' and 'con.'" Miller acknowledges that the word has "misleading overtones or implications," but his list of these can't be said to spoil his fun. The word *deconstruction,* he writes, "suggests something a bit too external, a bit too masterful and muscular. It suggests the demolition of the helpless text with tools which are other than and stronger than what is demolished. The word 'deconstruction' suggests that such criticism is an activity turning something unified back to detached fragments or parts. It suggests the image of a child taking apart his father's watch, reducing it back to useless parts, beyond any reconstitution." And here Miller, excited by his metaphors, seems to belie the idea that these "implications" are "misleading" after all. "A deconstructionist is not a parasite but a parricide," Miller writes, relishing his words. "He is a bad son demolishing beyond hope of repair the machine of Western metaphysics."

To the skeptical layman, as suspicious of jargon as the deconstructionist is suspicious of Western metaphysics, the sound of *deconstruction* suggests another possibility. Mightn't it be a *con* game concealing a *destructive* intent? An aspiring theorist would emphasize the pun with arch parentheses—*de(con)struction*—before rejecting it in favor of a more sophisticated example of parenthetical cleverness. Deconstruction is an *end-of-the-wor(l)d theory*. As a method of analysis, it seems invariably to entail a meditation on the ends of words—*end* in the combined senses of conclusion, aim, completion, and demise. There is an air of last things, a brooding sense of impending annihilation, about so much deconstructive activity, in so many of its guises; it is not merely postmodernist but preapocalyptic. It is a catastrophe theory inasmuch as it proceeds from the perception of an extreme linguistic instability that undermines the coherence of any statement—a breakdown in our collective confidence in the power of words to communicate ideas and represent experience. It announces or implies that a rupture has occurred, an irreparable break with the past, and that nothing can ever be the same again.

Deconstruction likes putting things in question—things like cause and effect, right and wrong, the idea that a text expresses a writer's intention rather than somebody else's hidden agenda, that individuals are agents of volition, or that there is an objective reality to which interpretations may be more or less faithful. Deconstruction would wipe the slate clean; it insists not that everything has been said but that nothing can be said—that words have reached their tautological ends. Surely no previous form of literary analysis paid so much attention to grammar and rhetoric—or devoted so much energy to showing that the grammar and the rhetoric of a given piece of writing can pull it in opposite directions. The logical outcome of such an analysis is that it confronts us with, in Miller's phrase, "the abyss of 'annihilation.'" Less sanguine observers call it nihilism.

An end-of-the-wor(l)d theory. The parenthesis in *wor(l)d* is meant to accomplish several things. It implies not only that *word* and *world* are reversible terms but that the relation of one to the other is . . . upside down. The word doesn't reflect or represent the world; the word contains the world, and not the other way around. Therefore, texts are self-referential—they refer only to themselves, not to anything outside themselves. There is no such thing as the real world; it is a text, subject to misreading, a "problematized" text that invariably resolves itself into an *aporia,* a terminal impasse. The writer, the reader, and the larger community are blotted out at a stroke, and all that's left is a succession of misleading signs, a parade of words beyond the power of humanity to control them. It is a paradox in keeping with the paradoxical sound of its name that deconstruction declares "logocentrism" the enemy. For deconstruction itself is centered on the relentless study of the *logos*—the Greek term for word, speech, discourse, and thought, but also, in *The Gospel According to St. John,* the word made flesh, the engendering word, reason incarnate, the rational principle presumed to exist in the universe.

CHAPTER 2

CRAZY ABOUT

DECONSTRUCTION

Were I not so frequently associated with this
adventure of deconstruction, I would risk,
with a smile, the following hypothesis: America *is* deconstruction.

—*Jacques Derrida*, MÉMOIRES: FOR PAUL DE MAN

Is the study of the humanities—that cornerstone of a liberal education—in trouble? Is the academic treatment of literature, art, and
culture in the broad sense, failing our students? It is easy enough to
find defenders of the status quo among the tenured beneficiaries of the
system. But the signs of malaise are everywhere. The enrollments are
down; the students have gone elsewhere. Jeremiads bewailing this or
that academic fashion are widely popular. Bleakly funny anecdotes of
ignorance circulate around dinner tables ("Asked to read the passage
aloud, the student stumbled over the unfamiliar Roman numerals, then
tentatively pronounced 'the battles of World War Eleven' "). The
fault can't lie entirely with the faculty. It may be that the collegiate
ignoramus who figures in such jokes is the product of inadequate
preparatory training; students today enter college at lower levels of
skill and achievement than did their predecessors. But surely there is
some connection between the demoralized state of the humanities and

the ferocity of the professorial debate on what the "humanities" are about and on whether "humanism" is a good thing. There is surely a connection, too, between the spread of college-level ignorance and the rise of academic theories intended not to perpetuate but to "subvert" (to use the word the theorists favor) our cultural heritage.

The defensiveness of university officials is not hard to account for, given the persistent criticisms to which they and their institutions have been subjected in recent years. Still, the terms used in defense of the status quo are often disquieting. A new species of academic bureaucrat has sprung up, invented to confute the criticisms made by Allan Bloom in *The Closing of the American Mind* and E. D. Hirsch in *Cultural Literacy*. The "executive director of university communications" at a major Ivy League institution writes a letter to the *Chronicle of Higher Education* assailing the idea of a "core" curriculum to be required of all students. He argues that a core curriculum would establish a hierarchy of knowledge and values and that such a hierarchy would be incompatible with democratic ideals. This is what he writes: "The very point of modern culture is that we will not believe a thing if its hierarchy is determined by an elite. Even this formulation is not strong enough in the contemporary world: It is not just that we don't believe in hierarchies, we *cannot* believe in them." This is an unusual perspective for a high university official to take. Does the writer mean to say that his is not an elitist institution? How does that square with the admissions department's proud boast that the school is one of the hardest in the country to get into, one of the most competitive, most prestigious, most exclusive? Then there's that other bogey word, "hierarchy"—as if the modern American university weren't the most hierarchical of structures, a stratification system by academic rank from lowly instructor to full professor, with the tenure line dividing the haves from the have nots. If there were no hierarchy, would grades be assigned? And, in the office of "university communications," would there be any need for the executive director to invoke his title? It gets curiouser and curiouser. The impulse to denigrate "hierarchy" is, or would be if it were taken to heart, profoundly anti-intellectual, since the making of a hierarchy—the subordination of some ideas to others in order of importance—is fundamental to rational inquiry. Yet "hierarchy" is almost always a pejorative term in academic discourse, and nowhere more so than at our elite universities. When the contradictions are so basic, one may reasonably conclude that the "crisis" is not the result of faulty perception, to be corrected by the resident flack, but that there is some essential confusion and self-doubt behind the ivy walls.

Certainly the crisis is acute in the field of literature. In the spring and early summer of 1989, the assiduous reader of periodicals could have come across five memorable articles examining aspects of the dilemma. Each was written by a critic of high standing. Robert Hughes in the *New York Review of Books* excoriated the "apocalyptic hype" that is the hallmark of fashionable critical theory. "To write straightforward prose, lucid and open to comprehension, using common language, is to lose face," Hughes wrote. "You do not make your mark unless you add something to the lake of jargon whose waters (bottled for export to the States) well up between Nanterre and the Sorbonne and to whose marshy verge the bleating flocks of poststructuralists go each night to drink." Frank Kermode in the Australian magazine *Scripsi* observed matter-of-factly that "there is an ever-increasing supply of books classified as literary criticism which few people interested in literature, and not even all professionals, can read." Irving Howe in the *New Republic* lamented the passing of "the common reader"—"almost as if that figure has been banished, at least in the academic literary world, as an irritant or intruder, the kind of obsolete person who still enjoys stories as stories and still supposes that characters bear some resemblance to human beings." In the *Hudson Review,* Clara Claiborne Park added the author to the list of figures made obsolete in the new academic order. Deconstructionists speak not of Shakespeare but of "Shakespeare"—the ritual use of quotation marks is meant to suggest the papier-mâché status of the designated author. If authors are reduced to the level of fictional characters, Park declared, that is not only "an intellectual heresy." It is "a concept that devalues human personhood and human pain." Finally, again in the *New Republic,* Tzvetan Todorov deplored the "dogmatic skepticism" he finds in the academy—the attitude that "there is no such thing as truth or objectivity." Todorov dramatized the danger by recalling that in George Orwell's *1984* Big Brother crushes the idea that reality is "something objective, external, existing in its own right." Through the agency of some ingenious torturing devices, Big Brother—that apotheosis of dogmatic skepticism—can prove that "reality is not external.

Reality exists in the human mind, and nowhere else." The editors of the *New Republic,* who set store by their catchy headlines, ran Todorov's piece under the title "Crimes Against Humanities."

No one is quite immune to the tendency to idealize the past, locating in some remote decade a mythical golden age of enlightened "common readers" and engaging literary critics. Yet there does seem to be something unique about the malaise affecting literary studies today. We are familiar with the concept of "cultural literacy" and the alarming evidence of ubiquitous student ignorance; we have heard the one about the sophomore who thinks that Toronto is in Italy, that Charles Darwin "invented" electricity, that the Great Gatsby was an underwater escape artist, and that Socrates was an American Indian chieftain. Reports from the academic literary front suggest that a more fundamental sense of literacy is also at stake—a decline in the general ability to read and to write. "Our students can't read, and we are failing to teach them," warns the judicious Denis Donoghue, a man not given to false alarms. "The ability to read, in the sense of construing or interpreting or following the play of the words in a poem or a novel, is now so rare as to constitute an abnormality." While the crisis cannot be attributed exclusively or even primarily to university English departments, it seems safe to say that the institutions of literary criticism have not been part of the solution.

Four decades ago, the poet Randall Jarrell could see the writing on the wall. Something odd was happening to the study of literature. Critics had begun to compete with poets and fiction writers; literature, little valued in the culture at large, would—if the trend were left unchecked—be endangered in the very institutions established for its sake. "People still read, still write—and well," Jarrell wrote, "but for many of them it is the act of criticism which has become the representative or Archetypal act of the intellectual." It's an irony Jarrell would have ruefully appreciated that posterity seems to have judged him a great critic and a merely good poet. He invested more of his heart and mind in his poetry than in the vivacious critical essays he wrote about the poets that he loved. Yet he understood that "the age of criticism" had arrived—and his own gifts as a poet, impressive though these were, paled beside the impassioned and pungent prose with which he surveyed his literary landscape. "The Age of Criticism," perhaps his most famous essay, seems in retrospect to have the flavor of a prophecy:

it is descriptive of the most extreme tendencies of Jarrell's time and uncannily predictive of the commonplaces of ours.

Too much ingenuity was going into critical essays, and not enough into stories and poems, Jarrell complained in "The Age of Criticism." So much of what passed for criticism "might just as well have been written by a syndicate of encyclopedias for an audience of International Business Machines." Who could want to read, who could hope to learn from, such "astonishingly graceless, joyless, humorless, long-winded, niggling, blinkered, methodical, self-important, cliché-ridden, prestige-obsessed, almost-autonomous criticism"? Yet criticism, pursued as an end in itself, had become the literary intellectual's archetypal act. It could no longer be taken for granted that criticism is "necessarily secondary to the works of art it's about"—it was, in fact, no longer self-evident that criticism had to be "about" anything. The nature of criticism itself had been distorted, obliging Jarrell to state his first principles: "Criticism *does* exist, doesn't it, for the sake of the plays and stories and poems it criticizes? Much of this criticism does not." Criticism was trying, it seemed, to supplant art and literature. Mindful of the greater glory attached to the sciences, some critics wanted to give their work the veneer of a chemical analysis. Pseudoscientific jargon was routine, and more care went into the development of a "method" than into anything that might make us better readers. It will soon reach the point, Jarrell predicted, at which "the most obviously absurd theory—if it is maintained intensively, exhaustively, and professionally—will do the theorist no harm in the eyes of his colleagues."

The specter Jarrell feared has long since materialized. The age of criticism gave way to the age of theory at roughly the same time that Vietnam made *postwar* obsolete as an adjective for the contemporary world. You can date the onset of the change to 1966 and a now-legendary academic conference held at the Johns Hopkins University. At the conference, which was meant to herald the arrival of structuralism, Jacques Derrida subversively declared that structuralism was finished—and *post*structuralism was born. The following year Derrida published three of his most formidable theoretical studies of writing, or *écriture,* aiming to unmask the assumptions of Western metaphysics. In May 1968—with Paris in a state of revolutionary uproar—Derrida was in New York declaring humanism the enemy in a paper entitled "The Ends of Man." At the same time, and with a much wider audience, Roland Barthes was making radical pronouncements about literature and the orgasmic "pleasure of the text." Vanguard English professors began to quote in their lectures from Barthes, Derrida, Michel Foucault, and other "revolutionary" French theorists.

On a grass-roots level, the domestic political upheavals of 1968 gave theory an added impetus in the United States. The turmoil at the Democratic National Convention in Chicago was repeated—on a modest scale and without the bloodshed—at the annual convention of the Modern Language Association, which took place in New York City that December. At the Americana Hotel, which served as the convention's headquarters, three activists—a professor and two graduate students—were arrested after a scuffle with hotel guards. The guards had tried to tear down a poster on which the words of William Blake appeared as a call to action: "The tigers of wrath are wiser than the horses of instruction." The incident sparked a mini-rebellion at the MLA convention, and it had a lasting symbolic significance. The war in Vietnam was radicalizing the profession. And what in literary studies was more radical than critical theory?

In the ensuing decade, the American lit-crit profession slowly but steadily shed its tweedy English image in favor of foppish French fashions. The result in time was a transformation of the very nature of literary studies. Thenceforth the study of literature could be primarily theoretical in outlook. Theory would reign where practical criticism once held sway. Practical criticism—the term coined by the British critic I. A. Richards in the 1920s—had been host to a great many different tendencies, but all of them involved the interpretation of a work, a novel or a play or a poem. Critical theory, the new king of the academic hill, seemed to issue a royal decree sending the work of literature into exile. There were always honorable exceptions, critics whose involvement with theory didn't preclude an engagement with specific authors and texts. But many professors were swept up in the intoxicating notion that criticism could be *autotelic:* it needed no object of study outside of itself. It could ignore literary works; it could treat them as specimens with no inherent value, symptoms of a syndrome rather than unique works of art; or it could use them as convenient points of departure for fanciful "interpretations" that bespoke the critic's ingenuity and were their own excuse for being. The particularity of the work in question was lost in any case. Criticism was no longer, properly speaking, criticism at all but *écriture,* a species of writing; it could revel in its liberated state, an autonomous entity, needing no subject to validate it. With the zeal of Nietzsche announcing the death of God a century ago, certain French critics proclaimed the death of the author; with the enthusiasm of a stripper determined to take everything off, a British neo-Marxist pronounced the death of literature; and more "graceless, joyless, humorless, long-winded, niggling, blinkered, methodical, self-important, cliché-ridden, prestige-obsessed" prose gushed out than ever before—with the difference that much of it no longer concerned itself with any actual novel or poem or play.

It would be an exaggeration to say that the present age of theory repudiates what was best about the age of criticism and magnifies its most questionable features, but it wouldn't be exaggerating much. Jarrell's own essays—the contagious enthusiasm with which he praised, the dash with which he scorned—testify to the passionate engagement with literature that was common once but is now long out of fashion. Chances are, if you majored in English between 1945 and 1970 you studied literature primarily under the precepts of what was then called the "New Criticism." Developed in the 1930s, widely disseminated by Cleanth Brooks and Robert Penn Warren in their textbook anthologies *Understanding Poetry* and *Understanding Fiction,* the New Criticism taught two generations of students how to read works of literature, what terms to use in their analyses, what characteristics to value (irony, paradox, complexity, and ambiguity), what to scrutinize (the tale, not the teller), what to disregard (the intentions of the writer, the impact of the work on its readers), and which periods of English literary history were most deserving of careful study (the metaphysical poets of the seventeenth century were in, the poets of the Romantic movement were out). The New Criticism was still "new" enough to raise hackles among self-styled traditionalists as late as 1948. That year the president of the Modern Language Association launched a polemic in behalf of "the common reader" against the New Criticism's "fetish" of complexity and ambiguity. But such rear guard actions did nothing to prevent the New Criticism's conquest of the profession—and its influence on postwar literature itself. At its best—in the work of such critics as R. P. Blackmur—the New Criticism made for tremendously effective pedagogy. Though many of the New Critics were instinctively patrician in their manner and values, there was something liberating and populist about their insistence on reading poems and novels without much, if any, reference to historical scholarship or biographical research. It meant that students didn't need to have had prep-school training, nor did they need to be amateur scholars; they simply had to be good readers. At a time when the ranks of college students were swelled by the GI Bill, this method of reading promised access to a great line of literary works. To all who were willing to work for the pleasure, the New Critics rendered the fruits of an immediate encounter with some of the canonical texts of English literature.

The New Criticism did have its polemical tendency—"to urge us," as Lionel Trilling put it, "to minimize the amount of attention we give to the poet's social and personal will." But Trilling, to whom this tendency went very much against the grain, objected to the New Criticism as a doctrine, not as a set of techniques applied to the formal analysis of literary works. The methods of the New Criticism were themselves quite useful, provided only that the study of a work's formal elements be not undertaken to the exclusion of historical and biographical considerations. Trilling, who put the methods of the New Criticism to use in several notable essays, always went beyond formalism to attend to the cultural implications of a work of literature, its ideas, its intentions, its effects. For Trilling, in short, the methods developed by the New Critics were far from incompatible with "the classic defense of literary study," in his formulation: "that, from the effect which the study of literature has upon the private sentiments of the student, there results, or can be made to result, an improvement in the intelligence, and especially the intelligence as it touches the moral life."

A good many of the New Critics, being poets themselves, had their priorities straight. Their critical energies were put at the service of literature—evaluating aesthetic success, enforcing critical discriminations, illuminating difficult works and making them accessible to the student. The emphasis was on close reading, with painstaking attention to what Blackmur called "language as gesture"—the ways writers charged their words with meaning. Literary works were admired as artistic totalities: a successful poem was a "well-wrought urn" or a "verbal icon." The myrmidons of literary theory, by contrast, would like to smash that particular icon—they repudiate the notion that art can have a transcendent value just as they dismiss Trilling's moral rationale for literary studies, and they insist that criticism need not take a "secondary" place to art. When Geoffrey Hartman presses "the reader-critic's claim to parity" with the creative writer, and adds that "literary commentary may cross the line and become as demanding as literature," he is rebelling against a constraint that critics of a previous generation never questioned. Of course, there is no reason a work of criticism can't itself aspire to being a work of literature. One thinks immediately of the lucidity, complexity, and brilliance of Trilling's essays in *The Liberal Imagination* and *Beyond Culture.* The prose produced under the dispensation of advanced critical theory, however, very often has little in common with either literature or criticism. Hartman himself, in a chastened spirit, once described the critic as "an overgoer with pen-envy." The whole vogue of literary theory may be an effort to compensate for what Hartman frankly called the critic's "inferiority complex vis-a-vis art."

In at least one way the New Critics did prepare the ground for the theorists of today. For the New Critics, a work of literature could be treated as an isolated textual experience, stripped of social and historical considerations. Literary theorists, going further, disregard not only the author's stated intentions but the very concept of authorship, and in all too many cases the primary text of concern to the theorist is the one he or she is writing. Barbara Herrnstein Smith's *Contingencies of Value* begins with a brief chapter about her classroom experience teaching Shakespeare's sonnets—about the ways in which her responses to the sonnets have changed over the years. The discussion serves as a springboard for Smith's theoretical disquisition on the merits of relativism; after these few pages, she offers no other example of how specific readers make sense of specific works. What the New Critics labeled "the intentional fallacy"—the reasoning that allowed the critic to disregard the author's testimony—has evidently been taken to a logical extreme. The author is dead, and so is the old-fashioned interpreter of literature. The theorist has risen out of the ashes of both, theorizing about everything—and nothing. E. M. Forster liked to tell the story of the young man who declared one day that he was a writer. That's very well, says his aunt, but what will he write about? "My dear aunt," says the young man, peevishly, "one doesn't write *about* anything. One just writes." Substitute *theorize* for *write* and you have an inkling of what's in store for that same literary aspirant in the university today. Though the office doors of resisting professors may sport signs on them saying "Theory: Just Say No," the ambitious graduate student finds out in a hurry that theory is where the glory is.

It is commonplace wisdom among job-seekers at MLA conventions that—as one told me at a recent gathering—"if you want to make it in the criticism racket, you have to be a deconstructionist or a Marxist or a feminist. Otherwise you don't stand a chance. You're not taken seriously. You're on the fringe. It doesn't matter what you know or don't know. What counts is your theoretical approach. And that means knowing the jargon, and who's in and who's out." His companion agreed, adding ominously that "to be a white male in academia today is like being a leper in the Middle Ages." Then the two of them went off to attend a session on "The Muse of Masturbation." There would be papers on "Clitoral Imagery and Masturbation in Emily Dickinson"—something called "clitoral hermeneutics" is in—and on "Desublimating the Male Sublime: Autoerotics, Anal Erotics, and Corporeal Violence in Melville and William Burroughs." I asked another conventioneer to help me decipher "clitoral hermeneutics." I said that I could grasp the clitoral part of the equation but that the implications for hermeneutics (that is, the interpretation of texts) struck me as elusive. My informant, an affably nondoctrinaire Yale graduate, told me that a synonym for this adventure in critical methodology is "ovarian hermeneutics." It is, she said, championed by those feminists who want to "valorize" the clitoris rather than the vagina in "the binary opposition of sexual discourse." Other feminists, my guide explained, deride the concept as "pseudophallocentric," since an emphasis on the clitoris might arouse old bugbears, such as the view of the clitoris as an inadequate penis. I still wasn't sure what any of this had to do with literary criticism or the teaching profession but took it on faith that the speaker in the conference hall was making some sort of theoretical statement when she declared that Emily Dickinson's poetic style was "clitoral." Gender now amounts to a formal dimension of a work of art. Or so I gathered in the corridors of the MLA convention.

It is the age of theory in the seminar rooms of America, and deconstruction is the paradigmatic theory of the age. Upon the users of its arcane terminology it confers elite status, and a methodology that can be universally applied. Less a coherent system of beliefs than a way of thinking, deconstruction casts skeptical doubt over the very concepts of coherence and system and belief. It dazzles the initiate with riddles and conundrums, paradoxes and reversals. Its skepticism is total; in effect it says (in the words of a Firesign Theater comedy routine) "everything you know is wrong."

Deconstructionists like putting things, as they say, *sous rature* ("under erasure"). A typical ploy is to print certain words or phrases in cancelled form, with slash marks running through them, as though to include and exclude them at the same time. Words for Derrida are "signs," but what is a sign? The answer he gives in *Of Grammatology,* by way of "challenging the very form of the question," is that "the sign ~~is~~ that ill-named ~~thing~~, the only one, that escapes the instituting question of philosophy: 'what is . . . ?' " The purpose of this typographical maneuver, which Derrida derives from Heidegger, is to indicate that the cancelled words, though inadequate, are the only ones available to the writer. It's a flashy gesture, and it makes an interesting point, though it can quickly become an annoying affectation. In a larger sense, however, putting things "under erasure" suggests an intellectual program that would apply a fresh wet sponge to the blackboard of received ideas. And the logic of self-cancellation—the idea of printing words with slash marks through them—is not merely a clever bit of typographical horseplay but a metaphor for a larger enterprise: the workings of a theory that revels in extreme doubt, boasts of its own contrarian stance, asserts ideas without necessarily subscribing to them, and regards moments of self-contradiction as supernally important.

Among those deconstructionists old-fashioned enough to write about honest-to-god literary works, there is a tendency to elevate linguistic and rhetorical considerations over all others, and a considerable amount of effort expended to locate the exact place where the work in question can be shown to contradict its own power to make a meaning. Readers interested in the moral dimension of a novel or poem, or in evaluating the degree of its artistic success, or in treating the ideas and the values it promotes, can forget it. What you get with deconstruction isn't knowledge but a reflexive suspicion of all sources of knowledge—a suspicion extended to art and culture more generally. A generation ago it was the fashion to declare that narrators are unreliable—that the "I" who tells the tale of *Wuthering Heights* or *The Turn of the Screw* may not be telling us the full story. That is a useful insight; among other things it reminds us that the author is not to be confused with his or her characters. Deconstruction extends that New Critical insight to another plane, jumping from unreliable narrators to duplicitous texts, as if authors were no more trustworthy—and no more real—than the characters they create. Authors, if properly deconstructed, are fictional entities, or they are the unwitting mouthpieces for a reigning ideology. Art is mystification, and the critic's job is to demystify it. This task gives the deconstructionist a heady rush: in deconstructing a text, the critic establishes his or her power over it. It is not only possible for the critic to know more about the text than its author did; it is also possible to expose that text as a house divided against itself. The author as an authority is dead; the authority has been transferred to the critic.

Readers educated with the precepts of the "New Criticism" were taught to prize ambiguity, complexity, and irony as cardinal virtues in a work of literature. The ambiguity of a passage spoke in its favor. It was the critic's task to elucidate the ambiguity and to show how it was resolved in the unified text; the analysis enriched the reader's experience of the text by deepening its meaning. For the deconstructionists, however, texts are not simply ambiguous but indeterminate—it is impossible for the theorist to decide which of several conflicting meanings is the right one. Meaning itself evaporates; the theory of indeterminacy suggests that interpretation is a futile or self-defeating exercise. In short, where "ambiguity" was a property of the text and supported the idea of meaning, "indeterminacy" is a property of the interpretation and argues in favor of meaninglessness.

For the deconstructionists, literature illustrates the fundamental instability of language as a medium for communication. Language is like a biological system, autonomous and beyond our ability to control it. The grammar of a given statement might be at odds with its rhetoric—the *how* and the *what* of a sentence can clash—as in the familiar linguistic paradox *this sentence is false,* a statement that can be neither true nor false, for its syntax points one way and its content the other. The trick is to apply this insight to literary works and expose them in the act of self-implosion. For deconstruction, according to one school of thought, is something that literature does to itself. "Great works of literature," writes J. Hillis Miller, "have anticipated explicitly any deconstruction the critic can achieve." Accordingly, if you look hard enough at a poem by Yeats, it can be shown to say the opposite of what it appears to say: in covert ways, texts contradict themselves, and deconstructionists are more interested in what is covert, or absent, than in what is there. The deconstructive analysis of a literary work nearly always ends in a moment of terminal uncertainty—or what deconstructionists in good standing call an *aporia*. Paul de Man, America's premier practitioner of literary deconstruction, likened the predicament to getting stuck in a revolving door. It's not a very comfortable situation, but that's only part of the problem: any critical methodology that virtually guarantees the same dismal result each time, ahead of time, seems cruelly and needlessly reductive of both literature and criticism.

Deconstruction is full of paradox. An antitheological theology, it examines the fallout from *the absence of a transcendental signified*—a complicated way of saying *the death of god*—yet it shrouds itself in cabalistic mysteries and rituals as elaborate as those of a religious ceremony. One of its aims is demystification—it is determined to show that the ideals and values by which we live are not natural and inevitable but are artificial constructions, arbitrary choices that ought to have no power to command us. Yet, like a religion-substitute, deconstruction employs an arcane vocabulary seemingly designed to keep the laity in a state of permanent mystification. Putatively antidogmatic, it has become a dogma. Founded on extreme skepticism and disbelief, it attracts true believers and demands their total immersion. No skeptic ever sounded more sure of himself than did Paul de Man, and no iconoclast sounds more worshipful than does a keeper of de Man's faith.

Which brings us to one more paradox: though it staunchly bears an adversarial relation to prevailing conventions and institutions, deconstruction in America is itself an institution and a convention. The vogue of deconstruction was short-lived in France; in England it never really took hold. It was in the United States that it found its most hospitable reception and took its most extreme form. The French critic Julia Kristeva observed in 1986 that a hard-line version of deconstruction had "become a sort of monopoly" in the high echelons of American literary criticism. "In America, the so-called deconstructionists think that, because ethics and history belong to metaphysics and because metaphysics is criticized by Heidegger or his French followers, ethics and history no longer exist," said Kristeva, whose own poststructuralist credentials are impeccable. When she lectures in America, she added, "somebody in the audience always asks why I speak about ethics and history when those notions already have been deconstructed. Not even the most dogmatic French deconstructionists ask such questions."

Shortly after de Man's death in 1983, Derrida tossed out the hypothesis that "America *is* deconstruction" (or that America would be "the proper name of deconstruction in progress," if only Derrida could bring himself to believe in proper names). The United States, he declared, "is that historical space which today, in all its dimensions and through all its power plays, reveals itself as being undeniably the most sensitive, receptive, or responsive space of all to the themes and effects of deconstruction." This was a point that Derrida's angriest critics could concede. Deconstruction in the United States had very quickly gone from an antiestablishment insurgency to an entrenched institutional power. Some deconstructionists even wondered out loud whether the subversive force of their theory was arrested by the speed with which it had been assimilated in the American academy. Perhaps some of them recalled the pedagogical dilemma that Lionel Trilling described in his famous essay "On the Teaching of Modern Literature" (1961). Modern writers engage in a quarrel with the culture at large but, as Trilling pointed out, when these same writers enter the required reading lists, their impact is cushioned by the academic structure of term papers and examination questions. The "terrors and mysteries" of modern literature had left Trilling's students unmoved: "I asked them to look into the Abyss, and, both dutifully and gladly, they have looked into the Abyss, and the Abyss has greeted them with the grave courtesy of all objects of serious study, saying: 'Interesting, am I not? And *exciting,* if you consider how deep I am and what dread beasts lie at my bottom. Have it well in mind that a knowledge of me contributes materially to your being whole, or well-rounded, men.' " Trilling sought to convey to his students the characteristic ideas of modern literature at its most disturbing; what deconstruction offers is a shortcut to the abyss. Deconstruction therefore hastens the process that Trilling called "the legitimization of the subversive." Just as students in the early 1960s didn't bat an eye when asked to ponder "the alienation of modern man as exemplified by the artist," so their counterparts today may cheerfully "reverse a binary opposition"—with, perhaps, as little grasp of the force of the proposition to which they have given their reflexive assent. To mouth the jargon of deconstruction does more to establish a student's academic standing than to "dismantle" any system of thought or action.

The function of criticism, it may be argued, is not to affirm the pieties of culture and society but to challenge them. The problem with deconstruction and its offshoots is that they substitute one set of pieties for another. In the age of theory, criticism doesn't need to get things right; "all readings are misreadings" is a contemporary shibboleth. Critics therefore have the license to take what liberties they like in commenting on a book. In practice, this has led to a proliferation of "theoretical" studies—books and essays that refer primarily to theories of literature and only incidentally (if at all) to literary works themselves. It has also led to many meticulous and minute dissections of given "texts" with a view toward demonstrating some a priori axioms. Literary works are routinely reduced to their linguistic components, their rhetorical stratagems laid bare. It is considered the height of naiveté to suppose that a character in fiction—and everything, including history, is a fiction—is anything but a "sign": a cipher signifying nothing or, perhaps, a mark of economic class or sexual "difference." It is retrograde in the highest degree to imagine that Shakespeare's heroes and Jane Austen's heroines resemble actual human beings and may therefore have something to teach us about the conduct of our lives. Mimesis as a project—literature as the representation of experience—is held to be a futile anachronism.

For the hard-line deconstructionist, not only is literature self-referential; its meanings are undecidable, as "indeterminate" as the velocity and location of a moving electron. Language has an autonomous life—words acquire and discard meanings as if they had minds of their own. Any text, any system of signs, can be shown to compromise itself from within. Here, for example, is the opening of the Gettysburg Address: "Fourscore and seven years ago our fathers brought forth on this continent a new nation, conceived in liberty, and dedicated to the proposition that all men are created equal." Most of us will have no trouble construing this statement or its "intertextual" relation to the Declaration of Independence, in which the phrase "all men are created equal" also appears; Lincoln means to exalt equality as one of the nation's founding principles. A deconstructionist, however, might pause over "our fathers brought forth" and "conceived," characterizing this trope as an attempt to appropriate for the patriarchal authorities the procreative power vested in the female body. "All

...n are created equal," but the deconstructionist might point out that "men" excludes women and other "marginalized" figures and that the document therefore promotes something other than full equality. "Government of the people, by the people, and for the people," Lincoln urged, but the deconstructionist may argue—as H. L. Mencken once did—that it was actually the Confederate states that fought for self-determination. At work in such exercises is a kind of perverse imperative. The critic must expose the text as one would expose a scam or a sham, for all texts are presumed guilty, complicitous with a Western philosophical tradition that the procedures of deconstruction are designed to discredit.

My own first exposure to deconstruction occurred before I made it my business to read Derrida, de Man, and their followers in depth and detail. I got a strong dose of the stuff during a year at Cornell University, where I held a postdoctoral fellowship in 1980. Many of the brightest graduate students had embraced critical theory. They could tell you what "phallocentrism" was, and how to "reverse hierarchies," and why it was a good idea to put some words "under erasure." A sympathetic and highly intelligent doctoral candidate told me in all earnestness that "meaning is fascist." Maybe he was quoting somebody, maybe it was his own phrase—but he said it with an air of assurance that implied it was common knowledge. Calmly he explained the logic of his position. We inhabit, he said, an indeterminate universe. Everything is mediated entirely through language—the only way we can know anything is by using words. And the words of any discourse constantly shift their meaning. Everything depends on interpretation, and no interpretation is more correct than any other. The proper attitude is to regard all interpretations as equally "not true and not false." To insist that a given piece of discourse means something specific and decided is to elevate one meaning at the expense of the others. It is to uphold a hierarchy of values, and that renders one guilty of a dictatorial urge. Fascism, in short.

On another occasion, I went with a friend and fellow writer to the Temple of Zeus, a basement snack bar favored by the literature faculty at Cornell. We sat with two well-known deconstructionists. One of them, who suffered from a severe case of writer's block, said he was working "on" plagiarism—he wanted to deconstruct the "hysteria" (his word) with which colleges treat plagiarism cases. The other man explained what made plagiarism a theoretical problem—what "problematizes" it. The author, you see, is dead. And with his or her elimination, the text enters the academic equivalent of the public domain. Since it belongs not to the writer but to everyone, the logic that labels plagiarism a vice is called into question. This, too, may be cast in the terms of a political allegory. The author, controlling the means of literary production, is the fat-cat capitalist. Readers who rebel against his authority (a pun that clinches the case) are the heroic proletariat, appropriating the language factory. "Private property is theft," the professor concluded, with the air of having said something quite original.

"Maybe," replied my writer friend, "you'd feel differently about plagiarism if you were the author of books." I admired his terse precision; for my part, I think I was a little too stunned to say anything. I had just completed a four-year stint teaching at Hamilton College, which takes pride in its student honor code. At Hamilton, as at most colleges and universities, plagiarism is equated with dishonesty and irresponsibility; a student who plagiarizes a term paper has committed a grave offense. Were honor and integrity, then, to be written off as "hysteria"? Were my interlocutors really intent on undermining our cultural condemnation of plagiarism, and if so, what would the practical consequences be? Perhaps their attack on the notion of plagiarism was a merely "academic" exercise. It made me think of the eloquent final paragraph in Lionel Trilling's book *Sincerity and Authenticity,* in which Trilling observes that proponents of the doctrine of madness—the view that madness is a liberating condition—don't plan to go crazy themselves. Trilling remarks that "it is characteristic of the intellectual life of our culture that it fosters a form of assent which does not involve actual credence." To see how this applies to the deconstructionists, you need only consult the leading journals in which critical theorists duke it out. When an article critical of Jacques Derrida or J. Hillis Miller appears, these exponents of deconstruction, in violation of their own edicts about authors and texts, will not hesitate to call their critics wrong—as if they, as authors, were in sole possession of the truth, which their own texts, unlike those of the hapless authors they deconstruct, are supposed to reveal.

In the literary magazine *Scripsi,* I came across a piece of epigrammatic verse by the Australian poet Laurie Duggan, who had evidently encountered some variant of the antiplagiarism rap. Duggan's poem is entitled "Pleasures of the Text":

> The editor of a magazine
> who denied "authorship" as
> more than a function of print
> sues a parodist for libel.

Given the possibility that a sincere deconstructionist is a contradiction in terms—sincerity is, after all, one more concept that awaits dismantling—I suspect that Duggan has hit upon the right ironic tone with which to discuss the whole phenomenon. It is surely a happy alternative to the apoplectic sputtering to which deconstruction has been known to reduce many otherwise highly articulate professors.

"America is crazy about deconstruction," says a European professor in *Small World,* David Lodge's send-up of jet-setting academic conferencegoers in the age of critical theory. "Why is that?" she asks. Professor Morris Zapp of "Euphoric State" has an answer. "Well," he says, "I'm a bit of a deconstructionist myself. It's kind of exciting—the last intellectual thrill left. Like sawing through the branch you're sitting on." This is no idle figure of speech: something about deconstruction makes it seem an inevitable trope. In his book *Beyond Deconstruction,* Howard Felperin evokes the same image to describe the contradictory impulses that deconstruction both embodies and elicits. Consider, as Felperin does, the undeniable fact that so many professors perceive in deconstruction a threat to their own tasks and enterprises. And then, the paradoxical contrary: that deconstruction through the 1970s and 1980s was the only available "market opportunity" in the lit-crit biz after the golden era of the old New Criticism. Consider, too, that the resistance to deconstruction divides itself into two groups, which dislike it for apparently conflicting reasons. Felperin's comment:

> The view of deconstruction as a nihilist plot is incompatible
> with the view of it as an elitist cult. Why would the high
> priests of a religion of literature want to abolish the source
> of their status and power? Such a state of affairs would be
> akin to the mafia lobbying for the extirpation of opium-

networks in south-east Asia, or to the venerable comic routine of a man sawing off the bough on which he sits. Deconstruction cannot, within Aristotelian logic at least, be what each of its chief polemical opponents has claimed—a priestly cult and a nihilist plot—at one and the same time. Or can it?

Felperin answers his own question by remarking that "within the current system of institutional politics, deconstruction may well seem elitist and conservative in relation to marxism, while in relation to our established formalism it may seem utterly radical." But to argue this way, Felperin acknowledges, would be "to play into the hands of deconstruction," which sets store on being "contradictory, perverse, multivocal, mind-boggling"—on being, or appearing to be, suspended in metaphysical space.

David Lodge writes as a bemused satirist of academic mores; Howard Felperin, as a critic who would separate the uses from the abuses of literary theory. But the image of the saw-wielding tree-dweller is found also in the work of a leading proponent of deconstruction. Jonathan Culler celebrates the activity in his book *On Deconstruction*:

> Deconstruction's procedure is called "sawing off the branch on which one is sitting." This may be, in fact, an apt description of the activity, for though it is unusual and somewhat risky, it is manifestly something one can attempt. One can and may continue to sit on a branch while sawing it. There is no physical or moral obstacle if one is willing to risk the consequences. The question then becomes whether one will succeed in sawing it clear through, and where and how one might land. A difficult question: to answer one would need a comprehensive understanding of the entire situation—the resilience of the support, the efficacy of one's tools, the shape of the terrain—and an ability to predict accurately the consequences of one's work. If "sawing off the branch on which one is sitting," seems foolhardy to men of common sense, it is not so for Nietzsche, Freud, Heidegger, and Derrida; for they suspect that if they fall there is no "ground" to hit and that the most

clear-sighted act may be a certain reckless sawing, a calculated dismemberment or deconstruction of the great cathedral-like trees in which Man has taken shelter for millennia.

This is a remarkable passage, not least because it is offered without the leaven of humor. Unlike dadaism, Derridadaism characteristically does its mischief with an air of solemnity. And we are not certain whether to laugh uneasily in response or to mount a volunteer rescue force to save the suicidal branch-sitters when they fall. The contempt for "common sense," the praise of "reckless sawing," the desire for "a calculated dismemberment or deconstruction of the great cathedral-like trees in which Man has taken shelter for millennia" *should* make us uneasy. Yet we must remind ourselves that the daredevilry is all sleight of hand—there's no need for a safety net if there's no ground to hit. Only in the never-never land of theory, where the law of gravity may be transgressed without penalty, can such reckless procedures be recommended. *The last intellectual thrill left.* It is possible that the comedian Ernie Kovacs hit upon the perfect comment on deconstruction when, in an episode of his television show, he sawed off the branch on which he sat while delivering a monologue unrelated to the action. Kovacs remained on the branch, which remained in the air, after he finished sawing. The tree had fallen down.

How did we get to this vertiginous depiction of the critic's lot? The transformation of literary criticism into vaporous critical theory happened in stages, not all at one time, and the present "mind-boggling" dispensation was anticipated a century ago by that masterly maker of paradoxes, Oscar Wilde. In question, then as now, was "the function of criticism at the present time"—a question to which the critics of every generation feel obliged to return. Matthew Arnold stated the classic position. The function of criticism, Arnold wrote, is "to see the object as in itself it really is." Proper observation was held to be a moral imperative; you endeavored to see things clearly and to see them whole, and you expected thereby to learn "the best that is known and thought in the world." Walter Pater presented an "aesthetic" alternative to the moral instrument Arnold had proposed. Arnold had proposed disinterestedness as a criterion for critical judgment; Pater insisted that subjectivity was inevitable and should not be scorned, and he revised Arnold's dictum accordingly. "In aesthetic criticism," Pater wrote, "the first step towards seeing the object as in itself it really is, is to know one's impression as it really is, to discriminate it, to realise it distinctly." Oscar Wilde in impish delight went further. Where Pater revised Arnold, Wilde deconstructed him—he turned Arnold upside down. Arnold had assumed that, as he put it, "the critical power is of lower rank than the creative." Not so, wrote Wilde. The "highest" criticism is "more creative than creation, and the primary aim of the critic is to see the object as in itself it really is not."

There is, as it happens, a measure of truth in Wilde's paradox. All you need to do is accept his equation of art and criticism—his identification of "the critic as artist," in Wilde's phrase. For what Wilde says about criticism is valid enough as a description of the poet's way of rendering an object. The poet, by the use of metaphor, makes us see the object "as in itself it really is not." To get us to see the pears on the table, the poet may show us nudes, viols, or bottles; Wallace Stevens shows us a hut standing beneath palms and we see a pineapple. The aim of art, what's more, needn't be the representation of an object in the first place; modern art doesn't characteristically ask to be judged on the basis of its fidelity to a model. But, and this is the crux of the matter, criticism is not art. To obliterate the differences between the two is to inflate the importance of criticism while puncturing that of art—a curious ploy, and a self-defeating one, since art is still capable of wielding a significant force in human affairs while criticism is busy retreating into obscurantism and obscurity. Literature, not criticism, is and always was the really dangerous activity; the death sentence on the author of *The Satanic Verses* is only the most violent recent reminder of that. But literature has received its walking papers in the age of theory—for the deconstructionist, it exists as something to be willfully misinterpreted if not ignored altogether. If our writers today operate largely in a critical void, surely some of the blame attaches to the academic theorists whose backs are turned to books other than their own.

To take Wilde's paradox as a practical dictum for literary criticism—to make us see things as they aren't—may be the license for a visionary program. In the age of theory, however, "to see the object as in itself it really is not" sounds suspiciously like uttering "the thing which is not"—the phrase that the noble horses in *Gulliver's Travels* use to denote a lie. And indeed a deconstructive "ethics of reading"— proposed by J. Hillis Miller in his book of that title—lays heavy stress on lying as a "universal principle." "Ethicity," writes Miller with characteristic clunkiness, "is a region of human life in which lying is necessarily made into a universal principle, in the sense that ethical judgments are necessary but never verifiably true." By rhetorical fiat, Miller reduces ethical judgments to the status of lies! His logic is circular and confused: it is based on the dubious proposition that everything not "verifiably true" is a lie, and on the implicit assumption that nothing is "verifiably true." (Holden Caulfield would call this the "everything is phoney" view of life.) Miller deconstructs "ethicity" by identifying it with falsehood—by seeing it as it really is not. The gesture is perverse in a way that calls attention to itself. The man sits on the branch, sawing away, and we half-expect him to fall but he doesn't—it was only a toy saw.

CHAPTER 3

ARCHIE

DEBUNKING

Only the sign is for sale.
—*Søren Kierkegaard,* EITHER/OR *(1843)*

Back to square one: What is deconstruction? Here are seven attempts at defining it. Perhaps the overlapping elements will tell us what we want to know:

> Deconstruction is the practice, in reading, of one who refuses to be lulled into the complacency of self, into believing in the stability of reference, or in the appearance of a seamless web of meanings. It is a debunking of the delusory tokens of meaning and reference.

> . . . the term invented by Derrida in the 1960's to describe analysis showing that the major structures by which we organize our thoughts are *constructions,* not natural and inevitable.

> . . . a form of commentary that shows the connection between the stated content of a piece of writing and the rhetorical system which controls it. The connection establishes a discrepancy between the content and the rhetorical system . . .

A deconstructive reading is an attempt to show how the conspicuously foregrounded statements in a text are systematically related to discordant signifying elements that the text has thrown into its shadows or margins, an attempt both to recover what is lost and to analyze what happens when a text is read solely in function of intentionality, meaningfulness, and representativity. Deconstruction thus confers a new kind of readability on those elements in a text that readers have traditionally been trained to disregard, overcome, explain away, or edit out—contradictions, obscurities, ambiguities, incoherences, discontinuities, ellipses, interruptions, repetitions, and plays of the signifier.

. . . the dismantling of conceptual oppositions, the taking apart of hierarchical systems of thought . . .

To deconstruct a discourse is to show how it undermines the philosophy it asserts, or the hierarchical oppositions on which it relies, by identifying in the text the rhetorical operations that produce the supposed ground of argument, the key concept or premise.

A deconstruction always has for its target to reveal the existence of hidden articulations and fragmentations within assumedly monadic totalities.

Five of these definitions were culled from proponents of deconstruction; the other two from critics who dissent for different reasons. What all the definitions have in common is the sense of deconstruction as a vigilant activity born of mistrust and suspicion. Deconstruction is presented as a negating force, a "debunking" or a "dismantling," the establishment of a "discrepancy." It proceeds on the assumption that what you see is never what you get. Meaning is "delusory" and the deconstructionist refuses to be taken in. A work's "stated content" is belied by its rhetoric; the "supposed ground of argument" has the solidity of quicksand, and the marginal elements of a text subvert or deny its "conspicuously foregrounded elements." Deconstruction exposes "hidden" contradictions, shows how texts "undermine" themselves, discerns "discrepancies" and brings them to account. Everywhere it confronts "hierarchical systems" and systematically takes them apart. The "structures" of our thought are regarded as man-made, artificial, "not natural and inevitable." Our values and our ideals are *constructed,* as if out of bricks and mortar—and are therefore subject in their turn to the wrecking ball. There are no truths, only rival interpretations—*constructions* in that second sense, as when we speak of a broad or strict construction of the Constitution. It is a tenet of deconstruction that our words give us away. Language's "hidden articulations and fragmentations" may belie a speaker's intention or reveal an unspoken assumption. If that is so, surely the deconstructive fondness for *text* and *construction*—rather than *book* or *idea*—is a giveaway. A book asks to be read; an idea, to be understood—but what is there to do with a text or a construction but to unravel or deconstruct it?

To deconstruct is to debunk—this primary sense of the word survives the translation from academic discourse to more popular forms of literary journalism. The word *deconstruct* appears in two separate articles in the *New York Times Book Review* of March 11, 1990. In one case it is used in disparagement; in the other, as praise. On page thirteen, Rosellen Brown uses the word to compliment Alison Lurie's treatment of children's literature in her book *Don't Tell the Grown-Ups.* Lurie has uncovered "the neoconservative and sexist subtext of Wil Huygen's acclaimed book, *Gnomes,"* and thus debunked it. Her "deconstruction" of a "superficially benign" children's book will, Brown writes, give "valuable aid and comfort" to all but the credulous. (Brown was perhaps unaware that Lurie has also deconstructed, in a witty essay, the language of deconstruction itself.) On page sixteen, meanwhile, Gertrude Himmelfarb uses the word with a fully negative valence in the course of praising the late John Clive's *Not By Fact Alone.* The "favorable reception" that Clive's essays on history have received—the book had just won the National Book Critics Circle Award in criticism—is, writes Himmelfarb, heartening for "people who are weary of some of the new fashions in history, and weary above all of the indecent speed with which one fashion succeeds another ('deconstructs' another, in the language of the latest fashion)." For Himmelfarb, deconstruction as an academic tendency is distasteful, but the interesting and perhaps surprising thing is that the word as she uses it describes substantially the same debunking activity that Brown commends.

To deconstruct is to debunk, systematically, rigorously, ruthlessly. The point was punningly made by Paul de Man in a famous feat of deconstructive exegesis. As a literary critic, de Man operated within a narrow and patrician range—his chosen authors were Proust, Nietzsche, Rilke, Rousseau, and several others on that order of greatness—but on this one occasion he turned to a television sitcom for his text. De Man describes an episode of *All in the Family* in which Edith Bunker asks her husband whether he prefers his bowling shoes laced over or laced under. Archie Bunker answers her with an impatient question: "What's the difference?" The question is a rhetorical one; Archie means to say that he doesn't care. And so he does a slow burn when Edith, taking his question literally, proceeds to explain the difference between the two ways of tying your laces. The example affords de Man a lighthearted way to demonstrate that rhetorical questions may be taken literally—and that even simple sentences may yield opposing meanings. To Archie Bunker, "what's the difference" announces an indifference to any answer that can be given; to Edith Bunker, on the other hand, it is a simple query for information. The potential for misunderstanding and confusion is an inherent risk in our use of language—or would be, if we were all like Edith Bunker. In de Man's account we are. It may be, de Man writes, "impossible to decide by grammatical or other linguistic devices which of the two meanings (that can be entirely incompatible) prevails." This notion of undecidability is at the heart of de Man's deconstructive program.

But de Man gets more mileage than that out of Archie Bunker; he uses him to pay a punning homage to that arch-punster, Jacques Derrida. For it appears that Derrida, too, asks "What is the Difference?" This is in fact one of the central questions with which Derrida investigates language. He starts with the premise that a word gains its meaning not because of a presumed identity with an idea or a thing but because of the word's *différence* from the other words in its linguistic system. But Derrida goes further. To describe the way language works, he proposes the neologism *différance,* a combination of the French word for "difference" and that for "deferral." In French you can't hear the difference between *différence* and *différance,* but the substitution of an *a* for the second *e* is Derrida's way of indicating that the meaning of words is always and incessantly deferred, never present. In de Man's conceit, Derrida is thus "a *de-*bunker rather than a 'Bunker.' " And since *arche* is the Greek word for origin, he is "a de-bunker of the arche (or origin)"—convinced as he is that language and thought lack foundation. The doyen of *différance* is, in short, hereby dubbed "an archie De-bunker."

I propose that we take de Man at his word and call deconstruction a fancy name for "archie debunking." Doing so risks missing the point of de Man's complicated joke—or deconstructs it by emphasizing the irreverence of the gesture, whatever the writer's intention may have been. Call deconstruction the academic science of archie debunking and you have cut it down to size. The phrase suggests that beneath the inflated rhetoric, the punning, the preening, and the publicity, something fairly simple and innocuously "academic" is going on. Maybe so. But right away the questions proliferate. What about the consciously "subversive" intent of deconstruction? What is it about archie debunking that beguiles some people and mortifies others? Does it threaten to unleash the forces of nihilism? Does that make it a radical phenomenon or a reactionary one? If it has caused a revolution in several academic disciplines, will that revolution last? Perhaps, as the philosopher John Searle has written, deconstruction's "rather obvious and manifest intellectual weaknesses" make it "fairly obvious to the careful reader that the emperor has no clothes." Is deconstruction, then, merely a fad that will fade, or is it a fit of fiddling while Rome burns? Is it well understood as an arcane parlor game, or is it perhaps a form of critical terrorism? Are we speaking of a priestly cult of true believers or a professional sect of overachievers? Deconstruction has been depicted, and reviled, in terms so various that they can't all be true. Or can they? The conflicting responses to deconstruction are in keeping with the spirit of contradiction it prizes—the spirit of contradiction implied in the name itself. As if to illustrate Derrida's theory of language, *deconstruction* has no essence; it means what you want it to mean—the virtue of the empty pot is that you can fill it with the liquid of your choice. What all the responses to deconstruction have in common is their emotional intensity; it is clearly not a phenomenon about which one can feel indifferent.

As befits an age of theory, it seems that everyone, with conscious or unconscious irony, has a pet theory to account for the rise of literary theory in general and deconstruction in particular. There is, for example, the Zeitgeist theory. According to this argument, deconstruction reflects some of the primary intellectual currents and anxieties of the age. "Both deconstructive literature and deconstructive criticism flourish," M. H. Abrams has remarked, "because they appeal to the temper of the times—a dangerous temper, one that worries me—in which we tend to be much more hospitable to negative modes of thinking and writing than to positive ones." Deconstruction capitalizes on the crisis of authority and the crisis of faith; it proposes a radical skepticism that suits the temper of a generation that came of age amid credibility gaps, hype campaigns, and spin doctors. The linguistic assumptions of deconstruction must rank high on any Zeitgeist checklist: that "the medium is the message" (McLuhan), that "the limits of my language mean the limits of my world" (Wittgenstein), that there can be no "unmediated" vision or idea, and that language constantly subverts itself. In an age of disbelief, deconstruction gives its adherents a program to enact rather than a body of principles to affirm. And in proposing a universal conspiracy in the history of Western metaphysics—a conspiracy that leaves nothing untainted—deconstruction has a further advantage. It promises an answer to everything. It is an ideology in the sense that Hannah Arendt gave to the term: an ism that "to the satisfaction of [its] adherents can explain everything and every occurrence by deducing it from a single premise." For Arendt, an ideology "claims to possess either the key to history, or the solution for all 'riddles of the universe,' or the intimate knowledge of the hidden universal laws which are supposed to rule nature and man." The description applies to the deconstructionists, who conduct their textual battles with the zeal of ideologues and whose "solution for all 'riddles of the universe' " is to reduce them to linguistic predicaments.

Then there is the professionalism theory: the idea that deconstruction exemplifies cult-formation as a method for prevailing in a profession noted for the bickering and the bitterness surrounding every last tenure decision. Whatever else it is, deconstruction is a movement, a network of like-minded professors who fiercely promote one another's works and use their institutional power to further the cause. For all their professed distrust of authority, deconstructionists show no reluctance to exercise the prerogatives of authority. Mastery of the jargon certifies the budding theorist's professional standing; initiates are rewarded with teaching appointments and prestigious postdoctoral fellowships. Deconstruction makes possible, moreover, a risk-free form of subversiveness. It gives its adepts a way to look daring while playing it safe—to mouth the rhetoric of the rebel while climbing up the tenure ladder to pluck the fruits of the system whose legitimacy they claim to question. The fictional Professor Zapp in David Lodge's *Small*

World explains the sense of *professionalism* at issue here. At an academic conference, Zapp has just delivered a paper on "Textuality as Strip-tease." There was no "point" to it, Zapp acknowledges, "if by point you mean the hope of arriving at some certain truth." And the point of the enterprise as a whole? It is, says Zapp, simply "to uphold the institution of academic literary studies. We maintain our position in society by publicly performing a certain ritual, just like any other group of workers in the realm of discourse—lawyers, politicians, journalists. And as it looks as if we have done our duty for today, shall we all adjourn for a drink?"

One often-heard explanation for deconstruction's institutional success is that its proponents are dogmatists while its opponents are pluralists who are willing to accommodate rival positions—and that in any battle between dogmatists and pluralists, the former have a distinct advantage. Some veterans of behind-the-scenes academic politics complain that too many humanists felt they could ignore the new creed rather than confront it directly, thus ceding the intellectual initiative to deconstruction's advocates, quick to sense an opening. But these explanations underestimate the resistance to deconstruction, the sustained efforts of its foes to refute it in print or on the academic conference circuit. While some antideconstructionists were intellectually overmatched, others brought to the task resources of mind and scholarship that equaled those of their opponents. M. H. Abrams, always a courtly critic, found complimentary things to say about Derrida in *Partisan Review* in 1979. But Abrams did not hesitate to characterize Derrida's theory as "suicidal" on the grounds that "his subversive process destroys the possibility that a reader can interpret correctly either the expression of his theory or the textual interpretations to which it is applied." In 1982, Frederick Crews warned readers of *Commentary* that "indeterminism as a movement bears implications that are both irrationalist and undemocratic." Walter Jackson Bate, the most formidable presence on the Harvard literature faculty, raised his voice in *Harvard* magazine that year. Deconstructionism, wrote Bate, involves "a nihilistic view of literature, of human communication, and of life itself." In 1986 Rene Wellek spoke out. Wellek had been the co-author of *Theory of Literature* (1948), a volume that helped pave the way for the vogue of literary theory. Now, upon the completion of his six-volume *History of Modern Criticism,* Wellek published an admonishing postscript. "Recent varieties of skepticism" could, he wrote, "lead literally not only to the 'deconstruction' but to the destruction of all literary criticism and scholarship." It is possible, of course, that the protests of Messrs. Abrams, Bate, Crews, and Wellek had the opposite effect from the one they intended. The protests were implicitly or overtly defenses of traditionalism, and an appeal to tradition may not play all that well with students, who are temperamentally inclined to align themselves with the forces of change, the new, the avant-garde. The point, however, is to dash the glib supposition that deconstruction owed its academic ascent to an absence of determined resistance. If anything, the critics of deconstruction were quite aggressive in pressing their case, perhaps sensing—as Robert Alter did—the "martial implications" of deconstructionist discourse, with its "warring forces of signification" and its ambition to prevail over "the resistance" to theory.

A likelier explanation for the rise of deconstruction dwells less on the weakness of the old guard and more on the zeal of the young Turks. The gurus of deconstruction have been remarkably successful at recruiting disciples and turning them into promulgators of the faith. "The deconstructionists are absolutely ruthless behind the scenes," a hard-nosed combatant at Cornell told me. "They are essentially fanatics. If you don't conform to their orthodoxy, there's something wrong with you. As in an inquisition, you are measured by your allegiance— you're found religious or you're burned." In the course of researching this book, I was to hear this same analogy, or variants on it, from teachers at so many other universities that it was hard to escape the sense of its ubiquity. One literature professor who has taught at Yale since deconstruction's halcyon days there observed in 1982 that deconstruction had become "a church" replete with hierophants and disciples. Changing his metaphor he added that "it has, in effect, put a laser beam in the hand of a spastic"—avid disciples were using the procedures and catchwords of deconstruction with mindless abandon. "Like any dogma, it relieves people of the burden of having to think for themselves. And that has become a paradigm for American university teaching: you don't have to know anything provided that you know the method."

Several professors active in the resistance to deconstruction consider the theory's novelty to be an important source of its appeal. By the 1970s the New Criticism had run its course; many of its chief practitioners had died or reached retirement age. At the same time, the tremendous expansion of universities in the 1960s had—in line with the demographics of the baby boom—given way to stagflation. Jobs and grants were suddenly scarce. "The sense that 'everything has been done' turns to panic as opportunities for appointment and promotion disappear," notes Frederick Crews. "Such a climate is ideally suited to nurturing a mania for theories, however poorly supported, that promise to multiply the number of allowable remarks one can make about literature." To this craving for novelty, add the Oedipal subtext of deconstruction: the rise of the theory supports the notion that every generation defines itself in opposition to the one before it, in metaphorical acts of parricide. "The real impetus of Deconstruction in America," in Robert Alter's opinion, "is a rebellion against authority in the strictly delimited sense of academic institution and critical tradition."

A popular sociological theory emphasizes deconstruction's nose-thumbing attitude, its scorn for institutions, its suspicion of received wisdom, its antagonism toward hierarchical orders—all of which may be seen to commend it to legatees of the turbulent 1960s. The theory has it that deconstruction is the academic revenge of the Sixties' generation, a sublimation of the radical impulses of that era into something resembling a "textual" revolution. The British Marxist Terry Eagleton states the case. "Post-structuralism was a product of that blend of euphoria and disillusionment, liberation and dissipation, carnival and catastrophe, which was 1968," Eagleton writes. "Unable to break the structures of state power, post-structuralism found it possible instead to subvert the structures of language. Nobody, at least, was likely to beat you over the head for doing so." The critic Morris Dickstein, who has written extensively on the cultural impact of the 1960s, picks up the theme. "As everyone knows," he writes, "it was the failure of the revolutions of 1968 that provided much of the impetus as well as the footsoldiers for the explosion of literary theory in the 1970s. Now the strategies of confrontation that had failed in the streets succeeded on the page. In the first, heady phase of Derridean deconstruction, every form of critical language was arraigned for its self-deceptions, its internal contradictions, its residue of dubious metaphysical assumptions."

There is something to be said for this analysis, though the phrase "as everyone knows" is Dickstein's sly way of acknowledging that the logic here may be facile. It looks right at first glance but not so right when you start testing it out. It would be incorrect, for example, to suppose that the acolytes of deconstruction were all of them militant radicals in the late 1960s. There *is* a relation between "1968" and advanced critical theory, but it is more ambiguous than straight cause and effect. David Bromwich pinpoints exactly what is glib in the reasoning "that what is happening now is the inward migration, on campus, of the leaders and followers of the student revolt." The difference is the difference between politics and academic discourse: "If I say in a lecture, 'The figuration of Prospero's last speech in *The Tempest* betrays a slippage from subversion to containment which the occlusive presence of Caliban tends to undermine,' I may, in some fantastic dialogue of the mind, be singing the equivalent of a Sandinista Wedding March, but what it means to you practically is, 'Look at a slightly different list of secondary works this time, and don't turn in the paper late.' " Yet Bromwich also locates the particle of truth that justifies the linkage between the generation of 1968 and what Bromwich calls "the institutional radicals" of today. "A single article of faith from the sixties has passed unchallenged into the eighties—namely, the idea that the university is a microcosm of society." That article of faith, in 1968, translated into campus demonstrations whose real target was not the university administration but the national government. In the age of theory, on the other hand, the institutional radicals can pursue their projects with, in Bromwich's words, "only the usual iconoclasm."

Though the deconstructionists would like to think of themselves as in cahoots with leftist literary critics, the latter regard the former with grave mistrust. It is possible to regard deconstruction as a species of harmless pseudoradicalism, for its invincible skepticism blunts its force as an instrument of dissent. Deconstruction, in Terry Eagleton's words, "is mischievously radical in respect of everyone else's opinions, able to unmask the most solemn declarations as mere dishevelled plays of signs, while utterly conservative in every other way. Since it commits you to affirming nothing, it is as injurious as blank ammunition." This is, perhaps, precisely the sort of radicalism that can flourish in a Yuppie climate. So Wolfgang Holdheim argues. Holdheim, who chaired Cornell's department of comparative literature for many years, characterizes deconstruction as an episode in the history of "the youth culture" rather than in the history of ideas. In Holdheim's analysis, deconstruction enables its adherents to retain some vestige of "Storm and Stress" radicalism while, in the pursuit of tenure, they obey the upwardly mobile imperatives of the Republican Era. Holdheim makes a convincing case. The twentieth century began "with the movement of the Wandervögel in Germany, and the youth culture of the 1960s and 1970s was a rather recent American version of the trend," he writes. The Vietnam war was the radicalizing event for the generation that came of age in the 1960s and early 1970s. The withdrawal of American troops from Asia coincided with a general belt-tightening in academic departments of the humanities, and in short order, the tendency toward political rebellion was replaced by its antithesis, the pyramid-climbing of Yuppieism. "But in the academy, with its 'radical' tradition, such a complete change of orientation cannot always be openly acknowledged, not even to oneself. What could be the answer to this dilemma? Meta-radicality, transcendent to the point of evaporation. The 'syndrome' furnishes this; it is the fitting ideology for the period when the academic youth culture is turning from revolt to careerism without clearly distinguishing the two."

To the post-Vietnam generation, new theories that purported to stand for "liberation" were bound to have an impact. At the MLA convention in 1976, Wayne Booth, whose book *The Rhetoric of Fiction* influenced a generation of literary scholars, shrewdly noted that "every version of the newer criticisms has promised some kind of liberation, whether from bourgeois political control or from the critical claims of the past or both." Booth gave several examples. Roland Barthes offered, in Booth's words, "freedom from boredom." Fidelity to the text's intentions would result in sterile repetition, whereas Barthes's recommended method of reading promised "novelty and creativity." Stanley Fish, the Duke University professor who is widely believed to be the model for David Lodge's Professor Zapp, made the ultimate statement of this position (which he would later retract). Fish asserted that critical theory "relieves me of the obligation to be right . . . and demands only that I be interesting": literary criticism as a personal liberation front.

It remains unclear whether and in what sense deconstruction really is as revolutionary as it claims to be. Critics of the theory will tell you that many of its most "original" insights were formulated decades ago. John Ellis in his book *Against Deconstruction* alternates between contesting deconstructive notions and proving that the valid parts of the theory could be gleaned—without the excess doctrinal baggage—in the works of linguists and philosophers who preceded Derrida by many years. In fact, Ellis contends, deconstruction is revolutionary not in substance but only by bland, baseless assertion. If a celebrity is someone who is famous for being famous, deconstruction "is revolutionary in being revolutionary; it is antitraditional in being antitraditional." That deconstruction fancies itself as revolutionary is abundantly clear; its advocates are ever-anxious to portray themselves as in the forefront of revolutionary change. When a leading deconstructionist proposes parallels between his practice and nihilism, we may wonder whether to consider this a display of shock-tactic exhibitionism rather than a heartfelt attempt at being "subversive." Is it merely the speaker's lack of true seriousness that we deplore—or is that lack of seriousness, that penchant for articulating "subversive" ideas without any real attachment to them, irresponsible in a larger sense? It is, in any case, easy to see why people who aren't enchanted by such gestures tend to regard deconstruction with unconcealed alarm.

In at least one of its manifestations, deconstruction's continuity with the student radicalism of the 1960s is apparent. In 1985, Duncan Kennedy of the Harvard Law School referred to the Critical Legal Studies movement as "a ragtag band of leftover 60's people and young people with nostalgia for the events of 15 years ago." Ken Emerson in the *New York Times Magazine* describes Kennedy himself as "the spitting image of a grad student circa 1968," down to his corduroy jacket and black jeans. Kennedy, who would like to turn Harvard Law School into a "counterhegemonic enclave," has advocated several measures that are radical by any standard—such as a lottery system for admission to the school and either the elimination of tenure or the granting of it to all professors. In Kennedy's words, "the ideology of the legal hierarchy is no more than a specialized application of the general meritocratic ideology of American society." One senses in such utterances the spirit of the rebellious 1960s; one hears in them the distinctive diction of deconstruction.

Of the various metaphors in currency for deconstruction, surely the most disturbing is "critical terrorism." The deconstructionists have done little to discourage the use of this handle, and it may be that they like it, relishing the tough-hombre image that the phrase conveys. The admittedly hyperbolic analogy between deconstructionists and terrorists appears to be based on several considerations besides the casual fact that both are features of the contemporary Zeitgeist. Both are, by temperament or by instinct, extremist. Deconstructionists have a reputation for ruthlessness and intransigence in pursuit of their agenda, when serving on faculty hiring committees and the like. The nearest thing in fiction to the deconstructive personality is the anarchistic professor in Joseph Conrad's *The Secret Agent:* a man of "pedantic fanaticism," who always carries a bomb with him and hopes to invent a "perfect detonator." Conrad's professor wants to destroy "public faith in legality." Critical terrorists—including but not limited to those associated with Critical Legal Studies—use different methods to reach the same end. They would like to blow up—metaphorically, of course—the legitimacy of institutions and traditions, canons of taste and judgment, and received values of any kind. And like terrorists, deconstructionists steel themselves to toss their bombs without regard for the comfort of bystanders—in this case, the authors and readers of literature.

Ironists may say that the danger is overrated—that the only people truly terrorized by deconstruction are other professors. Michel Foucault once described Jacques Derrida's prose style as an effort at "obscurantist terrorism." The idea is that the style is so obscure that it's hard to know what the author is trying to say, and this allows the *savant* to heap contempt on his critics by saying they have failed to understand him. There is no denying that the obfuscating jargon of deconstruction has proved useful for intimidating befuddled departmental foes. But to conclude that deconstruction is harmless except in the limited sphere of academic politics and debate is to overlook a simple but important consideration: that ideas, even specious ideas, have consequences, for good or ill, and that the academic arena is not ipso facto an insignificant one. Perhaps we should question the ease with which we habitually link the words *harmless* and *academic*—as if to say that the fictional Professor Zapp is right and there is no point in looking to academic discourse for something serious and substantial.

The ideas that deconstructionists articulate—with fervor if not necessarily with seriousness in the old-fashioned sense—do provide grounds for the terrorist analogy. There is, for one thing, the relentlessly nihilistic drive of deconstruction. It asks how we can know anything and answers that we can't—nothing can be known. And there is its real or metaphorical affinity with the projects of destruction and demolition, decentering and demystifying; Robert Alter wryly notes the critical theorist's affection for the *de-* prefix "with its presumably salutary suggestion of taking things apart." It may be argued that any act of analytical intelligence entails taking something apart. Perhaps. But deconstruction ups the ante. If we are to take the deconstructionists at their word, the task of taking texts apart is part and parcel of a more ambitious and more threatening endeavor: the dismantling of "the metaphysics of presence"—or what you and I would call Western thought.

As a critical methodology, deconstruction places its emphasis on tearing down a concept or a clause—on "putting it in question" or "problematizing" it, to use the approved jargon—without proposing anything new to take its place. Deconstruction's "thrust," writes the critic Sven Birkerts, "is to demolish the deeply-rooted conceptions of the Enlightenment, presumably so that the culture can evolve in new directions. Deconstruction itself offers no signposts for this evolution, only a method of taking things apart. In this, Deconstructionists are like members of a terrorist sect." Equally "terrorizing" is the deconstructive shift of attention from the content of a person's ideas to his or her hidden motives; you don't read a book, or even have a dialogue with it. You *interrogate* it. A book subjected to deconstruction is a structure waiting to be dismantled; an idea subjected to deconstruction is an idea whose legitimacy is cast in doubt, terminally. Thus Luc Ferry and Alain Renaut, in their survey of "The Philosophies of '68" in France, describe the workings of "the deconstructive will" with its underlying assumption that "all conscious discourse is really just a symptom that hides a deeper social or individual unconscious." If one follows this line, "it will be less important to pay attention to *what* someone says than to determine *who* he is, in order to know what he is really saying. One can imagine what strange idea of intellectual debate flows from this presupposition. The content of speech will be replaced by the person speaking and the determination of 'where he's coming from.' Once the 'real motives,' unacknowledged and unacknowledgeable by the speaker, have been uncovered, the genealogy then threatens to legitimize a disturbing brand of intellectual terrorism." Ferry and Renaut assert with some wonderment that such systematic practices managed to reduce French philosophy "to the point that it became blind to what can be called only its own idiocy."

One of the curious things about the resistance to deconstruction in the United States is that it unites critics from both ends of the political spectrum. Leftists, who regard literature and criticism as potential agents for social change, contend that the purer forms of deconstruction promote quiescence, not activism. What troubles them about deconstruction is not its putatively terroristic agenda but its penchant for heading off any discussion at the impasse. On this view, deconstruction leads not to action but to paralysis. It seems to entail a recoil from the world of material reality; it denies the relevance of history and biography. To the precise extent that deconstruction "brackets off" the social world—insisting that matters of life and death are to be regarded as linguistic predicaments—the tendency can be seen as conservative, ratifying the existing social order and discouraging political action. Deconstruction is regarded askance, moreover, as an elitist phenomenon. The deconstructors of "hegemony" are observed to be working toward their own hegemony, scorning their rivals as retrograde, reactionary, or even anti-intellectual. One Marxist critic discerned the trappings of a "hermeneutical mafia" at Yale. Presumably the dons of deconstruction go about their business by making people offers they cannot understand.

None of this brings any comfort to literary traditionalists, cultural conservatives, or others who disavow a left-wing political agenda. Such critics detect in deconstruction a radical enough impulse: the impulse to undermine institutions and ideas by asserting that they undermine themselves. Many observers think they detect the procedures and principles of deconstruction in the programmatic assault now in progress against the venerable idea of the canon—the notion that there exists a body of acknowledged masterworks with which the educated reader should become familiar. Allan Bloom is hardly alone in associating the techniques of deconstruction with the tendency to turn the great books into canon-fodder. The poet and critic Daniel Hoffman says he is moved to defend the novels of William Faulkner against "the rage to deconstruct canonical works, sweeping through academe like a self-replicating virus in a computerized information system." Nor is the fallout limited to the teaching of literature. In *Works and Lives,* Clifford Geertz cites "deconstructive attacks on canonical works" as evidence of the "pervasive nervousness" at hand in the study of anthropology. Geertz chose his words carefully. If the impact of deconstruction on a field of knowledge may be likened to that of a nervous breakdown, that seems rather the point of the exercise.

There is, in the practice as well as the theory of deconstruction, an urge to tear down boundaries—the boundaries, for example, separating one academic discipline from another. The application of deconstructive strategies to disciplines remote from literary criticism is not an accidental fact. For theorists weaned on the ideas and methods of Jacques Derrida, anything from a comic strip to the Pledge of Allegiance qualifies as a text, and any text is fair game for a deconstructive analysis. It is, Derrideans maintain, a vulgar error to observe a distinction between a literary text and any other kind—or between the text and the world. The world *is* a text and may be read, or deconstructed, as such. It becomes possible, thanks to this logic, to widen the scope of critical inquiry. That is far from a bad thing and not altogether a new thing. There is every reason to keep bringing intelligence to bear on science fiction and detective novels, Hollywood movies, and even TV commercials, which at the very least tell us things about ourselves that we ought to know, though knowing them might make us wince. A seminar devoted to "the deconstruction of everyday life"—in which the objects under scrutiny are designer jeans, radio jingles, tabloid journalism, campaign slogans, and contemporary supermarket design—becomes a real possibility and may well have its uses, sociological if not aesthetic. One deconstructionist may study tourism, the significance of souvenirs, the tourist's anxiety to avoid appearing like a tourist, and so forth; a colleague may devote himself to the semiotic analysis of cigarette smoking.

In chapter five of this book, I chart out some broad parallels between postmodernism in art and poststructuralism in academic thought. Yet I strongly resist the idea that approval of the former implies assent to the latter. One is in fact better able to appreciate what is valuable in contemporary literature or painting or music *without* reference to Derrida's theories. Moreover, all the happy talk about cross-disciplinary seminars on tourism may make deconstruction sound more cheerful and innocuous than it is. For the real effect of deconstruction has not been to widen inquiry but to narrow it. Not content with the perfectly sensible idea that much besides high literature is worthy of scrutiny, deconstructionists would obliterate the differences between Roger Rabbit and Henry James. The function of criticism is reduced to description and analysis; the task of evaluating works of art is left undone. Abandoned is one of criticism's foremost responsibilities: the making and revising of critical discriminations. The determination of a canon, a syllabus, a reading list of any kind, is stripped of all but political considerations, with results that are nothing if not arrogant. For most educated persons it would be difficult to dismiss the masterworks of Homer, Dante, Shakespeare, Cervantes, Milton, Goethe, Tolstoi—but not for the deconstructionist, who omits mentioning names but packages them all together as he patronizes a "conception of 'greatness' that, even in the 1980s, yields a corpus of works written by white males prior to 1920."

The characteristic assumptions of deconstruction—its profoundly antihumanist drift—have a nightmarish side. What happens if you deconstruct history? What happens if you accept the deconstructive dogma that, as Paul de Man put it, "the bases for historical knowledge are not empirical facts but written texts, even if these texts masquerade in the guise of wars or revolutions"? What happens when you deconstruct the subject, the self, the human protagonist? Tzvetan Todorov, a commanding figure among French structuralists, has grave doubts about the poststructuralist agenda. In an arresting phrase, Todorov writes that "it is not possible, without inconsistency, to defend human rights with one hand and deconstruct the idea of humanity with the other." Deconstruct humanity—reduce the autonomous self to the status of a fiction—and you are left with an entity no more responsible for its actions than a puppet manipulated by an unseen master. Gone is the existential hero, wearing a beret and trenchcoat, who would act upon his destiny; the deconstructed man, taking his place, wanders unprotected into a hard-hat zone where lethal beams have been known to fall. *Humanity deconstructed:* the phrase conjures up the fate of Winston Smith, George Orwell's hero in *1984,* who is made to understand, on penalty of torture, that the name of the game is power and that power consists in tearing human minds apart and reassembling them to suit the rulers' specifications.

Orwell coined the word *doublethink* in *1984.* The word, he explained, denotes the labyrinthine processes with which the mind may be made "to hold simultaneously two opinions which cancelled out, knowing them to be contradictory and believing in both of them, to use logic against logic, to repudiate morality while laying claim to it." That is not, as it happens, a bad description of the deliberately contradictory logic of deconstruction. There are times when deconstruction is precisely described as a form of voodoo literary criticism—it's seldom easy to tell where the nuances leave off and the double-talk begins. Barbara Johnson, one of deconstruction's more cogent advocates, demonstrates the logic in her book *A World of Difference.* See if you can follow: "Instead of a simple 'either/or' structure, deconstruction attempts to elaborate a discourse that says *neither* 'either/or,' *nor* 'both/and' nor even 'neither/nor,' while at the same time not totally abandoning these logics either. The very word *deconstruction* is meant to undermine the either/or logic of the opposition 'construction/destruction.' Deconstruction is both, it is neither, and it reveals the way in which both construction and destruction are themselves not what they appear to be." Using deconstructive logic you can undermine the ground rules that make debate possible—by "proving," for example, that what your adversary says is not what it appears to be. Not merely do you contest the premises or dispute the conclusions of your opponent's argument; you reject your opponent altogether as either a dupe or a mouthpiece for a set of "hidden articulations." If this is not exactly a terrorist tactic, it comes close. No wonder that clashes between deconstructionists and their critics sometimes resemble the exchanges between Alice and the inhabitants of looking-glass land—it's as though the debaters were playing with two different sets of rules. Each seems convinced that the other is being willfully obtuse, and there are bonus points to be earned for the most acid-tongued expression of contempt.

As *doublethink* is to logic in *1984,* so *Newspeak* is to language—and here again there is a parallel in deconstructive practice with its punning neologisms that mean contradictory things at once. "The key word here is *blackwhite,*" Orwell writes in *1984.* "Like so many Newspeak words, this word has two mutually contradictory meanings. Applied to an opponent, it means the habit of impudently claiming that black is white, in contradiction of the plain facts. Applied to a Party member, it means a loyal willingness to say that black is white when Party discipline demands this. But it means also the ability to *believe* that black is white, and more, to *know* that black is white, and to forget that one has ever believed the contrary." For those who equate deconstruction with critical terrorism, such passages from *1984* sound a stern admonition about the dangers of yielding to a system of thought that aspires to turn the word and the world upside down.

. . .

Even those who characterize deconstruction in relatively un-threatening terms—as, say, imperial nakedness or exhibitionistic paronomasia—will concur that in one area at least it has had a lethal effect. Opponents of deconstruction and related theories can't help dwelling on what these theories have done to language, in the name of a heightened awareness of the way language works. "The plagues of Egypt couldn't equal all the references to Freud and Jung and Marx and myths and existentialism and neo-Calvinism and Aristotle and St. Thomas that you'll sometimes see in one commonplace article," wrote Randall Jarrell back in "The Age of Criticism." One would like to send a postcard to heaven: Dear Mr. Jarrell, you ain't seen nothing yet. In the present age of theory, the names may have changed (though Freud and Marx remain on most lists) but the name-dropping tendency has gone to a new extreme. There may not be so many footnotes—critical theorists have a relaxed attitude toward the traditional proce-dures of scholarship. But even a commonplace article will yield a bonanza of diacritical marks: quotation marks around words held suspect, hyphens to break a word into its components, parentheses to expand a word like an accordion. This is writing that tries hard to be daring, playful, and experimental, but frequently succumbs to pure preciosity. Consider the desperate cleverness of the titles that professors give to the papers they deliver at academic conferences. You might come across the theme of "Class(room) Consciousness: Tradition and the Production of Cultural Literacy": a wave of the wand and, presto, Marx's analysis of class conflict extends to sophomores and juniors. Or you might—at the same MLA convention—take in a session on "S(e)izing Power: Gender, Representation, and Body Scale," where the parenthesis is meant to make the point that the slender body is one more unjustly "privileged" notion.

A professor with a flair for showmanship once amused his MLA audience by offering, for a fee, to convert any attempt at a critical essay into a publishable paper. It was hard to say whether the speaker was in jest; his project sounded eminently practical. So long as an essay makes the right noises—and these may be inserted by the hired manu-script-doctor—the content seems almost beside the point. A set of recurring code words needs to be sprinkled liberally over the prose, like ketchup over French fries. The first sentence should feature *hegem-*

ony; the second *itinerary;* the third *foregrounding;* the fourth, *privilege* used as a verb (for example, "the retrograde critic privileges the author"). There should be plenty of *de-* or *dis-* prefixes, beginning with *deconstruction* and *dismantling,* and as many *-ize* suffixes, such as *problematize, valorize, contextualize, totalize.* A good way to begin your *discourse* (you must always call it that) is with a nod toward Derrida, an allusion to de Man, and a determination to call into question some *binary opposition* or other. You are going to deconstruct the dichotomy of your choice: *male* and *female, nature* and *culture, center* and *periphery, speech* and *writing, presence* and *absence.* The reckless may opt for *truth* and *opinion;* the really reckless, for *truth* and *propaganda;* the semiotically-trained analyst of TV commercials may stick with *slender* and *fat.* Your task is to dismantle hierarchies and you do this by showing that the first term in any such set is implicitly—and unjustly—endorsed ("privileged") in Western philosophy. You don't call it Western philosophy, of course; you refer knowingly to "the metaphysics of presence." It would probably be a good idea to mention "the prisonhouse of language," too. You must remind your readers periodically that no escape from language is possible. Language has humanity in thrall; textuality is all.

Deconstruction is supposed to train us to see the hidden subtext in any piece of writing, no matter how straightforward it appears to be. Dwell on deconstruction's favorite jargon words, and you arrive at a subtext that is nothing if not oppositional. To be *subversive* is a plus. What is *marginal* to an experience may be more significant than what is customarily held to be *central. Itinerary*—as when a speaker, analyzing "AIDS discourse," refers to our culture's "anal itinerary"— suggests we are all tourists in our scripted lives. Any *hierarchy* is unjustly repressive. *Privilege* with its connotations of ill-gotten gains registers the deconstructive bias against the making of value judgments. The critic's role is not to evaluate works of literature but to see through them; to *privilege* art is a temptation that contemporary critics are perfectly able to resist. Alison Lurie provides a helpful gloss on *privilege:* "It is not popularity or traditional acclaim (economic success or aristocratic lineage, so to speak) that now determines the value of a text; it is the decision of the critic." Traditional values are suspect because they are the instruments of a *hegemony,* a means through which the holders of power reaffirm their power. *Text,* too, seems strategically chosen. It is, for one thing, a great leveler, since it serves equally well to describe the label on a soup can and an ode by John Keats—and reinforces the notion that these various "texts" are equal in importance. Moreover, *text* suggests *textile,* allowing for a metaphorical association of *reading* and *unraveling.* Finally, where *work* (short for *work of art*) carries a favorable overtone, *text* has a forbidding sound, smacking of schoolbooks and sermons. The reader is likely to associate *text* with *textbook;* to call *Anna Karenina* a text is thus immediately to label it an object of study rather than an aesthetic experience. As for the adversarial force of *deconstruction* itself, consider the image of a pile of rubble. Lurie says it best: "If someone came over to your house and said he was there to deconstruct it, you'd want to have him arrested."

It is easy to parody the jingle-jangle jargon of deconstruction, though rarely has it been done with the verve of the pseudonymous "Cosmo Dewlap" in the underground literary magazine *Exquisite Corpse:*

> Attacking the abyss of contemporary *écriture* like an aveng-ing, post-modern Clough, Braithwaite-Godolphin fear-lessly deconstructs the "poem" with such terrifying finality that it will no longer be honest (in the phenomenological sense) to attempt to write "poems" at all without arousing the contempt of the entire litero-*cum*-academico commu-nity. Having absorbed, in one swallow as it were, the devastating implications of the writings of Saussure, Benja-min, Lacan, Derrida, Barthes, Husserl, Foucault, and Jong, Braithwaite-Godolphin revels without apology in the slip-pages of meaning, indeed the total lack of *meaning* (in the old-fashioned sense) of words, phrases, even "poems" as a whole, undercutting the now-discredited falseness of the worn-out, shamelessly ideological English "grammar" for the *jouissance* and hard-won freedom of the bad-ass cowboy poet.

They're all here—the voguish phrases, the French fashions, the ironic quotation marks, the big words, the parade of names, and the unexam-ined assumption that to "deconstruct" works of art "with such terrify-ing finality" is the right thing to do.

What is saddest about the prevalence of this debased idiom is that the people who use it are the professionally appointed curators of our literature. "One has long been inured to such grossness in the use of the mother tongue by scholars in other disciplines," the scholar and poet Donald Davie has written. "What makes one weep is that such use of English is now not just tolerated but considered normal in the disciplines supposedly devoted to literature, that is to say, to language as a medium of art." Davie offers this example—"chosen, I assure you, virtually at random"—of the kind of "debased and yet pretentious Esperanto or dog-Latin" he deplores:

> We see in this rehearsal of "Foucault" that contemporary criticism cherishes the displacement both of dialectics by diacritics and of totalized organic representations of history by comprehensive graphs of affiliated disciplines in the epis-teme.

"Reading such jaw-breaking propositions," Davie writes, "we find ourselves echoing Ben Jonson when he objected to one of his contemporaries that he 'writ no language.'"

Professionalism is, no doubt, a contributing cause of the problem. The jawbreaking jargon of deconstruction functions as a badge of professionalism, ratifying the speaker's status and facilitating the performance of certain rituals, meaningless in themselves. Like the technological jargon of the military analyst, the theorist's gaudy patter confirms his or her expertise by reinforcing the layperson's sense of ignorance. Professionalism encourages obscurantism: it is easier to justify a steep medical bill when the diagnosis is vasomotor rhinitis and not the common cold. It is even possible that obscurantism is the academic theorist's revenge on society for having consigned him or her to relative obscurity—a way of proclaiming one's superiority in the face of one's diminished influence. The excesses of the deconstructive prose machine make it pardonable to wonder whether some practitioners are playing an intellectual confidence game, tricking out a pack of pseudoprofundities in polysyllabic armor. Nor does it seem overly cynical to suggest that the unreadable articles in scholarly journals are written and published primarily to demonstrate the writer's familiarity with the professional patois, in an effort to advance up the rungs of the tenure ladder. As against the professionalism in literary studies today, Donald Davie votes for the old-fashioned concept of the teaching "vocation" or "calling." Today, he notes, "no one reads Edmund Spenser or contemplates writing about him, unless he has first paid his dues to the Modern Language Association of America." Literature and literary criticism were both perhaps healthier when the accreditation system was less formalized and the field was home to " 'mavericks,' insisting on addressing to an illustrious shade like Spenser just those questions which the professional bodies had declared inadmissible."

The problem of professional jargon long predates the rise of critical theory. But the prose of deconstruction amounts to a pure statement of the problem: the prose of deconstruction seems deliberately aimed at the deconstruction of prose—the explosion of the idea that expository writing is meant to be understood. For the first thing one notes about the burgeoning literature of deconstruction is that most of it is frightfully hard to read; much of it seems to want to be unreadable, as if this were a positive value. For deconstructionists— and many of them are quite up-front about this—it's as though clarity of thought were a specious virtue, an aspect of the logocentrism they've been taught to deride. Certainly they proceed as though the proper use of language were not to impart information but to camouflage it, to preserve an air of mystery about the enterprise, and to keep outsiders at bay. David Grossvogel, who founded the journal *Diacritics* at Cornell in 1971, was asked why he resigned as its editor five years later. The journal was created, he explained, to give "a forum to various kinds of criticism that were becoming important and didn't have access at the time: Marxist criticism, psychoanalytic theory, and deconstruction." Five years later, Grossvogel reported, *Diacritics* had become "the entrenched journal of the poststructuralists. We had replaced one hegemony with another." Deconstruction was now "a religious creed, a political act of faith." And there was, Grossvogel grinned, one other reason for his disaffection. "I felt an editor should understand his own journal."

Jargon is the verbal sleight of hand that makes the old hat seem newly fashionable; it gives an air of novelty and specious profundity to ideas that, if stated directly, would seem superficial, stale, frivolous, or false. The line between serious and spurious scholarship is an easy one to blur, with jargon on your side. But what is most appalling about the academic addiction to prefabricated phrases is that they reveal an absence of thought and independence—the writer lets the prefabricated phrases do all the thinking, as if in illustration of the deconstructive notion that words manipulate us instead of the other way around. A study of contemporary academic jargon does have its uses, however, if only because it lets us measure the relative fashionableness of a doctrine or a dogma. And the perusal of professional journals and university press publications confirms the impression of deconstruction's dominant place in the jargon jamboree. Consider the role it plays in *Discourse and the Construction of Society,* a recent book by Bruce Lincoln, who is—the jacket copy informs us—a "co-founder of the Program in Comparative Studies in Discourse and Society" at the University of Minnesota. The book's title itself is like a combination of code words designed to advertise the writer's credentials as a theorist, able to cross disciplinary borders at a single bound. The book has all the characteristics of an unwitting self-parody, particularly in its immoderate love of *deconstruction*—here meaning something like *demolition* or *violent upheaval,* though Lincoln himself would be more likely to define it as *counterhegemonic inversion.*

Discourse and the Construction of Society reads rather like an ode to deconstruction. Lincoln is so charmed by the word that he sees it exemplified everywhere. The primary focus of his cross-disciplinary study "of myth, ritual, and classification" is on historical upheavals, crises, and anomalies—especially the bloodier sort—which signal, as Lincoln puts it in a typical formulation, "the deconstruction of established social forms and the emergence of new formations." Here are a few things that qualify as deconstructions: Aristophanes in Plato's *Symposium* divided people by sexual preference as well as by gender; in Lincoln's words, he "struggled to deconstruct" the "sociotaxonomic order." Victorious Royalists exhumed Oliver Cromwell's dead body and hanged it—"the ultimate act of deconstructing non-monarchic society." During the Spanish Civil War, the corpses of priests, nuns, and mummified saints were disinterred and exhibited before jeering crowds in Barcelona. The exhumations, Lincoln explains, "were a ritual in which the traditionally subordinate segment of Spanish society sought by means of a highly charged discourse of gestures and deeds to deconstruct the old social order and construct a new, radically different order in its place." (Translation: the exhumations were the rebels' way of saying that the church was as corrupt as the flesh of its deceased ministers.) One of the more notable aspects of Lincoln's book is the absence of Jacques Derrida's name in the index—fittingly, perhaps, since *absence* is one of Derrida's crucial terms. The fact that Derrida is nowhere cited confirms the extent to which the invention of deconstruction has escaped from its creator's laboratory. And if what Lincoln means by the word is not quite what Derrida had in mind, that seems perfectly consonant with deconstructive theory. Words have a life of their own, and few words demonstrate this more aptly than *deconstruction*.

A joke of the 1940s had it that the typewriters in the offices of *Partisan Review* were equipped with a special key that typed out the word *alienation* on command. Many word processors today are programmed to flash *deconstruction* on the computer screen, trailed by all manner of ready-made phrases. In Bruce Lincoln's case, the accompanying jargon is that of the sociologist. The writer who can say that the St. Bartholomew's Day Massacre in France in 1572 "effectively deconstructed" French society can also soberly commit this sentence to print: "Given the relation between schism and massacre, it is worth asking what factors lead toward the exercise of massacre as an option." *Massacre as an option!* A savage parodist would have a hard time producing a better example of what George Orwell had in mind when he warned about the "special connection between politics and the debasement of language." The problem of jargon, Orwell wrote, is that it can all too easily confer a bogus veneer of respectability on barbarous behavior. *The pacification proceeded according to plan. That is, the exercise of massacre as an option was never seriously considered. That is, we had to destroy the village in order to save it.*

A mild-mannered old-school English professor in David Lodge's *Small World* remarks that the word *theory* "brings out the Goering in me. When I hear it I reach for my revolver." So it is with the dreaded "D" word, too. It shows up regularly on blame-all lists of the evils that afflict mankind—as when an after-dinner speaker tickles his audience by remarking that "everything wrong with higher education may be summed up in one word: deconstruction." Deconstructionists charge, not entirely without reason, that the reaction against their insurgency has been marked by hysteria and hyperbole and is based on misunderstanding and anxiety. But it is disingenuous for a deconstructionist to sound a wounded cry, for deconstruction is predicated on the notion that misunderstandings are basic to language. Deconstruction *wants* to awaken anxieties; a stated goal of poststructuralist theory is to dismantle the repressive mechanisms of Western philosophy. Is it any wonder that those who do not share this view of Western thought should resist the new theorists? Paul de Man wrote a celebrated essay entitled "The Resistance to Theory." He meant something paradoxical by that phrase, but its primary sense is hard to mistake. In academe, you're either with the deconstructionists or you're part of the resistance. Between those who depend on deconstruction to earn them a living and those who would fight it every inch of the way, there can be no peace, only stalemate—the mutual animosity goes too deep.

In England, the repulsion of the poststructuralists left hard feelings all around. The decisive event occurred at Cambridge University in the winter of 1981. A young don named Colin MacCabe, whose work placed him squarely in the poststructuralist fold, was denied tenure in an acrimonious session of the faculty's appointments committee. MacCabe needed five of the committee's seven votes; he fell one short. Two professors who cast their ballots for MacCabe, Frank Kermode and Raymond Williams, were promptly ousted from the committee. "It is our job to teach and uphold the canon of English literature," said Christopher Ricks, the most prominent of the professors opposing MacCabe. MacCabe's supporters cried foul—it was, they charged, a "witch-hunt" organized by "reactionaries." The London newspapers made much of the imbroglio, which quickly acquired a symbolic significance: the dismissal of Colin MacCabe, leaving Cambridge with only one poststructuralist on its faculty, had become—or perhaps had been from the start—a high British verdict on deconstruction and related theories. In press accounts the outcome was presented as a triumph of English common sense over Left Bank abstruseness. Shortly after the incident, Kermode left Cambridge, where he had been King Edward VII Professor of English. He complained that his Cambridge colleagues were simply not sophisticated enough to handle the unsettling new doctrines coming from France. "Deconstructionism is, in part, a catastrophe theory, for behind it there is the assumption that the whole Western metaphysical tradition can be put into reverse," Kermode explained. "It is at this point that the orthodox, who dislike having to consider such unsettling propositions, man the walls with their dusty banners: principle, the imagination, the human world, though the most vocal of them are manifestly unacquainted with the first, lack the second and seem to know the third only by hearsay." Kermode had depicted himself as a mediator. In retrospect he felt that he should have known better. "There is a war on," wrote Kermode, "and he who ventures into no-man's-land brandishing cigarettes and singing carols must expect to be shot at."

No wonder, then, that writers in diverse contexts have fastened on *deconstruction* and won't let it go. The word means too many things to too many contending factions—it brings out the militancy in everyone. The word itself has become a sign of our times—a sign that no one can ignore—and that is itself a paradox and an irony, since deconstruction proclaims itself to be the study of signs: of language considered as a system of signs, and misleading signs at that.

Kierkegaard tells an anecdote in his book *Either / Or* (1843) that seems prophetic of deconstruction, its flashy gestures and enigmatic core. Kierkegaard tells the anecdote to illustrate the dismaying gulf— as he saw it in mid-nineteenth-century Denmark—between "philosophical discourse" and reality. Listening to philosophical discourse is, Kierkegaard writes, as misleading as seeing a sign in the window of a secondhand store. The sign says: *Trousers Pressed Here.* But if you were to bring in a pair of trousers to be pressed, you'd be in for a surprise. "For only the sign is for sale."

Kierkegaard's anecdote accurately expresses the deconstructionist's view of language. It is an article of the deconstructive faith that the relation between words and their meanings is anything but constant; language as a system lacks a vital center. It is pointless, therefore, to speak about meaning, since the meaning of any verbal construct does not and cannot precede the words themselves, and these are as duplicitous as the sign in the shop window—it may be that nothing stands behind them. *Trousers Pressed Here* refers only to itself; and because its existence is independent of the activity that it names, the sign in the window is a model for any literary text.

But while Kierkegaard's anecdote illustrates the radical linguistic insight at deconstruction's core, it helps make a further point—it seems to deconstruct deconstruction itself. It places the deconstructionist in the position of the store's proprietor, who perpetuates practical jokes and linguistic booby traps rather than useful goods and services. With his ostentatious sign, does he not dramatize the problem of "philosophical discourse"—its lack of apparent contact with reality? And we who wandered into the shop are left to wonder about what he's selling: is deconstruction itself but one more misleading sign, a check without sufficient funds on which to draw, a linguistic ruse? Is it a sign of our times because it's a sign for sale?

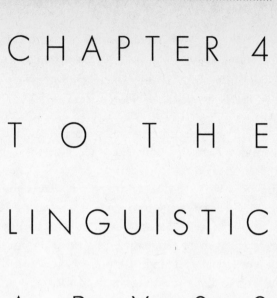

CHAPTER 4

TO THE

LINGUISTIC

ABYSS

The fall into the abyss of deconstruction inspires us with as much pleasure as fear. We are intoxicated with the prospect of never hitting bottom.

—*Gayatri Chakravorty Spivak,*
Translator's Preface, Derrida's OF
GRAMMATOLOGY

In one of his most notorious pronouncements, Paul de Man declared that "death is a displaced name for a linguistic predicament." This is, no doubt, the ultimate statement of the deconstructive credo. When we think we are talking about matters of life and death, we are merely having a "displaced" conversation about our inability to converse. Assumptions that once held true about speakers and listeners, words and meanings, have been thoroughly debunked. Sooner or later, therefore, the initiate into the mysteries of deconstruction must prepare to visit a linguistic abyss.

The age of theory is characterized by a general obsession with language and linguistics, and much of the theorizing in recent vogue requires familiarity with the groundbreaking work of the great Swiss linguist Ferdinand de Saussure. Compiled from lecture notes taken by his students at the University of Geneva in 1916, Sausssure's *Course in General Linguistics* remains the first word on the subject of French structuralism and its sequels. Published posthumously in 1916, the book laid the foundation for twentieth-century linguistics. It also predicted, and provoked, the career of present-day semiotics. "Contemporary literary theory comes into its own," wrote de Man, "in such events as the application of Saussurian linguistics to literary texts."

Saussure conceived of language as a system of signs rather than an orderly procession of meanings. One of his key insights is that the relation of words to their meanings is fundamentally arbitrary. The word *dog* has no intrinsic meaning; nothing in the word, its sound, or its shape on the page suggests a barking animal, any more than does *Hund* in German or *chien* in French. Language consists of signs, and signs are not independent entities that can be studied in isolation; signs can only be understood in relation to one another within a larger linguistic system. The meaning of a sign is a function of its *difference* from the others; *dog* means what it does in English because it is not *hog* or *bog*. And this is true for concepts as well. The terms we use have meaning, Saussure reasoned, not because they correspond to an external reality and not because they reflect ideas, but because of their differential status—their functional value within a system based on differentiation. It follows that the pairs of any culturally determined binary opposition define themselves in relation to one another. Some applications of this theorem are obvious. The meaning of the terms *Democrat* and *Republican,* for example, can be shown to depend on the system of differences to which they belong. The significance of the Democratic party platform in any given year would be lost on us if we didn't recognize it in the context of what the Republicans were saying at the same time. "Democrat," then, means what it does in relation to "Republican" not as an entity unto itself; and that relation is always in flux. It is possible for "Democrat" and "Republican" to switch their meanings altogether—the "Democratic" foreign policy line in one era may resemble nothing so much as the "Republican" line of an earlier era.

With his concept of *difference,* Saussure argued that the meaning of a sign is arbitrary and variable. But he did not mean by this that it was random or "undecidable," much less that it was divided against itself. In Saussure's terms, any sign consists of a *signifier* (the sound a word makes, its physical shape on the page) and a *signified* (the word's content). For language to work, the sign needs to be a united whole. For deconstructionists, however, there can be no point-to-point link between signifiers and signifieds; in place of Saussure's unified sign, they offer the vision of a shattered center, a split in the word itself. According to Jacques Derrida, the linguistic "chain of signification" is infinite—the signifiers and the signifieds never stay in the same place for long.

Saussure had introduced a distinction between two kinds of linguistic activity: he used the term *langue* to denote the structure or system of a language and *parole* to denote an individual's speech acts. "The linguistic system *(langue)* is necessary for speech events *(parole)* to be intelligible," Saussure wrote, "but the latter are necessary for the system to establish itself." Derrida fastens on the circularity of the logic here and concludes that "one does not know where to begin and how something can in general begin, be it *langue* or *parole."* Language, lacking a foundation or origin, entails "a systematic production of differences, the *production* of a system of differences—a *différance."* Thus is Saussure deconstructed with a pun.

In Derrida's brand of differential linguistics, the meaning of words is never present but is constantly *deferred,* since words *differ* not only from one another but from themselves. How do words differ from themselves? Part of the explanation is that there is an element of temporality in language, and therefore a word means something different each time it is used; Derrida's own style of exposition, prolix as it is, depends on the notion that every repetition involves variation. But Derrida's critique of Saussure is far more radical than that. For Derrida, nothing in language "is anywhere ever simply present or absent. There are only, everywhere, differences and traces of differences." Words are compromised at their root: the signifier and the signified come together like the accidental coupling of atoms that disintegrate into their components an instant later. Language is grounded on nothing. There is no nonlinguistic reality from which word-signs proceed and to which they must be faithful; there is, therefore, nothing to keep in check what Derrida calls the "infinite play of signification" that marks language in action. All that we have are texts, and all texts are indeterminate; any use of language breaks down—if you break it down—into a self-contradictory impasse. The possibility of knowing anything with certainty is cast into doubt; the capacity of language to tell the truth at the service of a speaker's will is radically wiped out. A vertiginous abyss has opened up where there once was solid ground.

Saussure foresaw a science of "semiology" (from *semeion,* the Greek word for sign) that "would show what constitutes signs, what laws govern them." While semantics concerns itself with the meaning of words, semiology would concentrate on the functional value of the signs independent of their content or meaning. This new science, Saussure wrote, "has a right to existence, a place staked out in advance. Linguistics is only a part of the general science of semiology; the laws discovered by semiology will be applicable to linguistics, and the latter will circumscribe a well-defined area within the mass of anthropological facts." With the emergence of French structuralism and semiotics in the 1960s, Saussure's prophecy was realized. Language, as Saussure conceived it, was now held to be the model for any sign-system. Applying this principle to psychoanalysis, Jacques Lacan gave it its most celebrated formulation: "The unconscious is structured like a language." Literary criticism could resemble a species of structuralist linguistics by other means, entailing the application of linguistic principles to all manner of texts—texts defined in the broadest possible way. You could, to equal advantage, offer a structuralist analysis of a beauty contest, a boxing match, a political debate, a myth, a ceremony, an advertisement, a dream. In each case, you studied not the stated content of the signs but their relations to one another; you emphasized the structure at the expense of that which it subtends. You could even conduct the analysis with something resembling scientific rigor. It was possible to elucidate the deep structure of, say, a James Bond novel and show how the conventions of the narrative function like the constants and variables of a mathematical equation. While the attempt to put literary criticism on the same footing as the scientific analysis, with diagrams and all, was far from an unmixed blessing, the integration of linguistics into the domain of literary criticism—and the widening of the scope of that domain—was potentially exhilarating.

Structuralism seemed to promise a major breakthrough in literary studies, as it had in anthropology before it. But it is an irony of academic history that structuralism in the United States was superseded before it could ever fully establish itself. Professors from France and the United States assembled at the Johns Hopkins University in the Fall of 1966 to celebrate the advent of structuralism in all the "sciences of man." Derrida was the conference's final speaker and made the most of the opportunity. Structuralism, he declared, was effectively finished. The paper he presented, "Structure, Sign and Play and the Discourse of the Human Sciences," launched the meteoric American career of deconstruction.

Derrida's paper focused on the linguistic loophole that, as he saw it, subverted Saussure and doomed any structuralist project to failure: for how could you study the structure of a text if that structure was collapsible, lacking a center or any kind of organizing principle to give it coherence? A vision of chaos—Derrida calls it "play"—replaces the concept of a unified structure. Fatally compromised is the confidence necessary for the interpretation of texts, whether conducted in a structuralist mode or any other: the confidence that the text will yield its meanings and its truths, if read with enough acumen and patience.

Derrida began his lecture by describing a momentous "rupture" in "the history of the concept of structure," a concept "as old as Western science and Western philosophy":

> This was the moment when language invaded the universal problematic, the moment when, in the absence of a center or origin, everything became discourse—provided we can agree on this word—that is to say, a system in which the central signified, the original or transcendental signified, is never absolutely present outside a system of differences. The absence of the transcendental signified extends the domain and the play of signification infinitely.

Language invaded the universal problematic. Henceforth no intellectual discussion could avoid a detour into the realm of linguistics. Not the content of an expression but the *means* of expression must occupy our attention. Derrida's military metaphor ("invaded") emphasizes the disruptive impact of the pronouncement. *The central signified, the original or transcendental signified, is never absolutely present outside a system of differences.* Nothing exists ahead of language or outside it; there are no things or ideas except in words. Words have an autonomous existence because they are grounded in nothing else. This heavy emphasis on absence leads George Steiner to propose the briefest and perhaps pithiest definition of deconstruction on record. Deconstruction, writes Steiner, can be defined as an elaboration of Gertrude Stein's famous remark about the city of Oakland: "There's no there there." There's no prime mover—whether you call it the "transcendental signified" or the presence of an ineffable God—that "underwrites" our utterances and gives them their meaning. *The absence of the transcendental signified extends the domain and the play of signification infinitely.* God is a supreme fiction and doesn't exist outside of language, "a system of differences." The dashed belief in a meaning that transcends the power of language to modify it—"the absence of the transcendental signified"—is like a translation of the death of God from theological terms to those of rhetorical analysis. If so, Derrida's concept of *différance* is surely the deconstructive equivalent of original sin: a fall, not from grace, but from pure, unmediated presence. It is not that words had meanings but lost them; the process of *différance* was at work "always already," in Derridean parlance. There is no escape from "the prisonhouse of language." There is only the prospect of infinite "play."

In the absence of a center or origin, everything became discourse. There are no facts, only interpretations, and no truths, only expedient fictions. It becomes possible for Paul de Man to declare that literature is everywhere; anthropology, linguistics, and psychoanalysis are merely branches of literature—but that is far from a consoling thought, since literature involves "the presence of a nothingness." In effect, the deconstructionist derogates everything else to the same level of fictionality to which he has already reduced literature. Interpretation, he insists, is doomed from the start; it is, in de Man's words, "nothing but the possibility of error." Under these circumstances, the proper function of criticism is "the deconstruction of literature, the reduction to the rigors of grammar of rhetorical mystifications." And with such pronouncements in mind, a whole school of literary criticism commits itself to doing deconstructive "routines" on literary works, displaying considerable ingenuity on the road to the foreordained dismal conclusion, the linguistic abyss that meets our gaze at the heart of any text.

. . .

Derrida warmly endorses the spirit of linguistic "play"—the "affirmation of a world of signs without fault, without truth, and without origin"—and his use of *play* seems calculated to produce a benign impression. There is certainly in Derrida's own writing an inveterate playfulness, a reliance on jokes and puns and fanciful etymologies to do the work of logical argumentation, and this may count as one mark of his originality. The wordplay in a Derrida essay is dizzying; in the amusement park of the higher criticism, the ride called Derrida offers the most thrilling twists, turns, reversals, and sudden jerks forward. But it is understandable for humanists—even those not maddened by Derrida's rhetorical antics—to register misgivings about the "rupture" he describes; free-play is hard to distinguish from free-fall. If everything is reducible to a linguistic predicament, and if language lies or can be made to lie, then the concept of objective reality has been fundamentally undermined—or deconstructed. Divide the *signifier* from the *signified,* and mere anarchy is loosed upon the world.

George Orwell's *1984* is the canonical text on the dangers of the denial of objective reality. The state's triumph over the recalcitrant individual is sealed when a broken Winston Smith is persuaded that his torturer's four raised fingers number five. What makes such mental manipulation possible is the state's control of language. We can hardly be expected to applaud the disjunction between words and what they refer to, if that is the condition that empowers a totalitarian state—such as the one Orwell describes—to falsify the past and alter the terms of our existence by eliminating some words and redefining others. Discourse, lacking a center, becomes an instrument of power, and so, in the land of Big Brother, war is peace, freedom is slavery, and ignorance is strength. I am not saying that Derrida or his followers find such a thought comforting; on the contrary, Derrida would like to believe that deconstruction fosters "the analysis of the conditions of totalitarianism in all its forms." I am simply suggesting that the belief in an exclusively linguistic universe leaves humanity more rather than less vulnerable to the forces of political tyranny. There is, in deconstruction, neither a safeguard against nihilistic despair nor an antidote to passive quiescence. Rather than provide a philosophical basis for moral judgment or existential action, deconstruction has the effect of silencing literature and language, leaving us an intellectual void. The danger of such a void is that it may be filled up by the next great dictator.

I was present at the 1986 convention of the Modern Language Association, which was held in New York City that year, and listened as a British professor—Stephen Heath of Cambridge University—demonstrated the ease with which deconstructive procedures can be used to serve a sinister political agenda. The session at which Heath spoke was entitled "Literature and Propaganda." Heath mounted a defense of propaganda. After noting that it is considered "a bad thing," as opposed to literature, "its antonym," he commented that "it should be easy to reverse this hierarchy," since propaganda is fundamental to "political action." Well, Heath was probably right in saying that the hierarchy that values literature over propaganda can easily be reversed. Isn't that exactly what tyrants do after they seize power? The loaded word once again is *hierarchy*. "Hierarchy" implies that truth in the realm of art may correspond to repressive authoritarianism in the realm of the polity—that it's all propaganda, or may be treated as such. The demolition of hierarchies is pursued as an end in itself, leaving us nothing to hold onto, nothing with which to resist the imposition of a new hierarchical order. The twentieth century's dismal chronicle of new hierarchies, established upon revolutionary new theories, does not make one welcome the prospect.

Postulate a disjunction between the word and the world, hold fast to it, and then assume the possibility—made the more imaginable by technology—that a government in control of the airwaves can create a false world out of words. What you end with, if you take the supposition far enough, is paranoia. The world of appearances may be a collective hallucination; deconstruct it and you find a fictional construct, valid only because people have been manipulated to credit it as real. This linguistic predicament—the disjunction between the word and the world—is taken to heart in a novel that is far less familiar than *1984* but, in its way, equally disturbing. *Time Out of Joint,* a science fiction classic, was published by Philip K. Dick in 1959 but written as if for an imaginary reader in the year 1997. Early on, the novel's protagonist, a man with the unlikely name of Ragle Gumm, approaches a soft-drink stand in the park. Suddenly Ragle sees the stand disintegrate into its component molecules, "along with the counter man, the cash register, the big dispenser of orange drink, the taps for Coke and root beer, the ice-chests of bottles, the hot dog broiler, the jars of mustard, the shelves of cones, the row of heavy round metal lids under which were the different ice creams." He watches it pass out of existence, all of it. In its place is a slip of paper, which Ragle picks up and reads. The words "SOFT-DRINK STAND" are printed on it in crude capitals. The stand, counter man and all, wasn't real. It was just discourse.

The shattering of the link between words and things results in a kind of linguistic schizophrenia, and Dick develops a brilliantly paranoid scenario for his hero. Very gradually, Ragle Gumm begins to realize that the town in which he lives, his family and friends, are part of a sham world designed to keep him pacified—a world where appearances are carefully maintained to preserve the illusion that the year is the relatively innocuous one of 1959. The authorities have gone to great lengths to deceive our man, for he is indispensable to their military plans. It is really 1997. The earth is at war with Luna—that is, colonists on the moon have staged an insurrection against the forces in command of the earth. Ragle Gumm spends his days solving a running newspaper puzzle—at least that's what he thinks he's doing. For two straight years, he has been the national champion of the "Where Will the Little Green Man Be Next?" contest. On the huge checkerboard diagram provided by the newspaper, Ragle locates the rank and file of the square on which the moving dot—the "Little Green Man"—will appear that day. Ragle is so good at this contest that he is able to make a living on his prize winnings. Naturally, people around him think he's a little odd: that a grown man should spend his time so idly! Ragle's peculiar occupation makes him a kind of allegorical representation of the sci-fi writer, of Dick himself. Just as the sci-fi novelist appears to indulge in a frivolous activity that turns out to have a prophetic dimension, so Ragle Gumm's puzzle-solving isn't so innocent as it looks. In fact, what he is doing—what he has an uncanny talent for doing—is predicting where the next moon-launched missile will hit; the rank of the square indicates the place, the file indicates the time, and the "Little Green Man" stands for the engine of destruction. If Ragle really knew what the contest meant, he might be less willing to oblige its sponsors; there's no guarantee that his sympathies would lie with the powers that be rather than with the lunar insurrectionists. So Ragle is kept in the dark, kept "happy," with a specially chosen "wife" and a whole environment designed to be as unthreatening as possible—to keep him in an artificial state of tranquility, in a

simulacrum of his hometown in that year of his childhood, 1959. The
state's astonishing power to manipulate Ragle Gumm's reality is based
on its control of the means of communication, its deployment of
words severed from things and images divorced from actualities. Our
man's nightmare is, in short, the fictional extrapolation of a deconstructive world-view. Assume that language (and all other sign systems
that function on the model of language) is fundamentally duplicitous,
and paranoia becomes a reasonable response to anything that advertises
itself as reality. When everything is phoney, when there is a breach
between word and thing, between image and substance, lying threatens
to become a universal principle.

On the way to discovering the truth about himself and his
circumstances, Ragle Gumm arrives at a statement of the linguistic
crisis that has made his predicament possible. It could stand as an
epigraph for deconstruction:

Words, he thought.

Central problem in philosophy. Relation of word to object
. . . what is a word? Arbitrary sign. But we live in words.
Our reality, among words not things. No such thing as a
thing anyhow; a gestalt in the mind. Thingness . . . sense
of substance. An illusion. Word is more real than the object
it represents.

Word doesn't represent reality. Word *is* reality. For us,
anyhow. Maybe God gets to objects. Not us, though.

It is an approved deconstructionist tactic to search far afield for
the telling analogy, and there is at least one further resemblance
between Dick's fictional nightmare and the intellectual movement that
Jacques Derrida set in motion. The plot of *Time Out of Joint* rests on
a conspiracy theory. In a crucial sense, this is true of deconstruction
as well. When deconstruction in America was young, Michael Wood
told readers of the *New York Review of Books* that Derrida sees a "vast
metaphysical plot" infecting Western thought from Plato to the present. The principal feature of Derrida's method is, Wood wrote, "a
patient and intelligent *suspicion*"—he interrogates a text in the spirit
with which an intelligence operative interrogates a captured spy. The
plot he is determined to unmask is "a doctrine of presence, a faith

holding that immediacy is value and indirection is evil." The doctrine has a name, *logocentrism,* and Derrida detects it everywhere. What are the attractions and limitations of such a universal conspiracy theory? Wood summed them up. "There are," he wrote in 1977, "obvious virtues in a plot you can find everywhere, especially if you enjoy your suspicions, but Derrida's thinking does at times remind me of those Hollywood movies which insisted on confronting nothing less than the whole human condition." Edward Said, the most eminent critical theorist on the Columbia University faculty, put the case less politely five years later: "It has always seemed to me that the supreme irony of what Derrida has called logocentrism is that its critique, deconstruction, is as insistent, as monotonous, and as inadvertently systematizing as logocentrism itself."

Nothing stays the same, and the search for a unified field theory of oppression has led to a new deconstructive catchall for the metaphysical conspiracy at the bottom of our woe. The trendy coinage is *phallogocentrism,* a merger of logocentrism and phallocentrism. The right-minded critic sets out to undo "patriarchal" assumptions. In particular, you want—as one enthusiast puts it—to deconstruct "singularity, embodied in the phallus, asserted in Logos, inscribed in an egotistical I." As a definition of phallogocentrism this has the virtue of concision; it also has the reassuring sound of rote phrases strung together. Yet here again it is hard to shake the suspicion that wordplay has taken the place of argument. It may be that only the logic of a pun links the self, the phallus, and the logos in this particular chain of negative signification. If that is so, the spirit of play makes it possible to arrive at a rather more mischievous definition of phallogocentrism. Perhaps it is simply the linguistic equivalent of an optical illusion— rather like the printer's error that closed up the space between the second and third words of the sentence "The pen is mightier than the sword," and chipped off the *s* of *sword.*

The time has come to debunk the debunkers and demystify deconstruction—and to ask what difference it makes. With its aporias and its binary oppositions, deconstruction is coated so heavily in jargon that one feels positively goaded to define the theory as a set of straightforward propositions. I propose the following group of ten. I do so with some trepidation, though I am cheered by the knowledge that genuine deconstructionists won't risk contradicting me—if, that is, they really do play by their own rules. For surely the proponents of Derrida, glorifying the reader's empowerment to bend texts to his will, must expect their own texts to be treated no differently from anyone else's. Or is that too optimistic an assumption? Is exercising the free-play of signifiers recommended only for dealing with other people's writing, and never for the sacred texts of deconstruction? If so, the deconstructionists will directly refute the idea that all interpretations are misinterpretations, that none should be "privileged," that the author's intentions are irrelevant, and that meanings are "undecidable" and texts unknowable.

My ten candidates for a deconstructive decalogue:

—*Between the signifier and the signified falls the shadow.* Deconstruction begins by tearing things asunder, or depicting them as torn. The word is severed from its meaning; the linguistic intention is separated from the linguistic event. This notion, if taken to heart, would introduce either *différance* or terror into all writing and all speech. It turns out that we are skating at the edge of a steep and slippery precipice whenever we talk, write, or think. J. Alfred Prufrock in T. S. Eliot's poem states the theme: "It is impossible to say just what I mean." Yet, as another Eliot character says, "I've gotta use words when I talk to you." Words are all that we have; everything is mediated by language.

—*Writing precedes speech.* This is one of the most fundamental of the hierarchical reversals that Derrida proposes. By arguing that writing is prior to speech, Derrida isn't pressing the patently false claim that the invention of writing historically preceded the ability of human beings to communicate through spoken language. Rather, Derrida's point is that speech is as devoid of "presence" as is writing— and that it would be incorrect to imagine that the things we say or write exist in some prior form in our minds. Speech is not the materialization of thought. On the contrary, speech behaves like writing inasmuch as we are equally alienated from our words in either case. "Writing in general covers the entire field of linguistic signs," as Derrida puts it in *Of Grammatology.*

From the point of view of strict logic, there may be less to this celebrated instance of the deconstructive method than meets the eye. There is logically no reason to say that speech is a form of writing if you simultaneously maintain, as Derrida does, a distinction between speech and writing. It would be more accurate simply to observe that speech and writing are both aspects of a larger entity, language. A professor who did his graduate work at Yale has this domestic analogy for what Derrida is doing here. It is as if, instead of saying "cats and dogs are household pets," Derrida were to insist that "cats are always already dogs" by expanding the definition of "dogs" until it becomes coextensive with that of "household pets."

Given Derrida's conspiratorial view of Western philosophy, his reversal of the speech/writing hierarchy is meant to have major implications. In one of his essays, Derrida observes that the word *pharmakon* in Greek means both "poison" and "cure" and that Plato in the *Phaedrus* uses the word to describe writing. This etymological conceit, abetted by some heavy textual free-play, permits Derrida to expose what he sees as the perennial ambivalence toward writing in Western philosophy. According to Derrida, speech has always been "privileged" over writing—that is, philosophers since Plato are supposed to have distrusted the written word and placed their confidence in speech. Written words, says Socrates in the *Phaedrus,* "seem to talk to you as though they were intelligent, but if you ask them anything about what they say, from a desire to be instructed, they go on telling you just the same thing forever. And once a thing is put into writing, the composition, whatever it may be, drifts all over the place, getting into the hands not only of those who understand it, but equally of those who have no business with it; it doesn't know how to address the right people, and not address the wrong."

It seems questionable to assume that this speech by Socrates puts Plato on record as "privileging" speech over writing. For after all, Socrates is a character in the *Phaedrus* and doesn't always speak for the author; in writing the dialogue, Plato may be said to have negated the gesture made by Socrates in the speech. Derrida himself has played on this irony. Nevertheless, in seeking to undo the real or alleged hierarchy of speech and writing, Derrida acts as if what is at stake is somehow a "liberation." It is as though the championing of writing over speech were a moral imperative. "The history of truth, of the truth of truth, has always been . . . the debasement of writing, and its repression outside 'full' speech," Derrida writes in *Of Grammatology*.

This "debasement," this "repression," is nothing other than the old nemesis, logocentrism. It remains a mild irony that the deconstructionists, for all their advocacy of writing over speech, favor the oral presentation as the ideal medium and the academic conference as the ideal forum for the exposition of their ideas.

—*Words speak us.* J. Hillis Miller laid down "the law that language is not an instrument or tool in man's hands, a submissive means of thinking. Language rather thinks man and his 'world,' including poems, if he will allow it to do so." Language does the talking for us. We're not in control of our words, but they control us. (A Marxist revision of this deconstructive dogma is that language speaks through us at the service of some repressive ideology or other.) What makes this one of the most radical of deconstructionist principles is that it blithely waves away the possibility of free will; for if language manipulates us, how can we assign responsibility for the statements we make? If writers, even great writers, are continually betrayed by their words, what does this say about the rest of the population? The implication is that we are merely passive conductors of language; the implication challenges the autonomy of the speaker. But then this, too, is a deconstructionist goal: to undermine the self as a concept or entity or, in proper Newspeak, to confront the Self with the Excluded Other and thereby to deconstruct it.

—*All the world's a text.* This is the principle of "wall-to-wall textuality." Everything is a text or may be considered as such; what's more, at no fixed point does the text leave off and something called reality begin. The rise of *text* as the noun of choice dates back to an influential essay by Roland Barthes, "From Work to Text" (1971). The change in vocabulary, as Barthes makes clear, means a change in the ground rules of literary criticism. *Work* implies good literature, *text* embraces all—a leveling impulse that does away with the value judgments that used to distinguish critical activity. Rather than evaluate the works of a given author, the properly enlightened critic plays with authorless texts. For the shift in terminology also signals a shift of authority. *Work* implies an author and *text* helps eliminate that unwanted personage. "The author is reputed the father and owner of his work," Barthes writes. "As for the Text, it reads without the inscription of the Father." *Works* are objects of "consumption" devoured by passive readers; *texts* are "polysemous," having plural meanings, and reading is an act of "practical collaboration."

Roland Barthes affirmed what he called "the pleasure of the text." He used the word *jouissance* to indicate the erotic dimension of reading; the appropriate response to a book is to read it like a playful lover rather than like a uxorious husband, with liberty rather than with fidelity. Jacques Derrida raised the importance of the text to a metaphysical quandary, a difficulty standing in the way of our knowing anything with certainty. "There is nothing outside the text"—*"Il n'y a rien hors du texte"*—he declared in *Of Grammatalogy*. It is a philosophical position that effectively dissolves all borders. It makes little sense to observe the distinction between truth and fiction, for example; both are subsumed under the heading of "textuality." Texts don't speak about the world but about other texts. There is, where meaning once was thought to reside, only an infinity of mirrors.

The concept of *textuality* is a good example of how deconstruction reflects and builds on the crucial assumptions of our cultural Zeitgeist. You find the concept endowed with a similar significance in the field of anthropology. "Doing ethnography," Clifford Geertz argued in *The Interpretation of Cultures* (1973), "is like trying to read (in the sense of 'construct a reading of') a manuscript—foreign, faded, full of ellipses, incoherencies, suspicious emendations, and tendentious commentaries, but written not in conventionalized graphs of sound but in transient examples of shaped behavior." Anthropological writings are interpretations in search of meaning rather than investigations in search of scientific laws. It follows that they are fictions, "something made," "something fashioned." But for Geertz the knowledge of the ineluctable textuality of all experience and all evidence doesn't lead to a deconstructive dead end. Geertz recognizes the threat to "the objective status of anthropological knowledge" but maintains that "the threat is hollow. The claim to attention of an ethnographic account does not rest on its author's ability to capture primitive facts in faraway places and carry them home like a mask or a carving, but on the degree to which he is able to clarify what goes on in such places, to reduce the puzzlement—what manner of men are these?—to which unfamiliar acts emerging out of unknown backgrounds naturally give rise." In the years since Geertz wrote these words, radical anthropologists have seized on the threat that he calls hollow as if it were the one indubitable fact that makes all others suspect.

—*The author is dead.* "Popular wisdom warns us that we frequently substitute the wish for the deed," writes the novelist and critic William Gass, "and when, in 1968, Roland Barthes announced the death of the author, he was actually calling for it. Nor did Roland Barthes himself sign up for suicide, but wrote his way into the College of France where he performed *voltes-faces* for an admiring audience." Barthes tolled the bell in his essay "The Death of the Author," naming that as the precondition for the wished-for "birth of the reader." For Barthes the demise of the author successfully completes a rebellion against authority. The elimination of "the Author-God" frustrates any attempt to "decipher" the text, and that, wrote Barthes, is a good thing. The text is to be "disentangled," not "deciphered," and this "liberates what may be called an anti-theological activity, an activity that is truly revolutionary since to refuse to fix meaning is, in the end, to refuse God and his hypostases—reason, science, law." There is something awry, William Gass notes, in the metaphorical linkage of authors and gods—an odd leap of logic that makes us balk at the assumption that the literary half of the analogy is as "liberating" as Barthes would have us believe. Gass explains:

> The idea of the death of the author does not match the idea of the death of god as perfectly as the current members of this faith may suppose, because we know—as they know—that there *are* authors; and we know—as they know—there *are no* gods. The death of the author is not an ordinary demise, nor is it simply the departure of belief, like an exotic visitor from the East, from the minds of the masses. The two expressions are metaphors which are the reverse of one another. The death of god represents not only the realization that gods have never existed, but the contention that such a belief is no longer even irrationally possible: that neither reason nor the taste and temper of the times can condone it. The belief lingers on, of course, but it does so like astrology or a faith in a flat earth—in worse case than

a neurotic symptom, no longer even *a la mode*. The death of the author, on the other hand, signifies a decline in authority, in theological power, as if Zeus were stripped of his thunderbolts and swans, perhaps residing on Olympus still, but now living in a camper and cooking with propane. He *is,* but he is no longer a god.

The "death of god" is the denial of a metaphysical belief; the "death of the author" is a denial of a material, historical, verifiable fact. The comparison between the author and God is a flawed one but is strategically employed to glorify the reader-critic's willful disobedience. Gass shrewdly suggests that the real point of convergence between the death of the author and the death of God lies somewhere beyond the two concepts—in the wished-for "death of the father." Undoubtedly this is the gesture that the word *phallogocentrism* is meant to perform.

While Barthes calls for the overthrow of the author as a way to replicate in literary terms the death of God, Michel Foucault sets out to demonstrate that the author never existed in the first place. According to Foucault, to identify a text by its author's name is, relatively speaking, a modern convention. "There was a time when the texts we today call 'literary' (narratives, stories, epics, tragedies, comedies) were accepted, put into circulation, and valorized without any question about the identity of their author." Foucault recommends that we regard the author not "as a genius" but as "an ideological product." He predicts that "the author-function will disappear" and that texts will then be able to "develop in the anonymity of a murmur." It need hardly be said that neither Barthes nor Foucault removed his name from the title pages of the books in which they pronounce their *requiescat in pace* for the author.

Deconstruction completes the assault. For Jacques Derrida, quotation marks make the point that "it would be frivolous to think that 'Descartes,' 'Leibniz,' 'Rousseau,' 'Hegel,' etc., are names of authors." What are they, then? Merely textual entities, fictive beings devoid of authority. Peter Mullen's parodic poem, "Deconstruction," is quite exact:

> D'ya wanna know the creed'a
> Jacques Derrida?

Dere ain't no reada
Dere ain't no wrider
Eider.

If the author is dead, and has been dead "always already," the author's life is irrelevant: deconstruction is a profoundly antibiographical theory. To note the boom in biography as a publishing category and as a literary enterprise is to note one more sign of the breach between the academic scene and the culture at large.

—*Presence is absent.* The deconstructive unmasking of "the metaphysics of presence" has a plainly antitheological charge. Where existentialism regarded "the death of god" as a starting point for a philosophy of moral action, deconstruction is curiously and needlessly absolutist; it suggests that an absolute ground for truth is indispensable and that in its absence, no moral judgments can be made. Apply this logic to the Ten Commandments, and you find that they deconstruct themselves. The argument goes like this: For the Ten Commandments to have any real moral force, you need to credit the authority of God. The various imperatives, the *thou shalt* and *thou shalt not* clauses, make no sense without the prior assertion of a God in whom these commandments originate. Therefore the Ten Commandments begin with an affirmation rather than a command: "I am the Lord thy God, who have brought thee out of the land of Egypt, out of the house of bondage." The voice of God—God's presence—precedes his commandments; it's the *is* that makes *ought* possible. "If God is dead, everything is permitted," wrote Dostoevski in *The Brothers Karamazov.* The deconstructive world-view is closer in spirit to Nietzsche's way of saying it: "Nothing is true; everything is permitted."

—*History is bunk.* Henry Ford summed up the orthodox deconstructive position with admirable succinctness. History is one casualty of the dissolution of philosophical boundaries. Since there is no history outside of texts, and texts are unstable in their meaning, history is rendered undecidable—as undecidable as literature. In effect, history exists within bracket marks. A programmatic skepticism toward all truth-claims promotes the view of history as either irrelevant to the study of a given text or as itself a scripted text, with no more substance than a movie. The double danger of such a view is that it would paralyze the will to act upon our destiny while at the same time it implies the possibility that the "texts" of our lives can be revised, erased, or interpreted out of existence.

For a fictional treatment of the wars-as-texts theme, turn to Philip K. Dick's *The Man in the High Castle* (1962), a masterpiece in the "alternative history" subgenre of science fiction. The novel is based on the premise that the Germans and the Japanese won the Second World War. The victors between them occupy the United States—the Japanese control the West Coast, the Germans the East—except for a slender nonaligned region in the mountain states. In a remote castle in this unoccupied zone lives a man named Abendsen, the author of a novel entitled *The Grasshopper Lies Heavy*. Though banned by the Nazis, *The Grasshopper* enjoys a lively underground existence. It is a most subversive novel—its premise is that Germany and Japan *lost* the war. Juliana, Dick's heroine, undertakes a pilgrimage to Abendsen's high castle and, after various crises and close calls, reaches her destination. She finds that the Abendsen house is not a castle at all but "a single-story stucco house with many shrubs and a good deal of garden made up mostly of climbing roses." The climactic revelation comes next. When Juliana and Abendsen meet, both are startled to learn that his book "is true." Despite all appearances to the contrary, Germany and Japan did lose the war.

The fragility of historical truth is a great theme for the novelist to explore, whether in the form of a prophetic warning or a paranoid fantasia. But when it is taught as serious doctrine—when the assault on "empirical facts" is made sober-faced, as though the knowledge were somehow liberating, as though it weren't standard totalitarian practice to substitute interpretation for fact in the rewriting of history—the deconstruction of truth is not so benign a phenomenon.

—*Goodbye to aesthetics.* Art is suspect because works of art are ideological constructions—as are governments, wars, and revolutions. Art has been corrupted by technology. Fascism can be understood as a triumph of the aesthetic ideology: the Nazis mesmerized the masses with images and illusions, the construction of a myth. Here the key text is Walter Benjamin's essay "The Work of Art in the Age of

Mechanical Reproduction" (1936). "The logical result of Fascism is the introduction of aesthetics into political life," Benjamin wrote. War itself could be treated as if it were an aesthetic spectacle. Fascism "expects war to supply the artistic gratification of a sense perception that has been changed by technology." Published in 1936, before the Nazis' state-sponsored violence ran its full course, Benjamin's analysis leaves out the more extreme forms of coercion of the fascist state—a state in which, to paraphrase W. H. Auden, the unacknowledged legislators of the world are the secret police. But while Benjamin's is a limited view of fascism, that hasn't stopped deconstructionists from harping on the dangers of "aesthetic ideology." The deconstructionist suspicion of art is thus put on a quasi-political footing.

Some theorists make the argument that art underwrites the authority of the powers that be. The view that regards the work of art as an autonomous entity is seen as a "bourgeois fiction" designed to mask the ways in which art is used to inculcate a dominant cultural ideology. For the so-called cultural materialists, who put deconstructive tactics at the service of Marxist objectives, art is a species of production, of interest as an object of study to the extent that it presents a microcosm of the economic structure of capitalism. The moral experience of a work of art, the ideas it expresses, the feelings it educates, are an obvious casualty of such critical programs.

—*Language, not knowledge, is power.* Humpty Dumpty in *Through the Looking-Glass* was an early forerunner of deconstruction. Words, he says, don't mean what you think they mean. Everything depends on who does the defining. In Humpty's own example, *glory* can mean "a nice knock-down argument." It follows that language is a mediator of power, not a repository of beliefs. For Humpty, words mean what *he* wants them to mean. "The question is," says Alice, "whether you *can* make words mean so many different things." "The question is," Humpty replies, "which is to be master—that's all." Like Humpty, the deconstructionists are preoccupied with power—they are inordinately fond of using words such as *power* and *institutions* and avoiding words such as *greatness* and *genius* and *wisdom*. Humpty even has a comment, or so it seems, on the prose style of deconstructionist critics. "Impenetrability!" he exclaims. Alice asks what he means. "I meant by 'impenetrability' that we've had enough of that subject."

. . .

—*What you see is never what you get.* You expect a text to represent the world, but the text is self-referential. You persist in regarding words as means toward an end, but you cannot escape the endlessly labyrinthine coils of discourse. Words point only to other words, to traces and differences, never to the real thing. The truth is what is absent, concealed, "marginalized," excluded, invisible. The late novelist Walker Percy defined a deconstructionist as an academic who claims that texts have no referents, but who leaves a message on his wife's telephone answering machine requesting a pepperoni pizza for supper. The message is a text, writes Percy, and the pizza is a referent. To extend the metaphor, it could be specified that the telephone answering machine in question has a self-erasing tape. The deconstructive critic should not be surprised if the pizza fails to materialize.

And that brings us to the Marxist/Freudian axis. In a Marxist model of knowledge, the superstructure—the tangible products of culture—camouflages and reinforces the hidden reality of class warfare. In a Freudian model, the manifest content of a dream is a cover or disguise for its latent meaning. In a deconstructive model, the text that is the world is similarly a camouflage. Like the Marxist's superstructure and the Freudian's manifest content, it is something to be seen through. The difference is that here, in contrast to the Marxist or Freudian schemes, there is no ultimate meaning to which one can penetrate. There is only the constant deferral of meaning, the infinite play of signification, and finally, the equilibrist's wire across the linguistic abyss.

CHAPTER 5

A KEY IDEA

A word that everyone snaps up, or a question
that has everybody excited, probably carries a
generative idea—the germ of a complete reorientation in metaphysics, or at least the
"Open Sesame" of some new positive science.
The sudden vogue of such a key-idea is due to
the fact that all sensitive and active minds turn
at once to exploiting it; we try it in every
connection, for every purpose, experiment
with possible stretches of its strict meaning,
with generalizations and derivatives. When
we become familiar with the new idea our
expectations do not outrun its actual uses quite
so far, and then its unbalanced popularity is
over. We settle down to the problems that it
has really generated, and these become the
characteristic issues of our time.

—*Susanne K. Langer,* PHILOSOPHY IN A NEW
KEY *(1942)*

Tales of the liberated signifier: Now that we have *deconstruction,* we
keep finding new situations in which the word makes perfect sense.
In an issue of *Newsweek* devoted to the escalating costs of the savings
and loan debacle, Jane Bryant Quinn notes that banks have begun
tightening their credit policies, though "it's still pretty early in the
deconstruction of the temple to see much evidence in the statistics."
A fashion reporter in the *New York Times Magazine* salutes Giorgio

Armani's new look in men's clothes for the 1990s: loose-fitting garments, to be worn with a slouch, in place of the power suits of yesteryear. She quotes an expert on cultural mythologies: what is going on is the "dismantling of Reaganist attitudes. And fashion participates in that deconstruction." The writer of the "Newsmakers" column in the *Philadelphia Inquirer* has an item about a "hyper-rich" Texas couple with a superfluous mansion on their estate. The couple had "the 6,600 square-foot house carefully dismantled, then reassembled" on the grounds of an institution for emotionally disturbed children. Juxtaposed is an anecdote about an American artist who bought two five-ton fragments of the crumbling Berlin Wall. The headline: "Deconstruction."

"Words in isolation have no meaning," Jacques Derrida has written. "What makes sense is the sentence. How many sentences can be made with 'deconstruction'?" Answer: no limit. Making up sample sentences is a game anyone can play. My hypothetical political columnist wants to recall the televised debate between the vice-presidential nominees in 1988: "When Lloyd Bentsen told Dan Quayle that he was 'no Kennedy,' Bentsen not only won the debate; he terminally deconstructed the air and pretension of the Quayle campaign." The theater critic is not to be outdone: "By putting the rant in the mouth of a discredited speaker, the playwright has it both ways—she gets to rant and to mock the rant at the same time. This is generally called 'having your cake and eating it, too.' But a high-sounding interpretation could be placed on this hedging of bets—to wit, that the dramatist intends to conduct us to the deconstructive abyss that awaits when equal and opposite meanings cancel each other out." The art chronicler will come across plenty of works on which to pin the tag of deconstruction. The French sculptors Anne and Patrick Poirier, he might note, specialize in pseudoruins—a fallen column here, a tomb entrance there—strategically positioned to suggest "the effect of a deconstructed marble temple." Then there's the foreign policy pundit: "Are the Soviet hardliners—the ones critical of Gorbachev's overtures to the West—left-wingers or right-wingers? The question is either unanswerable or meaningless, but asking it might have the beneficent effect of deconstructing the standard left-right dichotomy, which is so often misleading." Even the autocrat of the breakfast table can get in on the act: "On the front page of the *New York Times* today I read, 'K.G.B. Chief Says New Legislature Should Ride Herd on His Agency,' and in slightly smaller type, 'In Talk With Reporters, He Cites U.S. Over-sight System as the Model.' I paused over 'Oversight.' Did that mean overview—or error? Self-deconstruction!"

Though a deconstructionist might deride it as vulgarization, the popular use of the term *deconstruction*—the way it has entered the language—confirms that it is a "key-idea" in the sense that Susanne K. Langer had in mind in her book *Philosophy in a New Key*. "Every-one" has snapped up the word, using it with "possible stretches of its strict meaning"; it "probably carries a generative idea," if not "the germ of a complete reorientation in metaphysics." I believe this to be true; I believe that, for better or worse, deconstruction has codified some and modified other of the prevailing cultural assumptions of our time. I believe that deconstruction has at least a limited value for the practicing literary critic—if he or she disregards the metaphysical dogma and brings to bear on the reading of literature the heightened awareness of language that deconstruction promotes. Define it broadly enough, and there's no reason to shy away from the word—and several good reasons to use it. One reason is that literary criticism remains an art, not a science, and therefore the critic would be wise to borrow from any given theory or system of thought that seems to fit an individual case. The methods and categories of deconstruction, its profound skepticism and its spirit of high play, may help us to make sense of anomalies that would otherwise go unexplained. The decon-structive bias in favor of theory over practice is easily dispensed with, and the alarming aspects of the theory don't discredit all the insights it fosters. "We ought scrupulously to risk the use of any concept that seems propitious or helpful in getting over gaps," wrote R. P. Black-mur, one of the century's greatest literary critics. "Only the use should be consciously provisional, speculative, and dramatic." To the extent that the word itself has become a part of our language, moreover, it is unavoidable. The poet—whose concern, in Mallarmé's famous phrase, is to "purify the dialect of the tribe"—will not simply ignore *deconstruction* but will try to redeem it. Deconstruction has a name for this procedure: it's called a *recuperative* reading. A recuperative reading asserts the value of a discourse after methodically tearing it apart. And if the real gesture of *recuperative* is the clear implication that the discourse, prior to the critic's surgical intervention, is sick, then so be it.

One step toward recuperating deconstruction is to distinguish between the "hard-core" and "soft-core" varieties. These terms were introduced by Howard Felperin in his book *Beyond Deconstruction,* in 1985. Felperin classifies as soft-core the work of such critics as Harold Bloom and Geoffrey Hartman, who share affinities with the deconstructionists but retain features of a more humanistic world-view. Hard-core deconstruction, on the other hand, is hard-line, insistent, "thoroughgoing," and Jacques Derrida is its "doyen." Felperin defines it rather ingeniously by hunting down a precedent in ancient Greece. "The first work of thoroughgoing (what I shall later term 'hard-core') deconstruction to come down to us," Felperin writes, "is the fifth-century B.C. treatise *On Not Being, or On Nature* by Gorgias, the argument of which was summarized by Sextus Empiricus: 'Firstly . . . nothing exists; secondly . . . even if anything exists, it is inapprehensible by man; thirdly . . . even if anything is apprehensible, yet of a surety it is inexpressible and incommunicable to one's neighbour.'"

The "hard-core" and "soft-core" categories are invoked but defined somewhat differently in Stephen Moore's recent book about the impact of literary theory on biblical studies, *Literary Criticism and the Gospels.* Derrida exemplifies the "utterly pitiless, no-holds-barred style of deconstruction," which "can be called the 'hard' style," Moore writes. What Moore calls "soft deconstruction" is, on the other hand, "an American product, whose corporate headquarters might be said to have been at Yale University until Paul de Man's death in 1983." For Moore, in other words, Derrida is to "hard" deconstruction what de Man is to the "soft" variety.

My own sense of the terms "hard-core" and "soft-core" in this context comes closer to Felperin's version. By hard-core deconstruction, I mean precisely the academic orthodoxy associated with de Man and his disciples. It is "hard" in the sense of being putatively rigorous (or rigid, depending on your viewpoint) and defiantly difficult to follow. It is programmatic. It asks to be taken as something more than a critical method—something like an antitheological theology. By contrast, soft-core deconstruction is an elastic critical concept and is meant to be used with a lighter touch; a synonym might be "practical" or "applied" deconstruction. It differs from hard-core deconstruction in having a strictly provisional value and an utterly pragmatic function; its use does not imply the critic's subscription to deconstructive doctrine in any larger sense. Soft-core deconstruction may serve to describe virtually any form of critical interpretation that is concerned with the tricky relations between language and meaning, between what is said and what is hidden, in a text. It refuses the mandatory trip to the linguistic abyss but retains the sense of deconstruction as a devastating critique, an exposé, an unmasking—what the journalist is getting at in describing the effect of Lloyd Bentsen's showstopping line in his vice-presidential debate with Dan Quayle. Finally, soft-core deconstruction in this broad sense eschews the idea that reality is "inexpressible and incommunicable" but retains the deconstructive alertness to conundrums, logical contradictions, enigmas, and ironic reversals. Deconstruction in all its guises has certainly conditioned us to pay particularly close attention to those moments when, double-crossed by an author, we fall down a fictional trapdoor—with the result that we have to rethink the things that we have been taking for granted. It is surely not a coincidence that much of the art of our time, much of what is called "postmodernism," seems to place a high premium on just such shifts and reversals. If, in keeping abreast of new literary developments, criticism must continually come up with innovative tactics, the battery of devices associated with deconstruction will not fail to yield a value.

In its soft-core sense, deconstruction has proved itself to be a tremendously adaptable term. For the theatre critic, a new revival of *What the Butler Saw* might prompt the observation that Joe Orton's play "deconstructs"—meaning something a bit stronger than "undermines"—the institution of marriage and the concept of gender. A book reviewer notes the contradiction between a political journalist's spoken aims and his unspoken assumptions—the charting out of such discrepancies is called deconstruction. More significant is the application of deconstructive stratagems by a brilliant novelist. Chapter One of Philip Roth's *The Counterlife* ends with the death of a major character, who is—surprise!—alive and well in Chapter Two. The novel reverses its own premises midstream, reminding us that it is only a fiction. The novelist's *gotcha* gets us to revise our assumptions about narrative form on the one hand, and about the allegedly autobiographical character of Roth's fictional writing on the other. You can say, though Roth would probably resist the term, that his novel deconstructs the idea that a first-person narration seemingly based on the author's experience must be true to fact. He proves that it isn't so, but also makes us realize that we expect it to be.

The Counterlife is a terrific novel precisely because it is so radically skeptical of its own premises. It harnesses the full array of postmodernist tricks—the false-bottomed narrative, the multiplication of counterfeit actualities and alternative possibilities, "what-could-be having always to top what-is"—not as ingenious ends in themselves and not merely to serve an inquiry into the puzzling relations between fiction and reality. Rather, Roth interrupts his narrative and brings his characters back from the dead, letting them revise their speeches and their fates, for a purpose that can be characterized only as moral. The middle-aged dentist dies during heart surgery, or the same dentist recovers, abandons his New Jersey practice and family, and emigrates to Israel, where he joins the Gush Emunim settlement of a charismatic zealot: either scenario is valid not only as a metaphysical possibility but as a moral predicament. The dentist's initial dilemma, for instance, dramatizes the moral implications of Freud's argument in *Beyond the Pleasure Principle.* In the man's decision to undergo a life-endangering heart operation rather than continue to live without his sexual potency, we see the fatal alliance of Eros and Thanatos—the coupling of desire and danger, sexuality and death—and we see it as inevitable, irresistible, the self's anarchic refusal to subordinate its instinctive desires to the mandates of civilization. Civilization calls for self-preservation, yet the self insists on obeying its own wayward dictates. In submitting to the surgeon's knife, the dentist affirms the primacy of the erotic impulse. He pays for the decision with his life. End of chapter. But since this is fiction, there's no reason he has to stay dead—and so, when we turn the page, we intercept him en route to Israel, months after his successful recovery from surgery. In fiction, after all, both sides could have won the Civil War. If this counts as an example of applied deconstruction, I'm all for it.

Deconstruction's methods and concepts, used selectively and without doctrinal fervor, can sometimes bring us closer to the frequently enigmatic workings of some of our favorite books or films. The poet and critic John Hollander, a masterly teacher, demonstrates the pedagogical virtues of soft-core deconstruction when he observes that "Charlie Chaplin deconstructs public statuary in the opening frames of *City Lights.*" No other word will work so well to describe the effect of the brilliant sequence in which the tramp, played by Chaplin, sabotages the ceremonial unveiling of a new civic monument. The scene opens in a modern metropolis, downtown. In the background is the monument—a group of three statues—draped in sheets.

At the podium, speeches are delivered by pompous bigwigs. There is a fanfare of trumpets. Then the wraps come off, and there, to everyone's surprise, is the tramp, asleep in the lap of the central statue. He wakes up, tries to escape—and his trousers are impaled by the sword of the adjacent statue. A policeman in the crowd is outraged by these antics but, luckily for the tramp, the Star Spangled Banner is played at just this moment, and everyone, including the policeman, must stand at attention. What Chaplin has done in this sequence is to unveil an unveiling. By showing us the tramp comfortably sleeping in the statue's lap, Chaplin deconstructs the monument by turning it into its opposite. He makes us see the monument for what it is—cold and forbidding—by depicting it, for the moment, as welcoming and homey. The incongruity of the tramp's presence drives home the point. The monument is seen for what it really is when the tramp's trousers are impaled by the bronze sword. For now we recall that the statue is a monument to "Peace and Prosperity"—claims that are belied by the tramp's very existence in this depression year 1931. Humanized by the tramp, the statue signifies not "Peace and Prosperity" but the reality that it was meant to exclude—poverty and the threat of violence. Minus the tramp, it is merely a monument to human vanity and wishful thinking.

Something about the logic of Hollywood movies—the way they know that we know they're just movies—makes them apt agents of a deconstructive impulse. Movie logic has it that Claudette Colbert, the spoiled heiress in Frank Capra's *It Happened One Night,* is redeemed as a character when circumstances oblige her to rough it. Having run away from home, she is reduced to subsisting on strictly limited funds. Pursued by unscrupulous reward-seekers, she manages to escape undetected—in one memorable scene—by playing the part of the impoverished young housewife. Stripped of her customary resources and defenses, she is just vulnerable enough to fall in love with a man who could never belong in her social circle—the fired newspaperman played by Clark Gable. Gable aids her escape but, more important, it is through him that she realizes how little her happiness depends on her wealth. The paradox is that Gable's reward for teaching her this lesson is her hand in marriage, connubial bliss with, presumably, the lady's millions thrown in, though at film's end the couple is careful to keep up the appearance of penury by honeymooning in a motor lodge. The premise—you can be happy though poor—is immediately cancelled by the happy ending, which grants the hero the riches that make his happiness complete. It wouldn't really be a happy ending, as the audience well knows, if necessity and not choice took the honeymooners to that dingy motor lodge. Thus the film's outcome deconstructs its thesis, or revises it: the best things in life *are* free but only if you're a millionaire or if you marry one. It's not so bad, the film is saying, to be unemployed in the depression year 1934—if you're Clark Gable and you wake up in a bus with Claudette Colbert in your arms.

Another example: It's not too much to say that *The Maltese Falcon* deconstructs human desire and that it does so by separating the impulse from its ostensible object. Everyone in John Huston's movie, as in the Dashiell Hammett novel on which it's based, is after an allegedly priceless piece of avian statuary. The characters played by Mary Astor, Peter Lorre, and Sydney Greenstreet are positively obsessed with the black bird. It is not simply a matter of greed, for their infatuation with the falcon goes beyond the monetary value of the jewels encrusted beneath the bird's enameled surface—it is not what the statue can buy that confers the desired magic upon its possessor. The characters proceed as if possession of the trophy, though continually deferred, would justify any number of years spent on the chase. As the Fat Man (Greenstreet) says in Hammett's novel, " 'For seventeen years I have wanted that little item and have been trying to get it. If I must spend another year on the quest—well, sir—that will be an additional expenditure in time of only'—his lips moved silently as he calculated—'five and fifteen-seventeenths per cent.' " When Humphrey Bogart, as detective Sam Spade, calls the statue a "dingus," it is more than just a display of irreverent slang. *Dingus* deconstructs the object of obsessive desire, calling it by its proper name—in advance of the revelation that the sculpture is a fake. The black bird, when it finally turns up, yields neither gold nor jewels when its surface is scratched. It is a fake, and necessarily a fake, because the falcon exists only as a function of a never-ending fruitless quest. The object of desire need have no real value. Desire alone makes the falcon desirable. You can't ever possess the thing, for desire attaches itself to the quest, not the finding. In a model of deconstructive logic, the apparent fulfillment of desire is really its negation; and when Bogart walks down the stairs cradling the bird at the end of the film, he has exactly a "dingus" to show for his trouble.

Deconstructive logic, with the importance it places on paradox and self-cancellation, opens up interesting possibilities for the creative artist to explore. Philip K. Dick in his novel *Valis* (1981) makes a deconstructive move when he prints the same clause two ways:

GOD IS NO WHERE
GOD IS NOW HERE

The difference between God's immanence and his absence becomes a function of the typewriter's space bar—which is not to deny the magnitude of the issue. What it does prove is that contrary scenarios may be extrapolated from the same linguistic given—that language always contains the possibility of affirming mutually exclusive realities, substituting *either/and* for *either/or*. For the imaginative writer, the knowledge of language's generative power—and of literature's irreducibly linguistic essence—can act as a spur to creative activity. I write the word *therapist*. Then I introduce a space after the *e* and get *the rapist*. My task is to devise a fictional journey from one to the other—to generate a plot out of the drama within the word itself. Perhaps I can do the job in the form of a psychological thriller in which the notorious sex offender, always masked, is none other than the trust-inspiring Dr. Jekyll, whose psychiatric practice has prospered on a clientele of gun-shy women, victims of rape. With the villain's unmasking, *the rapist* has deconstructed the *therapist*. The self-cancelling nature of the word has led not to a philosophical dead end but to an imaginative possibility, one that enables us to reach further truths. For surely there's a sense in which the therapist in a psychoanalytic encounter can violate his or her client. And the reverse of that metaphor—the vicious suggestion that the rapist may be an agent of therapy—as surely exposes the secret, self-deluded logic with which the rapist justifies his misdeeds to himself.

Bruce Lincoln in his book *Discourse and the Construction of Society* goes overboard in his use of *deconstruction,* opting to use the term in cases in which there is no particular insight to be gained by it. But in his discussion of "anomaly as an instrument of revolutionary agitation," Lincoln does cite a pivotal historical episode that aptly illustrates the logic of deconstruction. When Louis XVI was tried and executed during the French Revolution, treason was the charge formally brought against him. The anomaly of the situation, as Lincoln explains, is that treason was defined in 1793 as a crime committed *against the king*. Again we confront a self-cancelling proposition—a deconstructive conundrum. If you could convict the king of treason, then *treason* would have to be redefined. Lincoln's point, and it's a good one, is that the revolutionary leaders Saint-Just and Robespierre aimed "not merely to convict one king, but to deconstruct kingship and its correlated sociopolitical order." Not so much the king but the *institution* of the king was on trial: the king had, in effect, committed a crime against himself—that is, a crime that discredited royalty. Here, Lincoln's use of *deconstruction* is warranted, because the anomaly of the charge brought against the king rhetorically expresses the Revolution's divorce of the law of the land from the prerogatives of the royal will—in a word, the deconstruction of the throne.

Other examples of soft-core deconstruction could be given, but I think these suffice to make the case. The word is a handy one to have, and the tactics that go with it—the tendency, for example, to focus one's attention not on the center but on the margins of a text or an event—can be fruitfully used. Hard-core deconstruction is something else again. It proceeds not from the love of literature but from the tacit assumption that literature exists primarily to illustrate the laws of a critical doctrine. Worse, it asks to be accepted in toto, not adapted into a critical instrument to be used with discretion. The hardening of a theory into dogma, wrote R. P. Blackmur, carries the danger of "fanatic falsification." It "arises when a body of criticism is governed by an *idée fixe,* a really exaggerated heresy, when a notion of genuine but small scope is taken literally as of universal application. This is the body of tendentious criticism where, since something is assumed proved before the evidence is in, distortion, vitiation, and absolute assertion become supreme virtues." Hard-core deconstruction flaunts this danger. It is accurately described as "a really exaggerated heresy," and given its claims to universality, it is not to be taken lightly. It has its consequences, not least on the way the humanities are taught in colleges and universities. One problem with the deconstructive approach is the conformism it promotes. In orthodox deconstruction, all roads lead to the same dismal antitruth. The text, any text, is an arena of contradictory impulses. Your job is to show how the text—by those contradictory impulses—undermines itself. You deconstruct it by revealing that it was all along an allegory of its own "unreadability." This is, ultimately, a sterile and pointless exercise.

Let me give two prime examples of hard-core deconstruction. Both are famous in literary criticism circles. The first dismantles William Wordsworth's poem "A Slumber Did My Spirit Seal." I quote the poem in full:

> A slumber did my spirit seal;
> I had no human fears;
> She seemed a thing that could not feel
> The touch of earthly years.
>
> No motion has she now, no force;
> She neither hears nor sees;
> Rolled round in earth's diurnal course
> With rocks, and stones, and trees.

The poem is generally classified as one of Wordsworth's "Lucy" poems—five brief lyrics that mourn the death of a girl—though her name does not appear in "A Slumber Did My Spirit Seal."

Because of its brevity and its popularity within the Wordsworth canon, "A Slumber" has for many years served as a test case for literary interpretation. The traditional view is that the poem is elegiac, an expression of grief recollected in the tranquility of mature wisdom. The space between the first and second stanzas of the poem acts as a bridge from the past to the present, from innocence to knowledge, from a carefree state of existence to a frank acknowledgment of mortality. The poem is so moving a lament because its grief is so restrained; it is so artistically satisfying because its economy and apparent simplicity go hand in hand with an exquisite patterning. Nor has the poem, brief though it is, been exhausted by critical commentary; fresh insights are still possible. One recent article dwells on Wordsworth's rhyme scheme. The rhyme of "fears" and "years" is picked up in the second stanza by "hears," and perhaps it is not an accident that the last word in the poem is a near anagram for "tears."

A rival reading stresses that Wordsworth, at the time he wrote "A Slumber," subscribed to a pantheistic philosophy. He held the belief that the dead return to the living life of nature, that "rocks and stones and trees" are alive in an elemental sense. The knowledge that the dead girl is "Rolled round in earth's diurnal course" becomes, according to this interpretation, an occasion for cheer rather than for lament. While I find this a difficult reading to accept, it is not outlandish. The case for the pantheistic interpretation has been made with care, and one finds oneself quarreling with the conclusion, not with the means used to arrive at it.

By contrast, the deconstructive analysis of "A Slumber Did My Spirit Seal" comes as a deliberate shock. It was undertaken by J. Hillis Miller precisely as an object lesson meant to illustrate the virtues of his "alternative mode" of literary study. A deconstructive reading, Miller explains, shows that "metaphysical assumptions are both present and at the same time undermined by the text itself." There is a "play of tropes" in any text and it "leads to a suspension of fully rationalizable meaning in the experience of an aporia or boggling of the mind." But since "the test of this hypothesis is the interpretation of the texts themselves," Miller will put it to work on Wordsworth's poem. He begins by summing up the traditional interpretation, and he does this quite competently. He is right to chart out the series of oppositions between the first and second stanzas of "A Slumber"; the poem does progress from slumber to waking, from past to present, from the girl as an innocent young thing to the inanimate "thing" she becomes in death.

Yet Miller's series of oppositions includes one that seems utterly foreign to Wordsworth's lines: Miller tells us that the poem presents "mother as against daughter or sister, or perhaps any female family member as against some woman from outside the family, that is, mother, sister, or daughter as against mistress or wife, in short, incestuous desires against legitimate sexual feelings." For Miller insists that the poem is "odder" than it looks, stranger and more enigmatic than traditional interpretations allow. The poet's "I" is absent in the poem's second stanza, Miller notes; perhaps "the speaker has lost his selfhood" as a consequence of Lucy's death. Miller maintains, moreover, that "an obscure sexual drama is enacted in this poem." He rather arbitrarily identifies Lucy as a stand-in for Wordsworth's mother, who died when the poet was eight years old; the dead girl "is both the virgin child and the missing mother, that mother earth which gave birth to the speaker and has abandoned him." And Miller discerns a disquieting nuance in the phrase "the touch of earthly years." As he sees it, the phrase designates "a form of sexual appropriation": "To be touched by earthly years is a way to be sexually penetrated while still remaining virgin." The upshot, for Miller, is that the poet is revealing his complicity and his guilt in Lucy's fate. "The poet has himself caused Lucy's death by thinking about it," Miller asserts. "Thinking recapitulates in reverse mirror image the action of the earthly years in touching, penetrating, possessing, killing, encompassing, turning the other into oneself and therefore being left only with a corpse, an empty sign." The etymological derivation of the name Lucy—it comes from the Latin root for "light"—impels Miller to take one final leap. The poem, he says, is an allegory of loss. But it is not a dead girl that Wordsworth mourns for; it is "the lost source of light, the father sun as logos, as head power and fount of meaning." In the absence of the logos, the meaning of the poem must continually oscillate: "Each word in itself becomes the dwelling place of contradictory senses."

Miller purports to illuminate Wordsworth's text, but look how far afield he roams. By an associative method that resembles the kind of exaggerated symbol-hunting that teachers used to discourage students from doing, Miller identifies the dead girl as both father sun and mother earth, a violated virgin child and a deceased mother. Where it suits his fancy, he introduces biographical information about Wordsworth, invokes psychoanalytic categories, and conjures up a complicated and somewhat incoherent family romance. In time-tested deconstructive fashion, he resorts to etymology—the etymology of a name that is nowhere mentioned in the poem itself. Yet on the basis of such speculative procedures and capricious moves, he does not hesitate to generalize broadly. The "loss of the radiance of the logos" is, he flatly declares, "the drama of all Wordsworth's poetry."

I have singled out this particular deconstructive routine for reasons that include but go beyond the ornery and bizarre turns that it takes. It is, for one thing, aptly described as a routine; Miller likes it well enough to have published it several times, in different forms and changing contexts. He first offered his "Lucy" interpretation in 1979 as part of a brief for deconstruction. He recycled it for a 1990 dictionary of literary terms, of which Miller was responsible for the entry on narrative. "To say that all narratives, including everything from 'A Slumber Did My Spirit Seal' to big novels like Anthony Trollope's *He Knew He Was Right* or Henry James's *The Princess Casamassima,* are no more than the exploration of a single figure or system of figures is to make a large claim," Miller admits. Yet it is a claim that he does not shrink from making. Miller is evidently convinced not only of the validity of his interpretation but of its universal applicability; he is sufficiently proud of it to offer it as exemplary pedagogy. And we in turn are invited to consider it as a characteristic rather than exceptional example of the deconstructive mind at work.

"A Slumber Did My Spirit Seal" furnished the battleground for one of the more memorable critical skirmishes in recent years. M. H. Abrams had previously clashed with Miller over the merits of the deconstructive enterprise. At a session of the MLA convention in 1976, the two men debated the issue, Abrams deploring the view that "no text, in part or whole, can mean anything in particular" and Miller espousing the notion that "nihilism is an inalienable alien presence within Occidental metaphysics, both in poems and in the criticism of poems." Three years later, their continuing quarrel prompted one academic wit to propose a Western, starring Abrams and Miller, called "Shootout at Hermeneutic Gap." Now, in reply to Miller's essay on Wordsworth's "obscure sexual drama," Abrams rose to the counter-attack. He wrote, he said, as "a traditionalist who has staked whatever he has taught or written about literature, and about literary and intellectual history, on the confidence that he has been able to interpret the textual passages he cited with a determinacy and accuracy sufficient to the purpose at hand." He examined the sequence of moves with which Miller deconstructed his initial construal of Wordsworth's poem into a "bewildering medley of clashing significations." He exposed the double-dealing inherent in Miller's method: a deconstructionist reading cannot "dispense with a determinate construal of a text, as a necessary stage toward disseminating what has been so construed." If deconstruction is routinely taught as a mode of literary study, Abrams wondered, will its adepts acquire a proficiency at construing texts or will the goal be "a display of modish terminology which never engages with anything recognizable as a work of literature?" It boiled down to a question of values. The traditionalist, wrote Abrams, reads a work of literature as "a human document—a fictional presentation of thinking, acting, and feeling characters who are enough like ourselves to engage us in their experiences, in language which is expressed and ordered by a human author in a way that moves and delights the human reader." The deconstructionist offers a poor substitute: "a set of conundrums without solution."

Miller's interpretation of "A Slumber Did My Spirit Seal" is vulnerable on one other point. Miller thinks he is proving deconstruction's ability to tap the "inexhaustible strangeness" of literary works.

He proves, however, that the pursuit of novelty leads in the end to boring sameness. For while Miller's sexual reading of the poem is certifiably strange, it is fully predictable that his analysis would terminate at the place where meaning oscillates, words turn into their opposites, and logos disappears. Miller disdains traditional criticism because, he charges, it "already knows what it is going to find." But as Abrams notes, the charge applies more to deconstructive criticism than to its alternatives. Traditional modes of reading, in Abrams's words, "have amply demonstrated the ability to find highly diverse structures of meaning" in a wide range of works. In contrast, deconstruction is "single-goal-oriented." Look for a mind-boggling "aporia" and that is what you will find.

My second example of hard-core deconstruction was presented by Paul de Man as one of several paradigmatic "readings" that indicate the direction he felt literary criticism should and would take. For de Man, literary criticism could be subsumed under the general heading of rhetoric. Rhetoric, he argues, "allows for two incompatible, mutually self-destructive points of view, and therefore puts an insurmountable obstacle in the way of any reading or understanding." How better to make the point than by analyzing a rhetorical question—a famous one, well-loved and frequently taught? Accordingly, de Man chooses "Among School Children," one of the most glorious of William Butler Yeats's poems. He will deconstruct it or, rather, show how it deconstructs itself into an undecidable "aporia." The particular focus of the deconstruction is on the poem's closing couplet:

> O body swayed to music, O brightening glance,
> How can we know the dancer from the dance?

For traditional readers, these lines affirm a powerful vision of unity. Yeats's question is sublimely unanswerable; you can't distinguish the dancer from the dance, because they are the inextricable halves of a unified whole—you can't have one without the other. The question is definitively rhetorical, meant to be posed but not answered, because in effect it answers itself. It is a fitting culmination to a poem that ponders the crisis conditions of mortality, old age, and the mocking of ideal "images" by seedy realities. Earlier in the poem, Yeats recalls a long-past day when he and his beloved had seemed as though blended together

> Into a sphere from youthful sympathy,
> Or else, to alter Plato's parable,
> Into the yolk and white of the one shell.

The Platonic parable Yeats has in mind occurs in the *Symposium* where
the theory is rehearsed that human beings were originally one sex, as
inextricable as the yolk and white of an egg, before they ran afoul of
Zeus, who divided them into man and woman; sexual attraction is thus
explained as a longing for the primordial unity. The unity at the close
of "Among School Children" recalls these earlier lines but transcends
them in a vision of heavenly glory. Body and soul are one, and this
harmony of spirit and matter informs the very processes of life. Here
is the last stanza, complete:

> Labour is blossoming or dancing where
> The body is not bruised to pleasure soul,
> Nor beauty born out of its own despair,
> Nor blear-eyed wisdom out of midnight oil.
> O chestnut tree, great rooted blossomer,
> Are you the leaf, the blossom or the bole?
> O body swayed to music, O brightening glance,
> How can we know the dancer from the dance?

De Man's commentary on these lines is elegant, brilliant, somewhat dandyish, and perverse. Flying in the face of the "traditional"
interpretation, de Man insists on taking Yeats's rhetorical question
literally. He wants to "know the dancer from the dance," to tell them
apart, for, as he sees it, the relation between the two—as between the
sign and that for which it stands—is always treacherously unstable. In
short, where readers have always seen unity, de Man discerns the
opposite. Rather than stating "the potential unity between form and
experience, between creator and creation," the last line of "Among
School Children" may be seen to dramatize a condition of epistemological uncertainty that threatens any striving toward unity:

> For it turns out that the entire scheme set up by the first
> reading can be undermined, or deconstructed, in the terms
> of the second, in which the final line is read literally as
> meaning that, since the dancer and the dance are not the

same, it might be useful, perhaps even desperately necessary—for the question can be given a ring of urgency,
"Please tell me, how *can* I know the dancer from the
dance"—to tell them apart. But this will replace the reading
of each symbolic detail by a divergent interpretation.
. . . This hint should suffice to suggest that two entirely
coherent but entirely incompatible readings can be made to
hinge on one line, whose grammatical structure is devoid
of ambiguity, but whose rhetorical mode turns the mood
as well as the mode of the entire poem upside down.

By turning the poem upside down, de Man achieves the force of a
tautology: he proves that the poem can be turned upside down. Ultimate unity gives way to ultimate meaninglessness. The dance as a
fusion of "erotic desire with musical form" disintegrates into the
naming of a linguistic disjunction, the rupture between the signifier
and the signified. Thanks to the duplicity of rhetoric, the ground can
be cut out from under any statement. Never shall the figurative and
literal meanings coincide; never can the dancer and the dance be one.
The remarkable thing about this deconstructive exercise is not that it
contradicts our experience of the poem but that it displays the critic's
monumental conceit; it depicts Yeats as no more than an unwitting
mouthpiece for the theories of Paul de Man. That is what opponents
of deconstruction have in mind when they castigate it for parading the
critic's superiority over the text. It is, in Blackmur's words, the sign
of "an *idée fixe,* a really exaggerated heresy, when a notion of genuine
but small scope is taken literally as of universal application."

I have now reached a turning point in this book. In the preceding
pages I have made a limited defense of soft-core deconstruction and
examined some of the ways and means of the hard-core kind. I have
shown how the word itself has entered our language. I have cited
definitions and descriptions of deconstruction and have tried to account for its rise in the academy, presenting the explanations most
frequently given. There is the view that suggests that deconstruction
needs to be understood in the context of the growing "professionalism" of literary studies. There is, too, the thesis that deconstruction and
related critical theories—with their revolutionary aspirations and their

"subversive" strategies—represent a sublimation of 1960s student radicalism. And there is the sense that deconstruction puts into play some of the crucial assumptions of our cultural Zeitgeist. The intellectual scope and ambition of deconstruction cannot be denied. It has aspired to supplant philosophy as the discipline of highest thought in the university, and its ideas have infiltrated far-flung fields; the theme of "today literary criticism, tomorrow the world" is, however improbable, common enough in academe today.

While it is not the only critical theory in vogue, deconstruction has left its mark on most of the others and done more than the rest to give the age of theory its characteristic "metalanguage." Deconstruction has a pragmatic value, offering the graduate student a certifiably new yet officially sanctioned way to approach familiar texts. It also has an apocalyptic dimension—it announces that the time is right for the destruction of metaphysics, that the end of the word is at hand. It is a fitting philosophy for a time when the written word is itself under assault—a time when the computer screen threatens to render the printed page obsolete and when, what's more, the spoken and written utterances of public figures meet with unprecedented skepticism and disbelief on the part of the intellectual population. Deconstruction is, in sum, a sign of our times, and nowhere more so than in the relentlessly skeptical gaze it turns on the signs that make up our language and our world.

Whether you opt for "nihilistic" or some less-inflammatory adjective, it is easy to see why hard-core deconstruction disturbs so many teachers and writers. The impulse of deconstruction is profoundly inimical to art (which it subordinates to theory), to biography and history (whose relevance it denies), to conventional methods of critical analysis (which it considers retrograde), and to any philosophy of action (since existential choices are always transmuted into irresolvable linguistic predicaments). Nor is deconstruction content to be merely one theory among many; the zeal of its disciples, and the rarity with which adherents deprogram themselves, indicate as much. Deconstruction has seduced some fine minds. It has also quickened pulses, awakened anxieties, and aroused ferocious conflicts that continue to get fought out in academic conferences, in the deliberations of hiring committees, and in the literary supplements of newspapers and magazines. The institutional ramifications of deconstruction are not to be underestimated. Yet more is at stake than the strutting and fretting of assistant professors on the right or wrong side of the tenure track.

That sense of high stakes, that constant controversy, explain why the posthumous case of Paul de Man quickly blew up into a major academic scandal in December 1987. At the time of his death four Decembers earlier, de Man was the acknowledged authority figure of American deconstruction—its most formidable theoretician, its most influential teacher, its purest practitioner. A cult of acolytes had formed around him. Admirers invoked his stern air of authority. Opponents respected his intellectual power, sometimes grudgingly, sometimes not, but always with the sense that de Man *needed* to be refuted and could not simply be ignored. Of the significance of deconstruction, de Man himself had little doubt. Shortly before his death in December 1983, de Man and J. Hillis Miller were discussing the polemical battlefield that literary criticism had become. "The stakes are enormous," de Man told Miller, and Miller would repeat the phrase on more than one occasion. No one realized then that the battle over de Man's texts would soon be transferred to the treacherous terrain of history.

For it was as if de Man had left behind a time-release knowledge capsule, whose contents began to leak out in December 1987. What neither de Man's adulators nor his detractors suspected in his lifetime was that the Belgian-born scholar had begun his career as a literary journalist writing for pro-Nazi publications during the German occupation of Belgium in World War II. As late as November 1942, de Man's articles were appearing in *Le Soir,* which had the largest daily circulation of any Belgian newspaper—and which was edited by a Nazi-appointed staff anxious to toe the political line laid down in Berlin. In America, de Man made no public mention of his disreputable past, though he had become a public man, with a wide following, and though he exercised, in his teachings and writings, a kind of moral authority over his disciples. To the jolting substance of the disclosures themselves was thus added the enigma of de Man's silence. Was it evidence of bad faith, or was a subtler explanation required? What moral could be drawn from de Man's silence—given the charge, frequently lodged against him, that hard-core deconstruction sets out to silence language?

The case of Paul de Man became a cause célèbre for many reasons.

There was, first of all, the darkness of the historical nightmare it conjured up. The case dramatized—yet again—the evident attractions of fascist ideology for certain upper-class European intellectuals in the 1930s. By a quirk of historical coincidence, the de Man revelations occurred against a backdrop that threw its sensational features into relief. There had been the uproar surrounding President Reagan's ceremonial visit to Bitburg, the German military cemetery where the bodies of Nazi SS officers lay buried. There was the capture of Klaus Barbie, the "butcher of Lyon," whose trial in France brought to the fore the whole sorry memory of French collaborationism in World War II. There was the remarkable case of Kurt Waldheim, who managed to win election as president of Austria in spite—or possibly because—of the scandalous revelation that he served in a German military intelligence unit that perpetrated atrocities in Yugoslavia. There were, too, periodic disclosures concerning the alleged anti-Semitism of this or that famous cultural figure in the decade preceding the Nazi Holocaust. It became widely known, for example, that Stravinsky was a fan of Mussolini and a confirmed anti-Semite.

It seems increasingly clear that World War II is the moral, political, and philosophical cornerstone of our time. When we address abstract or hypothetical questions concerning guilt and justice—the question, for example, of a citizenry's complicity in its government's misdeeds—we instinctively reach for examples provided by the Second World War. And though the first-hand memory of those events may fade as the survivors age and die, the traumas of the war endure, hanging over the consciousness and conscience of the generation born after Hitler's demise; each new headline—the capture of an escaped war criminal here, the unmasking there of a world "statesman" as a forgetful ex-Nazi—acts like the repressed memory that returns in savage nightmares and triggers off a painful morning-after of breast-beating and recriminatory debate. At the time the de Man scandal broke, European intellectuals were greatly preoccupied with the still-pressing need to come to terms with the Nazi past. What was the proper relation to have with that past? In Germany the reigning intellectual controversy—called the *Historikerstreit,* or "historians' conflict"—centered on the place of the Holocaust in German history. Was the attempted destruction of the Jews a uniquely heinous set of crimes, or could it—should it—be "relativized"? The revisionist view, denying the uniqueness of the Nazi genocide, treats it in the context of other national atrocities, such as those perpetrated by Stalin in the Soviet Union. The implicit issue in the debate is the burden of historical guilt borne by Germany. If the Holocaust is "relativized," that burden is immediately diminished.

In France, at the same time, the publication of *Heidegger and Nazism* by the Chilean scholar Victor Farias precipitated an incendiary debate about the Nazi commitment of Martin Heidegger. Previously, many people had rather wishfully assumed that Heidegger's involvement with National Socialism was a short-lived flirtation. Farias made the case that Heidegger embraced the Nazis out of conviction and not as a career compromise. Propagandizing for Hitler's revolution, Heidegger hoped to be Germany's intellectual *Führer*. During his ten-month tenure as rector of the University of Freiburg, he carried out the Nazis' racial policies, which resulted in the eventual expulsion of all Jewish professors. He signed his correspondence with an enthusiastic "Heil Hitler!" and affirmed his allegiance to Hitler with these words: "the Führer himself, and he alone, is the German reality of today, and of the future, and of its law." Though he stepped down as rector in February 1934, Heidegger remained a dues-paying member of the Nazi party right up to the end of the war. After Germany's defeat in 1945, friends implored him to repudiate Nazism. He chose instead to reaffirm "the inner truth and greatness of this movement (namely, the encounter between global technology and modern man)." Though he refused to discuss the annihilation of the Jews, in a lecture in 1949 he likened "the manufacturing of corpses in gas chambers and extermination camps" to the mass-production of agricultural goods. While many of these facts had long ago entered the public record, Farias shaped a coherent indictment out of them. He also opened the door to new revelations, which followed the release of his book. A letter written by Heidegger in 1929 came belatedly to light. It warned against the "growing Jewish influence" in modern German thought and recommended fighting it with forces "emanating from the soil."

In France, where devout Heideggerians had worked long and hard to keep the master's philosophical writings separate from his Nazi activities, Farias's book shifted the terms of the debate. Amid the ample evidence of the duration and depth of Heidegger's commitment to Nazism, it would no longer be possible to minimize it as a brief and inconsequential episode. Moreover, the evidence strongly suggested a connection between Heidegger's philosophical antipathy toward humanism and his embrace of Hitler. One Parisian commentator went so far as to describe Nazism as "the political translation" of Heidegger's antirationalist philosophy. Heidegger used the ideas he propounded in his philosophical writings—notably in *Being and Time* (1927)—again in 1933, only this time to commend Nazism as "a return to roots" that would arrest the "spiritual decline" of the West. In France, in Jane Kramer's phrase, "the vedettes of the apocalypse" conduct a continual intellectual debate in newspaper columns and magazine articles. In Paris in 1988 the storm over Heidegger's reputation dominated *le discours.*

The simultaneity of the Historikerstreit and the Heidegger and de Man controversies suggested more than the return of a repressed nightmare. Though de Man was not a thinker of the stature of Heidegger, and though de Man's relation to the Nazis was more tenuous and of far shorter duration, it was tempting to see the Heidegger and de Man controversies as rough parallels. A prominent theme in both cases was the betrayal of the intellectuals—the reminder that intellectual sophistication in itself offered no bulwark against the blandishments of a barbarous regime. A second parallel was the sheer amount of verbiage—and the shrill tenor of that verbiage—that both the Heidegger and the de Man cases generated in their respective locales. De Man's *Le Soir* file unleashed a blizzard of news reports, feature articles, and critical essays—many of them polemical in the extreme—on the meaning of the revelation. It seems fair to say that no previous set of perishable, forty-five-year-old newspaper articles ever received the kind of elaborate critical scrutiny that de Man's articles commanded in 1988 and after. A third parallel, and the really distressing one, concerned the reaction of Heidegger's followers in France and de Man's in the United States. In both cases, the faithful went to great lengths to deny the truth, or the relevance, or the significance, of the charges brought against their man. And since Heidegger was a major influence on Jacques Derrida, the tactics of obfuscation and deconstructive doublethink figured as prominently in the debate on Heidegger as they would in the scandal of Paul de Man. Derrida scornfully wondered whether Victor Farias, who had spent years building up his dossier on Heidegger, "has read Heidegger for more than one hour." For Derrida, Heidegger's "terrifying" and "perhaps unpardonable" postwar silence—his failure to acknowledge his Nazi ties or to condemn the Nazi genocide—had the beneficial effect of obliging "us" to confront what he had evaded. Philippe Lacoue-Labarthe, one of Derrida's Parisian allies, strove mightily to salvage Heidegger's reputation. Heidegger's "merit," wrote Lacoue-Labarthe, "is to have yielded for only ten months" to Nazism. In fact, as we know from Farias's book, Heidegger's "ten months" lasted for decades. But according to Lacoue-Labarthe, the real problem with Heidegger's early philosophy was not that it was antihumanist but that it didn't go far enough in its enmity toward humanism. "Nazism is a humanism," Lacoue-Labarthe declared. In the de Man affair as well, such outrageous pronouncements, made invariably with a straight face, were common.

When the debate over de Man's past was at its most intense, Barbara Johnson, a de Man protégée, asked an apt though somewhat disingenuous question: "Beyond the fact that Nazism is always news and that people love a fall, what is it that transforms this archival revelation into an *event?*" You can begin to answer the question by focusing on the irony, the melodrama, and the pathos of the situation. Had the story featured a lesser luminary, or had the buried secret been more mundane, it would never have caused such tumult. A news item's potential for controversy varies in direct proportion to the intensity of the shock it delivers. And in de Man's case the shock was powerful indeed. The story caught everyone off guard. De Man's personal reputation was above reproach; about the last thing people expected to find in his closet was any kind of Nazi connection. Had he killed a man the shock could not have been so great. The specter of the swastika! Wasn't deconstruction supposed to be an instrument to be used against totalitarianism—or, in decon-talk, against "totalizing" structures and ideologies of any kind? The ironies were pointed. De Man had gone so far in expunging pathos from literary studies—yet here were revelations that inescapably brought pathos to the fore. The writer had strenuously eliminated biographical data from consideration—"Considerations of the actual and historical existence of writers are a waste of time from a critical viewpoint," he asserted—yet here was a biographical fact that could not be overlooked or shrugged off by the most ardent disciple. A number of critics recalled that de Man had once characterized his methods as "totalizing (and potentially totalitarian)" in a typically convoluted, paradox-filled sentence. "Technically correct rhetorical readings may be boring, monotonous, predictable and unpleasant, but they are irrefutable," de Man declared, leaving it in no doubt that the readings he had in mind were his own.

"They are also," he went on, "totalizing (and potentially totalitarian) for since the structures and functions they expose do not lead to the knowledge of an entity (such as language) but are an unreliable process of knowledge production that prevents all entities, including linguistic entities, from coming into discourse as such, they are indeed universals, consistently defective models of language's impossibility to be a model language." What did he mean when he wrote that? And what did the writing mean in light of his newly disclosed past?

Above all, the case of Paul de Man reignited the debate over deconstruction, introducing new evidence that would have to be sifted, weighed, judged. On the one hand, you couldn't use one man's youthful mistakes to indict a critical theory that began many years later—and in another man's mind. "That's reading history backwards," said one longstanding opponent of deconstruction, judiciously. Yet de Man's own brand of deconstruction necessarily implicated his wartime language and his silence thereafter precisely because it focused on language and silence. Were there continuities within the body of de Man's work, or were his later writings a tacit repudiation of the pro-Nazi world-view of the newspaper for which he wrote in the dark days of World War II? Commentators pointed out—with many an *alas* and an *I told you so*—that de Man, in his most influential book, had obsessively trained his skeptical gaze on the very questions of guilt and confession that his posthumous case seemed to raise. What sense would we make of these passages now?

In the following chapters, I propose to tell the Paul de Man story in the light of what we learned, as one damaging disclosure chased another, in the months after the scandal broke. I will examine the *text,* if I may appropriate the term, of de Man's life. I want to approach it as if it were a text, for several reasons and to several ends. Full of enigmas and unexpected paradoxes, the text of de Man's life requires unraveling. The story itself is fascinating. It resembles a novel marked by ironic reversals, gothic secrets, and explosive revelations, and the riddles it poses may well bear on our understanding of deconstruction. De Man's life is almost made to order for a world-view holding that language is "an unreliable process of knowledge production." The text of de Man's life teases us with what cannot be known, compelling us to make extrapolations and conjectures, since he never owned up to what he had done, much less explained why he had done it. Yet something about the text invites us to interpret it and even supplies us with a key—de Man's own critical vocabulary seems curiously apposite to his case. De Man was the author of a book entitled *Allegories of Reading,* and his secrecy about his past invites us to read his intellectual development as an allegory in which some morals are clear and others less so. The existence of de Man's wartime journalism has unquestionably had the curious effect of forcing everyone, friends and foes alike, to revise their entire understanding of Paul de Man; in that sense, the reflux of de Man's past is precisely understood as a case of self-deconstruction—a point at which the entire contraption comes tumbling down, just as the vision of unity in Yeats's "Among School Children" founders, in de Man's analysis, on the observation that the dancer *can* be known from the dance.

The philosopher Stanley Cavell and the poet John Hollander—who were de Man's colleagues at Harvard University's Society of Fellows in the mid-1950s—are among those who have tried, with some urgency, to refute de Man's interpretation of "Among School Children." In separate essays, both Cavell and Hollander argue that a literal reading of Yeats's last line *is* possible but would take a different form from the subversive one de Man proposes. Cavell and Hollander point out that to *know from* can mean to *tell apart,* but it can also mean to *infer.* Therefore, the literalist of the imagination might ask not how we can *distinguish* the dancer from the dance, but how, appealing to the dance as our source of knowledge, we can come to *know* the dancer. It is a fine distinction but a real one—the difference, in Cavell's words, between "the reading of despair" and "the reading of hope." The purpose of the exercise is not to quibble over Yeats's sublime poem but to press home the possibility of knowledge against "the threat of skepticism" that de Man's reading represents. "The importance to me of preserving in Yeats's words the asserting and the questioning of knowing," Cavell writes, "is that I am interested in the possibility of art as a possibility of knowing, or of acknowledging. This means to me an interest in its confrontation with the threat of skepticism, with the possibility that the world we claim to know is not the world there is." The debate over the dancer and the dance was always epistemological, not aesthetic, centering on the question of whether anything can truly be known. De Man preached "the reading of despair." Would the belated discovery of his wartime past reinforce or contradict that view?

Perhaps, in extending the analogy into the biographical sphere, we should identify de Man as the dancer and deconstruction as the dance. The question—"how *can* we know the dancer from the dance"—then becomes as "desperately necessary" and "urgent" as de Man said it was. De Man's secret past may be, in deconstructive lingo, an example of the peripheral episode that throws light upon the center; de Man's youthful journalism, a marginal footnote to his mature deconstructive enterprise, may provide a key to unlock its secrets. And the response to the affair on the part of those most affected by the information—the deconstructionists themselves, still in the flush of victory, suddenly thrown on the defensive—will tell us much about them. It will serve as a practical test, a case of theory running up against the hard material existence of an undeniable historical fact.

It is possible, as one wag has put it, that "the dogma of deconstruction has had its day"—that it will forever be modified by the posthumous shock it received on that December day in 1987 when de Man's wartime behavior was reported in the *New York Times*. How peculiar and how poetically just it would be if so antibiographical a theory of literature should be vanquished by the discovery of a ruinous biographical fact. But rumors of deconstruction's demise have in the past proved premature, and for now, de Man's discipleship continues to provide a paradigm for other academic cults and sects that elevate critical theory and seem either indifferent to art and literature or actively hostile toward them. The scandalous revelations have not ended the controversy surrounding deconstruction, just lifted it to a further level of complication. Like the grin of the Cheshire cat that survives the animal's material disappearance, de Man's ambiguous smile—often remarked upon by his colleagues—lingers in the air. The posthumous text of his life is still in progress.

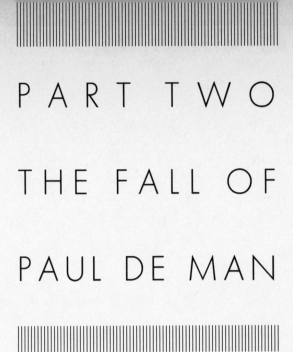

PART TWO

THE FALL OF

PAUL DE MAN

CHAPTER 6

THE FALLEN

I D O L

In a profession full of fakeness, he was real.

—Barbara Johnson, at a memorial service
for Paul de Man,
Yale University, January 18, 1984

To his academic confreres, Paul de Man was an exemplary figure, an inspiration and a model worth emulating. His was the fortunate immigrant's tale: a survivor of Hitler's Europe—a refugee or a resistance fighter; the details weren't clear—who came to America and rose from penurious obscurity to a position of high intellectual eminence. He was the Yale professor with the sweet and gentle manner, the intensely dedicated following, the reputation that transcended the academic cloister, and the originality of mind to spark something resembling a revolution in the field of literary criticism. Attractively modest of bearing, ferociously skillful in debate, de Man was America's archdeacon of deconstruction.

At the time of his death in December 1983, de Man was, in Frank Kermode's words, "the most celebrated member of the world's most celebrated literature school." Published tributes to his influence sometimes took on a hagiographic cast; the professor's disciples may as well have been speaking of Saint Paul de Man. Shoshana Felman: "He did not seek leadership, yet he was naturally at once an intellectual leader and a human guide." Ellen Burt: "He had himself no time to waste being seduced, disquieted, or threatened by women. And thus no time to waste vindictively barring them from effecting a full entry into the profession. He seemed to have no time to waste barring anyone from entering the profession. His time was devoted to giving us time, to work." Barbara Johnson: "It seemed to me paradoxical that people would accuse him of anti-humanistic beliefs, or anti-people beliefs, when he was the most pro-people person that I had ever met—in ways that were truly effective, and not in ways that made people feel good, or made people believe that he was on their side when he wasn't: he never failed people."

Even nondisciples spoke of de Man's "ethical" and "benign" presence in their graduate training. An almost spiritual aura is said to have enveloped him. With his monastic devotion to the exegeses of texts, he seemed to embody intellectual seriousness as a moral ideal. One word that comes up again and again in adulation is *rigor*—"his intellectual rigor" (Ellen Burt), "his forgiving rigor" (Andrzej Warminski), "the rigor and honesty of his thought" (Barbara Johnson). A second recurrent term of praise is *authority*—"the extraordinary intellectual authority he exerted on his friends and colleagues, at least on me" (J. Hillis Miller); "Paul disclaimed his own authority, yet none had more authority than him" (Shoshana Felman). It was this authority and this sense of intellectual rigor that de Man gave to the theory that is immediately and invariably associated with his name.

Having done his graduate work at Harvard and held teaching appointments at Cornell and Johns Hopkins, de Man joined the Yale faculty in 1970. In the decade that followed, that university established itself as—depending on your view—the trendiest or the most advanced center for literary studies in the English-speaking world. Yale was where the great transformation of literary criticism took place— where "practical" criticism as an ideal and a method gave way to the ethereal domain of literary theory. At Yale in the 1970s were gathered the three "boa-deconstructors"—Derrida, de Man, and Miller. Derrida held a series of visiting appointments at Yale, and the man most responsible for bringing him there was de Man. De Man was, at various times, chairman of the university's French and comparative literature departments. Very soon after his arrival in New Haven he became, in Barbara Johnson's phrase, "the center of theoretical gravity" at Yale. Miller's primary role was to publicize and promote the new dispensation. A tireless campaigner, Miller was unabashed in his admiration for de Man, whom he tended to cite with the awed reverence of a vice-presidential running mate.

Thanks largely to the efforts of de Man and Miller, deconstruction gained its initial foothold in the United States. De Man provided the theoretical model. The central essay in his *Blindness and Insight* (1971) combined an homage to Derrida with a critique of Derrida's reading of Rousseau. The essay had the effect of sponsoring Derrida to an American audience but also of tailoring his methods to the exigencies of an American academic specialty: literary criticism. Where Derrida had deconstructed Rousseau, de Man countered by saying that Rousseau had deconstructed himself; authors, according to de Man, have already known everything he says about them. In practice, this notion enabled de Man to put his own ideas in the mouths of the authors he studies, but it also enabled him to reconcile deconstructive theory with one traditional aspect of academic literary studies—the concentration on texts. "There is an impact of Derrida which is, in a sense, purely pedagogical," de Man commented. "As far as I'm concerned, I'm often mentioned as the one who is much responsible for that, since my work is, in a sense, more pedagogical than philosophical: it has always started from the pedagogical or the didactic assignment of reading specific texts rather than, as is the case in Derrida, from the pressure of general philosophical issues." Adapting Derrida to the field of literary studies, de Man obtained for deconstruction what it never fully or only fleetingly enjoyed in France: an institutional base of operations and a home in the academic disciplines devoted to English and comparative literature. "The accommodation or appropriation of deconstruction in the United States is producing something that is specifically American," Miller told an interviewer with some pride in 1986. "As Derrida keeps saying, he has more power and influence here than he does in France. Deconstruction is really an American thing."

The "Yale School"—the term frequently applied to de Man, Miller, Geoffrey Hartman, and Harold Bloom—was always a misleading concept, implying an intellectual affinity that obtained primarily between de Man and Miller. (Derrida was frequently omitted from discussions of the "Yale School" on the grounds that he was neither American nor a permanent member of the Yale faculty.) In contrast to Miller and de Man, Hartman and Bloom were, respectively, mildly and strongly ambivalent about deconstruction. Hartman, justly famous for his wit and erudition, had a flair for the telling pun; it was he who captured the anarchic flavor of deconstruction by dubbing it "Derridadaism." Bloom, a brilliant and prolific maverick, had written a quartet of studies that deidealized the whole question of literary influence; the author of *The Anxiety of Influence* (1973) made a powerful case for the thesis that the influence of one writer upon another was not a benign passing of the torch but rather a fierce struggle resembling an oedipal rite. Both Hartman and Bloom expressed misgivings about deconstruction and especially about its indifference to, and exclusion of, the experience of human pathos in literature. Writing about himself in the third person, Hartman observed that "Bloom and Hartman are barely deconstructionists. They even write against it on occasion. For them the ethos of literature is not dissociable from its pathos, whereas for deconstructionist criticism literature is precisely that use of language which can purge pathos."

Bloom went further to distance himself from deconstruction, telling an interviewer in 1985: "I have no relation to deconstruction. I never did have, I don't have now, and I never will have. Nothing is more alien to me than deconstruction." If some surveys of deconstruction make a place for Bloom nevertheless, it is partly to emphasize the disruptive impact he has had on received ideas about literary influence. According to Bloom's reasoning, every great poem is haunted by a predecessor and by a sense of its own "belatedness." The successful poet gains his originality only by "creatively misreading"— and hence vanquishing—his literary father. These ideas, advanced in *The Anxiety of Influence,* caused an intellectual sensation and made Bloom—as he likes to say, half in jest and half in pride—"the pariah of the profession."

There is one substantive point of connection between Bloom and deconstruction. It could be said that de Man helped Bloom refine his theory; Bloom borrowed from de Man's deconstructive studies in rhetoric, most notably when he expounded the view that rhetorical figures in a text correspond to psychological defense mechanisms in the psyche of the author. In a review of *The Anxiety of Influence,* de Man anticipated this development. Bloom's psychological drama of poetic fathers and sons was, de Man suggested, "a displaced version of the paradigmatic encounter between reader and text." Bloom had described six "revisionary ratios," six stages in the poet's struggle to overcome his master's influence. De Man contended that each of the six "ratios" could be traced back to "the paradigmatic rhetorical structures in which they are rooted." What Bloom called *kenosis,* for example, de Man characterized as "the figure of a figure, in which the one deconstructs the universe produced by the other."

Following through on these suggestions, Bloom dedicated his next book, *A Map of Misreading,* to de Man. But Bloom firmly resisted the most challenging statement in de Man's review. "We can forget about the temporal scheme and about the pathos of the oedipal son," de Man had written. "Underneath, [*The Anxiety of Influence*] deals with the difficulty or, rather, the impossibility of reading and, by inference, with the indeterminacy of literary meaning." In fact, however, Bloom continued to address precisely what de Man thinks "we can forget about." For Bloom's theories are predicated entirely on assumptions that would be anathema to the proper deconstructionist; his passionate intuitiveness is on the other end of the spectrum from deconstruction's linguistic reductiveness. Bloom casts his lot with Ralph Waldo Emerson's "Self-Reliance" and affirms the centrality of the ego; he celebrates the act of interpretation instead of documenting "the impossibility of reading." Far from eliminating the author, Bloom focuses on the conscious and unconscious impulses of the individual poet, whose struggle for originality of being and expression is taken as emblematic of the human condition. "There cannot be a method, except for yourself," Bloom has said. "Deconstruction is not a method; it is the highly idiosyncratic personality and mind of the late Paul de Man and of Jacques Derrida."

Long before the revelations of de Man's wartime past, Bloom coupled a warning about deconstruction with a declaration of what literary criticism should be but seldom is. It is worth quoting at length for its eloquence and its critique of the deconstructive world-view:

> Jacques Derrida is a close personal friend of mine. The late Paul de Man was very dear to me. I have great admiration for them both, intellectually. But I consider their actual influence on subsequent criticism to be highly pernicious. And though I'm very fond of Geoffrey Hartman and Hillis Miller, I do not approve of deconstructive criticism or any of the modes of what I would call formalist criticism. I

would say that all these European modes, finally, are too far away from the experience of reading a poem or the experience of reading a story or the experience of reading a novel.

I increasingly feel that criticism must be personal, must be experiential, must take the whole concern of men and women, including all its torments, very much into account, must offer a kind of testimony. Emerson taught me—he says very beautifully—that the reader or student is to consider herself or himself as the text, and all received texts whatsoever, be it the Bible or Shakespeare, simply as commentary upon ourselves. This is what the great critics have always done. If I were to be asked who are the finest critics in the English language, I would always have said Dr. Samuel Johnson and William Hazlitt and John Ruskin and to only a slightly lesser extent Emerson and Walter Pater and the divine Oscar Wilde. Precisely because they are critics in whom one hears the full cry of the human. They tell one why it matters to read. They do not give one mere linguistic problematics. They do not substitute philosophy for our *agon* and struggle with the author and with the text. They remember always that high literature is written by personalities, by suffering human beings and not by language, and is read by suffering human beings. They know that literature is a question of ethos and logos but also of pathos, and their criticism is not just logos but also has ethos and pathos in it.

On at least one celebrated occasion, however, Bloom and Hartman made common cause with deconstruction. With little apparent reluctance, the two men joined Derrida, de Man, and Miller on the title page of a volume entitled *Deconstruction and Criticism*. Published in 1979, the book—comprising essays by each of the five Yale professors—did nothing to dispel the notion of a "Yale School" and everything to confirm its ascendancy. Years later, Bloom would make the wittily outrageous remark that the book's title was his "personal joke, which no one can ever understand: I meant that those four were deconstruction, and I was criticism." But in 1979 the book's impact was unambiguous. Together with de Man's *Allegories of Reading,* also published that year, it signaled the moment of deconstruction's triumph in the American academy.

The prestige and influence of the Yale critics, individually or as a group, could be measured by the sharpness of the backlash they aroused. And to the extent that there *was* a "school" and that its headquarters were at Yale, it was de Man who was most often singled out as, for better or worse, its leading spokesman and ideologue. "Assuming there is a Yale Mafia, then surely there must be a resident Godfather," Frank Lentricchia wrote. "One is forced to finger Paul de Man, who exhibits qualities that may earn him the role of Don Paolo, *capo di tutti capi.*" (Lentricchia's own eminence in lit-crit circles may be inferred from the cinematic nickname that he has received in turn: one critic has called him "the Dirty Harry of contemporary critical theory.") Lentricchia pointed to "the tone of respect, even reverence," with which the other Yale professors referred—or deferred—to de Man in their published writings. What was it about de Man that earned him such devotion? Lentricchia thought he saw the answer in de Man's prose—not so much in his matter as in his manner. De Man's rhetoric, appropriately enough, gave him away. The confidence with which he made his assertions was rather strikingly at odds with the doctrine of extreme skepticism and doubt he was doing so much to advance. Here was a critic, Lentricchia wrote, who "presumes to tell us not only what literature has been but also what it must be." In short, de Man commanded "the rhetoric of authority":

> In the manner of a don whose power is assured and unquestioned, de Man has found it necessary to speak only sparingly; in comparison to his prolific lieutenants he is almost invisible. We know that according to certain dark traditions the don need not speak often, nor elaborately, because when the don speaks he speaks with total authority, and it is de Man's "rhetoric of authority," as I'll call it, which has distinguished his criticism since its earliest days. This is a critic who has always given the impression of having a grip on truth. Even while, in *Blindness and Insight,* he was telling us that there was no truth, or if there was, that it could never be known, he spoke transcendentally of the "foreknowledge we possess of the true nature of literature."

Unlike Hartman, whose prose, in its pursuit of the labyrinthine ramifications of a point, is the very model of the
scholar's descent into the inferno of self-consciousness; and
unlike Bloom, whose emotionally pressured and strident
style gives away a critic not altogether confident of how
what he proposes will be received, de Man has not had to
speak in anything but a cool and straightforward manner.

Lentricchia's analysis has acquired a pressing new relevance in the
aftermath of the posthumous publication of de Man's wartime writings. More than one of de Man's former students recognized the tone
of Olympian authority with which the youthful de Man wrote about
the future of Nazi-occupied Europe. It was the same "rhetoric of
authority" that Lentricchia found in de Man's *Allegories of Reading.*
The book's keynote essay displayed de Man's style "at its most intimidating," Lentricchia wrote, offering as his prime example de Man's
assertion that "the whole of literature" would bear out his theory of
rhetoric. "There is absolutely no reason why analyses of the kind here
suggested for Proust would not be applicable, with proper modifica-
tions of technique, to Milton or to Dante or to Hölderlin," de Man
asserted in *Allegories of Reading.* "This will in fact be the task of
literary criticism in the coming years."

De Man himself could not help being ruefully aware of the
resentment that his views aroused. "Deconstruction, as was easily
predictable, has been much misrepresented, dismissed as a harmless
academic game or denounced as a terrorist weapon," he wrote in the
preface to *Allegories of Reading,* "and I have all the fewer illusions
about the possibility of countering these aberrations since such an
expectation would go against the drift of my own readings." Barbara
Johnson professed herself to be "startled by the vehemence of de Man's
critics. His work is viewed, both from the left and from the right, not
just as misguided or useless, but somehow almost as evil. Radicals see
in his writing a conservative plot to talk literary critics out of participating in social change. Conservatives see in it a nihilistic desire to
cancel out human meaning altogether." Johnson connected both positions to de Man's "central insight": that language "cannot itself be
entirely 'human.'" Beyond its surface meaning there are hidden messages, and even beyond these, Johnson writes, there is a "residue of
functioning—which produces effects—that is not a *sign* of anything,

but merely the outcome of linguistic rules, or even of 'the absolute randomness of language.' Not that language is always absolutely random, but that we can never be sure that it isn't."

For all the controversy surrounding deconstruction in general and de Man's exposition of it in particular, there was never any denying the esteem in which he was personally held as a teacher, a thinker, a man. In the wake of the *Le Soir* disclosures, Geoffrey Hartman was asked to comment on charges that de Man, as the leader of an academic cult, was extending the fascist cult of leadership, with all the ruthlessness that this implies. These perhaps overheated charges were made by more than one professor without love for de Man or for deconstruction. Hartman replied with a ringing defense of the de Man he knew and admired:

> De Man made students see the seriousness of what they were doing. By the sheer power of intellect he made people see the importance of literature without any recourse to the context of manners and morals. He made them aware of the intricate logic of rhetoric; he made us understand why figurative language was a necessity, not a defect, and if it was a defect, a necessary one. It is extraordinary how many students admired de Man and imitated him. It had something to do with the strength of what he was doing: he would strengthen their intellectual discipline. He did not attract by flamboyance but by rigor and severity. He pierced an intellectual issue to the bone. After he spoke you realized he touched something essential. He was absolutely not personalistic. He had negative charisma. It is not that he was flamboyant. He was modest in his bearing. He wasn't ruthless at all. He was absolutely honest in his intellectual opinions. Someone with that power of intellect often leaves literature behind, abandoning it for philosophy. For de Man it didn't work that way. He demonstrated the seriousness of literature as a discipline.

One can imagine a movie of de Man's life as conceived at the time of his death from cancer in December 1983. It would have been an American success story, another chapter in the twentieth-century saga of European intellectuals who fled their bloodied native ground and flourished on American soil. A brilliant young man of letters emigrates from Belgium to the United States in 1948. Toiling obscurely in a Doubleday bookshop in Grand Central Station, he meets and gets taken up by various New York intellectuals, including the novelist Mary McCarthy and the editor of *Partisan Review,* William Phillips. He impresses many with his breadth of cultural knowledge, his ironic manner and aloof charm; people are eager to help him. A letter from Mary McCarthy to the poet Theodore Weiss, then chairman of the English department at Bard College, results in his first teaching job. At Bard he marries one of his students. They are so poor, and he so unassuming, that to make ends meet they uncomplainingly spend the summer picking berries and apples in the Hudson Valley. They move to Boston where he gets a job teaching in a Berlitz language school; on the side he translates articles from three languages for Henry Kissinger's journal, *Confluence.* Again friends assist him; de Man's austere passivity prompts Ted Weiss to write a letter to Harry Levin, a co-director of Harvard's prestigious Society of Fellows.

Though de Man, born in 1919, was a good ten years older than the average candidate, he was admitted to the Society, given a three-year appointment with a stipend, few teaching responsibilities, and the opportunity to master the old "New Criticism" at the side of one of its leading figures, Reuben Brower. De Man's colleagues at the Society of Fellows were an impressive lot: the philosopher Stanley Cavell, the poets Donald Hall and John Hollander, and the linguist Noam Chomsky were among those who would go on to make formidable reputations for themselves. "Politics was the lingua franca of the Society," Donald Hall recalled years later. There were nightly discussions, and "only Chomsky totally refused to talk politics"—Chomsky who, of all the Fellows, became the most overtly political during the Vietnam war and since. "One thought of Paul as 'a man of the left,' in a pompous phrase that we used," Hall said. "It was known that he worked in the *Résistance,* although he did not talk about it."

De Man spent the rest of the 1950s working on his doctoral dissertation at Harvard. He went to Cornell to teach in 1960, and held other professorial appointments at the University of Zurich and at Johns Hopkins later in the decade. It was in the 1960s that he began publishing articles of unusual depth and subtlety in the nonacademic intellectual press as well as in scholarly journals. Casual readers of literary criticism could come across his work in the *New York Review of Books,* where he published an extraordinary essay on the poetry of Friedrich Hölderlin, and in his introduction to the widely used Signet edition of John Keats's *Selected Poetry.* In 1971, newly arrived at Yale, de Man published his first book. He was nearly fifty-two at the time, an age at which most scholars of distinction have already published three or four books. But this was no ordinary first book: Geoffrey Hartman hailed *Blindness and Insight* as "the most subtly argued book of its kind I have ever read," and among adepts of literary theory it quickly achieved the status of a classic. The book even prompted enthusiasts to track down the articles de Man had not collected in the volume. One such article, "The Rhetoric of Temporality," acquired renown as "the most photocopied essay in literary criticism." Students passed it around, and more often than not the copy was heavily underlined with an exclamatory "wow" or two in the margins. "You could save your dope money for a month. That essay could blow your mind several times over," a Yale graduate told me. David Bromwich offers a more sober assessment. De Man's essay, Bromwich writes, "argues that two dogmas have shaped critical thought about the literary object since the early decades of the nineteenth century: the conception of irony as a fixed perspective, and of the symbol as a fusion of image and idea which cannot be found in allegory." Bromwich's judgment: "After one has read this essay, one's sense of the uses of irony can never be quite the same, and there seems to be very little point in ever talking of the symbol again, except for the historical purpose of exhibiting the preoccupations of a school."

In the opening essay of *Blindness and Insight,* de Man announced with "mock sensationalism" that the rules "that governed the discipline of criticism and made it a cornerstone of the intellectual establishment have been so badly tampered with that the entire edifice threatens to collapse." He had no hesitation in proposing "a radical relativism" as a solution to the crisis: "There are no longer any standpoints that can a priori be considered privileged, no structure that functions validly as a model for other structures, no postulate of ontological hierarchy that can serve as an organizing principle from which particular structures derive in the manner in which a deity can be said to engender man and the world." This, in short, was the deconstructive credo, and it was accompanied by similarly oracular pronouncements: "Sign and meaning can never coincide." The structure of a literary work is like that of a chair, which "in no way depends on the state of mind of the carpenter who is in the process of assembling its parts." "Considerations of the actual and historical existence of writers are a waste of time from a critical viewpoint." "Literary texts are themselves critical but blinded, and the critical reading of the critics tries to deconstruct the blindness." "The bases for historical knowledge are not empirical facts but written texts, even if these texts masquerade in the guise of wars or revolutions." "Instead of containing or reflecting experience, language constitutes it."

An unlikely guru, de Man was celebrated for his scrupulous "intellectual honesty"—as measured by the fastidiousness of what he called his "technically correct rhetorical readings." The prose exposition of his ideas often seemed to double back on itself, as if the author were scrutinizing the very position he was advancing. "The Resistance to Theory," for example, deplores the conventionally understood "resistance to theory in this country." "As a matter of fact," de Man writes, "the arguments in favor of the legitimacy of literary theory are so compelling that it seems useless to concern oneself with the conflict at all. Certainly, none of the objections to theory, presented again and again, always misinformed or based on crude misunderstandings of such terms as mimesis, fiction, reality, ideology, reference, and, for that matter, relevance, can be said to be of genuine rhetorical interest." Yet at the conclusion of the essay de Man makes the paradoxical and somewhat startling claim that "nothing can overcome the resistance to theory since theory *is* itself this resistance." De Man claims for literary theory in general a meticulous attention to rhetorical detail and an ability to resist what it advocates. What it proves in the process is "the universal theory of the impossibility of theory." The argument is either tremendously subtle or it is a case of wanting to have and to eat one's cake simultaneously, and its exposition in de Man's concluding sentences is a chain of paradoxes: "Yet literary theory is not in danger of going under; it cannot help but flourish, and the more it is resisted, the more it flourishes, since the language it speaks is the language of self-resistance. What remains impossible to decide is whether this flourishing is a triumph or a fall."

In person, de Man was charming and he was suave, perhaps never more so than when he elegantly parried a thrust at a big-name academic conference. He disarmed people with his European accent and delivered a piercing retort with no sacrifice of decorum. Geoffrey Hartman likened him to the fencer in the *New Yorker* cartoon who neatly cuts off his opponent's still-smiling head and says "touché" after the fact. Donald Hall picks up the same image: "I was very fond of Paul . . . and when he cut off your head, it was *he* who was smiling. Paul could say the nastiest bloody words, and never make you mad, because he did it in a sort of gentle way. But he was of course cutting your head off. A very good arguer he was. And there was something *utterly* forgivable about him in person." Others spoke about de Man's shoulder-shrugging irony and ever-present twinkle in the eye. At academic conferences he had the knack of deflating what the previous speaker had said. On one such occasion, a well-known critic addressed himself passionately to Keats's "Ode to a Nightingale," emphasizing the poet's repetition of the word *forlorn* in the last two stanzas of the poem. *"Forlorn,"* de Man said when it was his turn to speak, "sounds like *foghorn* to me"—the dismissiveness of the remark camouflaged by its air of levity. A colleague at Cornell, where de Man taught in the 1960s, recalled his ability to defuse a tense situation with a wry pun. It seems a comely female graduate student was going over the professors' heads and charming the male dean to get her way in a departmental dispute. The colleague was furious but de Man was all witty aplomb, a master of detachment. "Oh yes," he smiled. "Miss G——: the face that launched a thousand scholarships."

Frank Kermode distinguishes the followers of Paul de Man from the students of an earlier generation, the "Modernist" generation for whom Lionel Trilling was a revered mentor. Kermode recalls Trilling's essay "On the Teaching of Modern Literature": "Trilling's students, when he introduced them to the abyss of the Modern, gazed into it politely, said 'how interesting!' and passed by." Though Kermode neglects to indicate what the proper deconstructionist says when placed in the same predicament, it is well known that avant-garde literary theorists pride themselves on their ability to stare unflinchingly into the abyss. They do so in earnest emulation of the master's example. Alert to the reigning trends in Continental criticism, de Man reported on "a dangerous *vertige,* a dizziness of the mind caught in an infinite regression." There were no truths. They had all become texts, duplicitous texts, fictions within fictions within fictions. If you examined a text closely enough, you inevitably arrived at a point where it deconstructs itself. Suddenly the ground beneath you has given way, and you must brace yourself for a fall from a vertiginous cliff. On the lit-crit conference circuit in the early 1980s, it was frequently said of Paul de

Man that he was "the only man who ever looked into the abyss and came away smiling."

When de Man died in December 1983, Yale went into mourning. A. Bartlett Giamatti, then president of the university, declared that "a tremendous light for humane life and learning is gone and nothing for us will ever be the same." A festschrift in de Man's honor—entitled *The Lesson of Paul de Man*—was lovingly assembled and brought to press. Jacques Derrida dedicated a book, *Mémoires: for Paul de Man,* to his friendship with the deceased. And in the context of academic politics, de Man remained the standard-bearer of the deconstruction party. When J. Hillis Miller succeeded to the presidency of the Modern Language Association in 1986, he used the occasion of his presidential address to echo "The Resistance to Theory," de Man's "already classic essay of 1979." Employing an argument familiar to students of psycho-analytic theory, Miller reasoned that the resistance to critical theory— "the violence and irrationality of the attacks on theory"—confirms that it is active, threatening, in fact triumphant. "The resistance to theory as the resistance to reading has now taken the strange form of the almost universal triumph of theory," Miller asserted, offering the example of "the recent program of the Midwest Modern Language Association, which met in Chicago this past November. Almost all the papers, panels, and sessions of that convention were overtly and one might say aggressively theoretical." Though he spoke as the titular head of a pluralistic, many-sided profession, Miller was unabashed in his partisanship. He took the highly unusual step of naming some of the young scholars he felt were most likely to succeed in the profession; de Man's protégés heavily freighted the list. As for Miller himself, the impulse to ape de Man's rhetoric of authority proved irresistible. "I affirm," he said, "that the future of literary studies depends on main-taining and developing that rhetorical reading which today is most commonly called 'deconstruction.' "

Baseball players must wait five years after their retirement to become eligible for induction into the sport's hall of fame. It took de Man next to no time at all to enter the lit-crit equivalent. De Man was enshrined at a memorial service at Yale University's art gallery a few weeks after his death. On a snowy January day, when travelers were warned to stay off the slippery roads, hundreds gathered to salute their colleague and teacher. Read through the testimonials delivered that day—they form the first section of *The Lesson of Paul de Man*—

and you come away with the inescapable feeling that the man was truly beloved. His disciples took pains to frame their eulogies in an exact, unsentimental way that would have met with his approval, and his colleagues issued rallying cries to the faithful. Derrida, not given to understatement, said, "As we know already but as we shall also come to realize more and more, he transformed the field of literary theory, revitalizing all the channels that irrigate it both inside and outside the university, in the United States and in Europe." Miller, the proselytizer par excellence, made the most grandiose assertion: "If I may dare to say so, the future of literary studies depends on reading Paul de Man as best we can, on being true to his example as a reader and as a continuator of the long tradition of literary study to which he belonged."

"The last thing he probably would have wanted to be was a moral and pedagogical—rather than merely intellectual—example for generations of students and colleagues," said Barbara Johnson at that somber and tearful gathering, "yet it was precisely his way of *not* seeking those roles that made him so irreplaceably an exception, and such an inspiration." The late de Man "never sought followers," Johnson told her fellow mourners, yet "people followed him in droves. He was ironic toward discipleship; the country is dotted with his disciples. His impact was so profound and so specific that it is possible to determine from people's work not only *that* he was their teacher but also *when* he was their teacher—what he was working on when they passed their time beside him. He was the implied reader driving literary critical pens in every university in the country." It was not simply a question of intellectual eminence; rather, it was intellectual vigor—disinterested, dedicated, without false pretenses or hidden agendas—that made de Man an exemplary model. De Man was genuine in the full honorific sense of the word. As Johnson put it, "In a profession full of fakeness, he was real."

"Yale Still Feeling Loss of Revered Professor," the *New York Times* reported in 1984, supplementing its routine obituary with a eulogistic campus-mood piece. A bereft J. Hillis Miller told the *Times* reporter that he had faithfully attended de Man's graduate seminar, "just because something was going to happen there that I didn't want to miss." Professor de Man, the reporter concluded, "came to represent an ideal that attracts would-be scholars, an ideal of intellectual fellow-ship, a detached but passionate exchange of ideas without politics and posturing." The adulation—and the widening ripples of de Man's intellectual influence—continued for four years after his death. Then came the catastrophic revelations. Long ago and far away, the revered professor had done the unmentionable—something that, at any rate, he himself neglected ever to mention afterward. The *Times* broke the story on December 1, 1987. On the lead page of its second section was a photograph of de Man and the headline: "Yale Scholar's Articles Found in Nazi Paper." In his native Belgium during World War II, de Man had written for a newspaper under Nazi supervision; in his American years, he failed to make account of what he had done.

The scandal had to do with words and with silence, with what de Man wrote in Belgium and what he didn't say in America. Perhaps it wasn't coincidental that de Man's own critical practice dealt on an abstract plane with words and with silence—and that there had long been those who felt that de Man's theory had the effect of silencing language. Did de Man's insistence on language's "unreliability" con-ceal the wish to lay the blame for his youthful journalism on language? In fiction there is the occasional character who enjoys a lively posthu-mous existence by dint of having drafted a will requiring prospective heirs to perform extravagant feats. The successful legatee must, for example, solve a riddle—as in Harry Mathews's novel *The Conversions* (1962), in which an eccentric millionaire poses three riddling questions in his will (such as "When was a stone not a king?") and stipulates that the bulk of his estate will go to the person who answers them correctly. By concealing the facts of his youth, de Man assured for himself and his works a similarly lively posthumous fate. The belated discovery of his wartime journalism had the effect of requiring his students to reconsider his entire mature oeuvre in the light of the belated revelations. Derrida, for one, used the occasion to exhort his followers to reread de Man; now more than ever, Derrida wrote, "to read de Man, from A to Z" is "unavoidable." A minor irony was that the arch debunker of origins and ends assumed he had a firm hold on what "A to Z" now entailed for Paul de Man. Leave that inconsistency aside, and you're left with a sharper irony. For de Man's party, history is bunk—but now history was debunking de Man. The discrepancy between what he said he had done during the war, and what the archives show he had actually done, was a gap created not by the "unreliability" of language as a medium but by an exercise of will, a conscious act of dissembling.

A further irony was that the publication in America of de Man's wartime journalism—in 1989, long after the publication of de Man's deconstructive writings—had the effect of making the early seem late, of reversing their order of priority. What had happened was the biographical equivalent of a *chiasmus*—the rhetorical figure in which the elements of a sentence occur in a crisscrossing pattern. To appreciate the irony, you need to understand that the chiasmus was a trope greatly favored by de Man and his fellow deconstructionists, who invest it with considerable significance. The trope is not at all unusual. Using the structure of a chiasmus, I may introduce two terms—roses and violets, in that order. Then I proceed to discuss violets first, roses later. Karl Marx may have been the first to allegorize the chiasmus— that is, to use this figure of speech as a way of conducting an argument. John Hollander detects the logic of a chiasmus in *The Poverty of Philosophy,* Marx's rebuttal of a book by Proudhon entitled *The Philosophy of Poverty.* For the deconstructionists, similarly, the chiasmus serves to describe a working procedure—a way of instantly turning the tables. What else is the characteristic deconstructive project—"the reversal of binary oppositions"—but the movement of a chiasmus? And now, with the belated discovery of de Man's wartime writings, you had an unexpected new illustration of the trope. The writing he had done first was read last—and compelled a retrospective reassessment of everything he had written in the interval.

The case of Paul de Man instantly divided itself into three sets of questions, each corresponding to a specific time period. The first concerned the period from 1940 to 1942—years when Belgium was under the heels of the Nazi occupation. What exactly had de Man (then between the ages of twenty-one and twenty-three) said and done? Was it as bad as it looked? The answer was distressing: neither de Man's academic allies nor his sparring partners could have suspected the extent of his fascist involvement, or its duration, or the repugnance of the things he said in print. Other questions were more difficult to answer. Was de Man a fascist by ideological conviction, or was it sheer careerist opportunism that prompted the budding young literary critic to grab the chance to write for *Le Soir,* a national newspaper—albeit one committed to a Nazi party line? Why did he stop at the end of November 1942? Was it fear of assassination by the underground (the fate of a fellow *Le Soir* reviewer), or was it a matter of belated scruple? How did he escape the wrath of the court when the war was over? Was he pardoned because of his youth?

A second set of questions concerned the years of de Man's eminence at Yale. How were people to understand his failure to acknowledge his wartime writings? Was it, as it seemed, a matter of shrewd self-protectiveness? If so, how did that square with his previously unimpeachable reputation for integrity? What deepens the enigma is that de Man must have realized that his wartime journalism would surface one day. He knew, after all, that his cult would outlive him; his cancer had been diagnosed as terminal. He could not help being aware of his disciples' devotion. Several were writing books about him; at least one had begun to assemble an exhaustive bibliography of his writings. Given all that, it was surely only a matter of time before the fugitive pieces turned up. Yet de Man, when he adverted to his war years at all, told people that he'd gone to England and worked as a translator, or that he'd studied in Paris, or that he'd joined the underground in France—three palpable falsehoods.

A third set of questions—the most incendiary ones—concerned the present. Journalistic accounts of the case inevitably raised the intractable philosophical dilemma of whether, and to what extent, a writer's actions should modify our understanding of his ideas. Did de Man's wartime words, and his subsequent silence about them, confirm or contradict his analysis of language and writing, meaning and truth? It was possible to conclude that the theory he so artfully spun out was somehow an alternative to confession, or a justification for *not* keeping silent at a time when words had the force of actions. One result of de Man's secrecy about his past was that his admirers and cohorts were left holding the bag when the scandal broke. How they responded to the revelations—and the accusations and recriminations filling the air—would itself become part of the story. Predictably, there were some who set about to deconstruct the most notorious of de Man's wartime articles to show that they subverted their own spoken intentions. Others suggested, more reasonably if not quite convincingly, that de Man's later work was, as Geoffrey Hartman put it, a "belated, but still powerful, act of conscience." Still others blamed the media as the messenger of evil tidings—and reserved their ire for the professors from whom the media learned the story. Deconstruction was clearly on the defensive, and that gave its detractors an opening they could seize. Seize it they did.

The academic equivalent of a guerilla war broke out in the pages of the *Times Literary Supplement* and the *Chronicle of Higher Education,* the *New Republic* and the *New Criterion,* the *Village Voice* and the *London Review of Books.* In the debate precipitated by the sudden rash of disclosures about de Man's early life, one could see the truth in the old adage that the ferocity of academic politics varies inversely with the material stakes involved. But one also felt that one might just possibly be witnessing a critical turning point in the history of an idea. Back in 1984, Geoffrey Hartman observed that deconstruction was sometimes belittled as "cliquish, another fashionable wave that will pass. Yet," he added in rebuttal, "even in America the movement associated with de Man and Derrida is felt to challenge more than a particular set of institutionalized values such as nostalgia for a Common Reader or a Public Style or a Unified Sensibility. The spirit of criticism embodied by de Man seems to threaten the institutionalization of criticism itself." To *challenge,* to *threaten,* remained the operative words now that the *Le Soir* papers were on the table—only now it was deconstruction that was challenged and felt threatened. The case of Paul de Man, spreading like a media brushfire, made clear just how deep ran the animosity to the spirit of criticism embodied by deconstruction's fallen idol. A Columbia professor quipped: "Deconstruction turned out to be the thousand-year Reich that lasted twelve years." The prediction would be proved or disproved in time. The speaker's bitterness was real in either event.

The case of Paul de Man was always more than an ordinary scandal in academe. De Man's "negative charisma," or some other unexplained complexity, made him seem representative, as though there were an allegorical dimension to his career as a critic. In the face of the biographical facts, it is possible to contend that de Man's life really was exemplary after all—though not in the way his disciples would have wished. He was, in some rough sense, like a Citizen Kane who died without saying "Rosebud!" and dropping a snow-filled paperweight. But despite his silence and his dissimulation, the evidence de Man left behind proved far less perishable than the boyhood sled consigned to the flames at the end of *Citizen Kane.*

CHAPTER 7

THE STOLEN

EVENING

The war will only bring about a tighter union of these two things that were so close from the start—the Hitlerian soul and the German soul—to the point that they will become a single and unique power. This is an important phenomenon, because it means that one cannot judge the fact of Hitler without at the same time judging the fact of Germany and that the future of Europe can be envisioned only in the framework of the possibilities and the needs of the German spirit. It is not merely a matter of a series of reforms, but of the definitive emancipation of a people that finds itself, in its turn, called upon to exercise hegemony in Europe.

—*Paul de Man, in* LE SOIR, *October 28, 1941*

The discovery of Paul de Man's wartime journalism was made in the summer of 1987 by a young Belgian scholar named Ortwin de Graef. A de Man devotee, de Graef had set out not to damage the master's reputation but to deepen it; he was preparing a doctoral thesis on the critic he regarded as "arguably the most challenging writer on literature to have emerged in the past few decades." With scholarly zeal, de Graef pursued his archival researches, tracking down defunct journals and combing pages of yellowing newsprint. What had de Man written as a university student in Brussels? Was there anything in his Belgian years that might shed light on his subsequent career in the United States? De Graef was prospecting for the odd nugget of ore, some shining hint of the originality and brilliance that were to come. He happened upon paydirt of another color and texture.

De Graef's initial discovery consisted of ninety-two articles with de Man's byline in the pro-Nazi newspaper *Le Soir,* Belgium's most widely read paper during the German occupation. Over a quarter of a million French-speaking Belgians read *Le Soir* daily through October 1942, in large part because of its respectable prewar reputation. It was, in fact, something like a national newspaper of record. Editorially, it had an anti-German posture that commended it to Belgium's francophone community, the Walloons, but that changed abruptly when the Nazis overran Belgium in May 1940. The invasion began on the tenth of May. Following the May 16 edition of *Le Soir,* the newspaper's owners suspended operations and fled the country, as did most of the editorial staff. Belgium surrendered unconditionally on May 28. The fall of France a few weeks later dashed the hope that the paper could be published in exile from its Paris office.

The German invaders lost no time in exploiting this situation. One of the first things they did upon occupying Brussels was to seize *Le Soir* and make it over, staffing it with editors and writers judged politically correct by the exacting standards of Berlin. By June 13 *Le Soir* was back in circulation, despite the fact that no one formerly on staff was willing to continue under the new dispensation. The newspaper became, inevitably, an instrument of Nazi thought control and an agent of the German propaganda machine. "By choosing Germany we choose Europe," wrote Raymond de Becker, *Le Soir*'s editor-in-chief at the time Paul de Man wrote for it. "Victorious Germany will expel England from the continent and will assure peace for a long time." So heartily hated was *Le Soir* during the occupation that it came to be known derisively as *Le Soir volé*—"The Stolen Evening," stolen by the Nazis and by those who would collaborate with them. Yet it remained the citizenry's chief source of news.

In the demoralizing aftermath of Belgium's military collapse, the paper's influence was not to be underestimated. "Everybody reads quisling papers for information, but with all his bristles out against propaganda," wrote Anne Somerhausen, who kept a journal through the war years in Brussels as an act of resistance. *"Le Soir,* the biggest pre-war daily, was illegally taken over in June 1940 by a quisling staff," she noted, "yet it is read as much as before the war, or more." The nation had been humiliated militarily, was being bled of its labor and its resources, and was struggling with severe shortages of food and clothing; the Germans controlled not only the means of production but the media of communication and information, and they were nothing if not efficient at getting their message out. The defenseless Belgians—defeated, leaderless, and hungry—were in a spiritually vulnerable position. The people, Somerhausen wrote, were "like a defeated flock without a King"—King Leopold III had surrendered to the Germans and was now a virtual captive of his palace, a prisoner of war rather than a symbol of resistance. "We are apathetic. We try not to think beyond today. We shall be an easy prey to German propaganda," Somerhausen worried in July 1940. It was possible to read *Le Soir* and to dismiss the falsehoods it perpetrated, as Somerhausen was able to do. It was possible by the end of November 1942 for resistants—buoyed by the British success at El Alamein and the German setback at Stalingrad—to turn a defiant and vengeful eye on the "quisling press." But in the period when Paul de Man wrote for *Le Soir,* the war's ultimate outcome was far from clear, and the battle for the hearts and minds of the Belgian population was being waged in earnest by the Germans and their surrogates.

Assisted by Tom Keenan, de Man's American bibliographer, de Graef eventually determined that de Man published, in all, no fewer than 170 articles in *Le Soir volé.* Ten other pieces by de Man turned up in *Het Vlaamsche Land,* a Flemish-language daily similarly tarred with a collaborationist brush. With bilingual ease and an air of confident authority, the linguistically gifted and intellectually precocious young man had addressed himself to both of his nation's main ethnic groups: the Dutch-speaking Flemish (approximately half of the population) and the French-speaking Walloons (nearly thirty-five per cent). He knew he was writing for a wide national audience, and he knew, too, that both papers were stridently pro-German—as they would have to be to pass muster with the occupation authorities. De

Man had just turned twenty-one when he signed on as a cultural correspondent for *Le Soir* in December 1940. Not until the end of November two years later did he stop.

For the full two-year period of his association with *Le Soir,* de Man advanced the Nazis' cultural agenda in ways small and large. At best he was a defeatist, certain that destiny favored the Germans, and an opportunist, who didn't see why his country's humiliation should stand in the way of his career. At worst he was "a fascist, an anti-Semite, and an active collaborator with the Nazis during the German occupation of Belgium"—the judgment reached by John Brenkman after a meticulous analysis of de Man's contributions to *Le Soir.* "The results of the inquiry are incontrovertible," Brenkman asserted. "De Man responded, consistently and actively, to an entire range of ideological imperatives associated with European fascism and political imperatives specifically dictated by the Third Reich." One of the notable points about Brenkman's indictment is that he hardly fit the stereotype with which the deconstructionists attempted to discredit those professors who refused to whitewash de Man. It could not be said that Brenkman wrote out of an ignorance of deconstruction. The Northwestern professor had some years before published an analysis of Ovid that Jonathan Culler proclaimed "a classic deconstructive reading."

The charitable view held by those who knew and liked de Man in his American university career is that his wartime fling with fascism must have been motivated by careerist self-advancement—an understandable if not, under the circumstances, a pardonable impulse in a young man of twenty-two or twenty-three. Yet so constant was his apologia for the Germans that his motivation for joining *Le Soir*—whether he did it out of opportunism or conviction or a mixture of the two—seems a subsidiary question. Too many of de Man's articles exhibit an unmistakably ideological cast; he acquiesced in the Nazis' "new order" as if it were an inevitable and irreversible condition. The later de Man, in his years as a Yale eminence, insisted that history was a province of literature; the young literary journalist, in his active critical practice, had it the other way around—he insisted that literature serve the makers of history. His "literary" columns are always implicitly and often overtly political. The German "revolution"—for that is how de Man characterized the conquest of his country—was treated not only as a fact of history but as the uppermost fact to be kept in mind when surveying the cultural life of Belgium in 1941 and 1942. Collaboration with the enemy, de Man declared, was nothing short of "a necessity."

It is important, when setting the historical record straight, to distinguish among varieties of collaborationism, though any form of rapprochement with such a barbarous invader must strike us today as, at the least, unsavory, misguided, and timorous. The form espoused by de Man was more drastic than the fence-straddling "wait and see" policy—known as *attentisme*—adopted by some of his compatriots. A "wait and see" collaborator wasn't actively working toward a German victory in World War II; rather, he assumed it to be the likeliest historical scenario and determined to make the best of it. There were, as with other forms of collaborationism, varieties of attentisme, some less objectionable than others. In Belgium, easily the most notable and the most controversial instance of the "wait and see" attitude was that exhibited by King Leopold III. A brief summary of his case will help put de Man's into the proper historical perspective.

In May 1940, days after Hitler launched his invasion of Western Europe, Belgium's military defeat loomed as a near certainty. The king of Belgium had a crucial decision to make. He could have decided to flee, as both the king of Norway and the queen of Holland fled their conquered lands; he could have elected to preside over a provisional government-in-exile, the course of action recommended unanimously by his cabinet. He did neither. Though the ministers of the Belgian government did, in fact, go into exile, Leopold chose instead to stay behind. Rather than lead an incipient resistance, he authorized a complete capitulation, ordering his armies to lay down their arms in compliance with the German demand for an unconditional surrender. The king's actions were a blow to the national morale—coupled as they were with pronouncements from Leopold's chief adviser exhorting the people not to resist the conquering Germans. The king's decision to defy his cabinet created a rift between throne and parliament that would, in time, precipitate the gravest constitutional crisis in Belgium's history. For the duration of the war Leopold remained in Nazi-occupied Belgium—as if the throne itself were held captive—until the Germans evacuated him to Germany after the liberation of Belgium in September 1944. Though the king was evacuated against his will, for years afterward Leopold's critics associated his forced departure with the simultaneous flight of hard-core collaborators. Nor could the king's critics bring themselves to forgive him for having visited Hitler at Berchtesgaden in November 1940. Leopold had made the trip in the hope of repatriating Belgian POWs and alleviating food shortages. He gained nothing from this attempt at supplicating the dictator, but left behind the image of a royal humiliation.

The Belgian sovereign could plausibly claim that in accommodating the Nazis, he was trying to act in his nation's best interests. He could be convicted of poor political judgment—a grotesque set of blunders indeed—but his motives were not necessarily ignoble. Yet his "mild" form of collaborationism was serious enough: his behavior during the occupation—and particularly in its first days—made him a despised figure in much of his land. By ordering his troops to lay down their arms eighteen days after the ferocious Nazi blitzkrieg began, Leopold felt he was preventing their needless massacre. Good military arguments could be marshaled to support this view—though one indubitable consequence of the Belgian capitulation was that it left the British and French armies in a perilously exposed position. Recriminations were swift in the aftermath of the calamity that the British army managed miraculously to avert at Dunkirk. In London on June 4, in the great speech in which he vowed that England would fight on the beaches and on the landing grounds and never surrender, Churchill vented his ire. He recalled that the Belgians had foolishly maintained their neutrality—a policy of benefit only to the Germans—long after Hitler gave evidence of his bellicose aims. The British had responded to the Belgian sovereign's belated appeal for aid, Churchill told the House of Commons, only to have Leopold turn around and leave them in the lurch: "He and his brave, efficient army, nearly half a million strong, guarded our left flank and thus kept open our only line of retreat to the sea. Suddenly, without previous consultation, with the least possible notice, without the advice of his Ministers and upon his own personal act, he sent a plenipotentiary to the German Command, surrendered his Army and exposed our whole flank and means of retreat."

In fact, Leopold made his decision not merely *without* but *against* the advice of his ministers—with consequences that extended well beyond the realm of military strategy. To the extent that a constitutional monarch is a figurehead of authority, the king's acquiescence in his captivity had a distressing symbolic significance. There are times when exile seems synonymous with resistance, and the Nazi conquest of Europe was one of those times. But a constitutional monarch is not just a figurehead; he is a working partner in the government, with well-defined limits to his executive power. Acting unilaterally, Leopold had set himself at odds with his own parliamentary government—and thereby raised the whole question of his initiative, his prerogatives, and, finally, his fitness to rule. Either parliament or the king had, in practical political terms, been rendered illegitimate by the king's decision to remain in occupied Belgium—particularly as the king made it clear that he reserved the option to form a new government under the German occupation. Parliament would be casting doubt on its own legitimacy if, after the war, it simply welcomed back, with no questions asked, a monarch who had so clearly exceeded his constitutional bounds. Nor were his countrymen universally eager to forgive their sovereign. Unwilling to flee Belgium under the Nazi occupation, Leopold found himself obliged to take refuge in Switzerland after the war. His conduct—and the larger questions it raised about the proper relation between king and parliament—was hotly debated in his absence. Not until 1950 did he return to Belgium, and then under the least propitious of circumstances. A plebiscite recalled him to Brussels by an uncomfortably slim margin; a little less than fifty-eight percent of the electorate voted in his favor. Angry demonstrators, protesting his return, chanted "Leopold to the gallows!" as they marched down the streets of Brussels. Half a million workers went on strike; barricades went up; there were outbreaks of violence. The threat of revolution and civil war ended only when the king abdicated in favor of his son on August 1, 1950. It was as if the institution of the monarchy itself could be maintained only on condition that Leopold remove himself from the picture.

Was the condemnation of Leopold III too severe, given the defense that could be mustered in his behalf—that his motives were good even if his policy was misguided, and that he stood falsely accused of "treating" with the enemy? Historians are divided on the question. But David Littlejohn's comment seems apt:

> The king's enforced abdication may have been unjust but it was not unjustifiable. A king, by the nature of his position, must be a focal point, a symbol of national unity outside and above politics. Once he becomes involved in controversy, even by implication, he becomes a divisive

force and vitiates the essential function of his high office. Leopold *had* become involved in politics. Nothing he could do or say could alter that. Perhaps an inversion of Boulay de la Meurthe's well-known comment on the execution of the Duc d'Enghien would be the most appropriate verdict on the abdication: it was worse than a crime, but it was not a mistake. Belgian unity could be restored only by the substitution of a new and untarnished symbol.

"Wait and see," the shorthand rationale for Leopold's disastrous wartime policy, was a way of hedging one's bets in favor of the likelihood that Germany's victory in Europe was assured and would be permanent. The historian E. Ramon Arango explains the logic. "If the Germans should be victorious Leopold hoped to gain the maximum advantage for Belgium, and his behavior during the occupation was designed to accommodate himself to this eventuality," Arango writes. "One can imagine that Leopold reasoned like this: the Belgian government fights with the Allies while the King is a prisoner of the Germans. He will do nothing to aid the aggressor, but he will do nothing to offend him. Irrespective of who is the victor, that victor will have a Belgian friend, or, in the case of Leopold, if not a friend, at least not an avowed enemy. This was the policy of *attentisme,* 'wait and see,' 'wait and profit.'" More than one of Belgium's ministers of government were outraged by what they saw as the king's faintheartedness; some called it treason. As Belgium fell in May 1940, Paul Henri Spaak—Belgium's once and future prime minister, who would play a major role in the reconstruction of postwar Europe—accused Leopold of "a total collapse of a certain moral sense." Spaak spoke in uncompromising terms of his horror, and that of his colleagues, at learning that the king was planning to accept a political role for himself under the German occupation. "The King," he said, "had a certain number of radically false ideas":

1) The Belgian army should fight only on Belgian soil.

2) The French and British Allies had been defeated and the war was over. Peace is going to be made and consequently it is necessary to change cards and seek, as far as possible, the favor of him who will be the victor.

As I have said, these are completely false, mistaken ideas.
. . . We were aware of the reasons which the King wanted
to take advantage of. We found them mad, stupid, more:
criminal, because they indicated in the King a total collapse
of a certain moral sense which shocked us.

Spaak addressed the king directly. "You were bound from the moment
that you allowed thousands of French and British soldiers to be called
on our behalf and come be killed in the defense of Belgium. If you
abandon their cause, you will be a traitor and will be dishonored."
What Spaak called "the reasons which the King wanted to take advantage of" were the idea of a separate peace and the avoidance of useless
bloodshed at the expense of a unilateral capitulation to an invading
force: the calculations of attentisme.

Yet for Paul de Man in 1942, attentisme was unacceptable primarily because it didn't go far enough. Something bolder and more
affirmative was demanded by the prospect of German hegemony in
Europe. So far as de Man could see, the Germans had history on their
side: "the current of history," as he put it in one of his articles, "which
continues to flow without bothering about the reticence of a few
individuals who persist in not understanding its power." And it was
history, the pressure of "the overbearing reality," that condemned
attentisme as "untenable." Reviewing (and recommending) a book by
the notorious French collaborator Alfred Fabre-Luce, de Man coupled
a critique of attentisme with praise for "those rare perspicacious minds
who have grasped" the power of history. The task of this fascist elite
is "to combat the inertia and hostility of the masses"—to overcome
any resistance to the irresistible Nazi future. History will vindicate the
proponents of collaboration. "Later it will turn out that they were the
precursors of a unanimous will."

Some de Man loyalists initially downplayed the importance of
his wartime journalism on the grounds that a number of his cultural
notices had little apparent political content. There was something
dubious about this argument to begin with, and what made it especially disingenuous, coming from advanced literary theorists, was that
it flew in the face of their own insistence that even "literary" language
has an ideological dimension. They, of all readers, might have been
expected to understand that even the least political of de Man's book
reviews and literary "chronicles" assisted the Nazi propaganda ma-

chine. De Man gave a veneer of intellectual respectability to the stolen newspaper. In his precociously hierophantic style, he lent support to the idea that art and culture might flourish under a fascist dictatorship; he helped launder the image of Nazi Germany, and he did so at a time when his defeated compatriots were most susceptible to the techniques of mass-persuasion. The argument, in any case, proved academic. For when all 170 of de Man's *Le Soir* articles were laid out together, it became clear that a good many of them were quite overtly political. De Man wrote warmly of the major collaborationist authors of Belgium and France: men like Alfred Fabre-Luce, Pierre Drieu la Rochelle, Robert Brasillach, Pierre Daye, and Bertrand de Jouvenel; men whose names appeared on the recommended list of the *Propaganda Abteilung Frankreich,* the German agency in charge of the mass indoctrination of the French. Such noted collaborationists served a double propaganda purpose: they helped deter resistance in the occupied lands and at the same time they reinforced the resolve of the Germans. De Man explained these authors and, in the explaining, endorsed their vision of Europe. In the tart words of one present-day expert on the period, Jeffrey Mehlman of Boston University, de Man "plugged the Nazi hit-parade."

As past masters of propaganda, the Nazis understood the power of ideas and images, specious ideas and spurious images, repeated until they passed for truths in credulous minds among a demoralized and divided populace. Belgium was a divisible entity to begin with; its Flemish and Wallonian populations spoke different languages—Flemish (Dutch) and French—and coexisted in the mutual distrust of two rival cultural communities. And certainly during the bleak early days of World War II, Belgium was a demoralized nation. To the Nazis' *Propaganda Abteilung,* the occupation of Belgium thus presented a golden opportunity: the people could be considered at least potentially receptive to a propaganda effort determined to inculcate the view that a new order had arrived, would last a thousand years, and represented a change for the better from the decadence of prewar Europe.

German propaganda during World War II laid heavy stress on the image of "fortress Europe": the idea that Germany stood as civilization's bulwark against the barbarian hordes of Russia and the soulless materialists of the United States. In his journalism, de Man promoted this view of things implicitly and sometimes quite openly—as when he saluted the valor of the German soldier and sang the praises of the poetry that was coming from Mussolini's Italy. Among the most damaging of de Man's articles were those that surveyed "the present revolution" in Europe. In April 1941 de Man described the German occupiers as "more dignified, more just, and more humane" than the victorious French had been in 1918. The war that resulted in Belgium's subjugation wasn't merely "an economic and national struggle," he argued in August 1941. It was "a revolution"—a revolution "that aims at organizing European society in a more equitable manner." He referred to the German triumph as if it were permanent, a fait accompli to which resistance would be pointless. The war was over and the new Nazi order had begun. Germany had "the will to unify a set of regions that have one and the same racial structure, but which its enemies ceaselessly endeavor to divide," de Man wrote in March 1942. He promoted the infamous "blood and soil" ideology of the Nazis—the conviction that a nation's culture is inextricably bound up with its racial purity and with the ideals of duty and sacrifice. "A sincere artist," he wrote, "can never renounce his proper regional [character], destined by blood and soil, since it is an integrating part of his essence, which he has to utter." To de Man, fascism was a force for cultural and national renewal. "We are," he wrote in April 1942, "entering a mystical era, a period for faith and belief, with all that this entails in suffering, exaltation, and rapture." Germany would point the way: "the whole continuity of Western civilization depends on the unity of the people who are its center." There was indeed much to be said in favor of the "irresistible necessity" of collaboration with the German occupiers.

David Littlejohn, in his book *The Patriotic Traitors,* divides French collaborators into two broad categories. The majority favored "only that degree of cooperation with the occupying power necessary to secure for France a tolerable life in the 'New Order' "; a more radical (and smaller) group of collaborators not only acquiesced in but actively welcomed a German victory. In affirming the "irresistible necessity" of collaboration, de Man seems to have crossed over from one category to the other. Perhaps, as Littlejohn implies, such crossings-over were inevitable: "The tragedy of those who collaborated because they felt it was in the best interest of France is that they were driven more and more into the camp of those who collaborated because they thought it was in the best interests of Germany." Borrowing Littlejohn's terms, John Brenkman contends that de Man's arguments—abstract though they are—put him in league with the "German victory" collaborators as opposed to those in the "French survivor" camp. The former embraced fascist ideals for ideological, not pragmatic, reasons. And de Man's commitment to the notion of historical necessity was expressed in ideological terms. "Hitlerism," he argued in his *Le Soir* article of October 28, 1941, was far from an aberration in German history. On the contrary, "the Hitlerian soul and the German soul" were "close together from the start," and the war will only bring about "a tighter union" of the two. The triumph of Hitler promised "the definitive emancipation of a people that finds itself called upon to exercise, in its turn, hegemony in Europe."

De Man came to praise the literary spokesmen for French collaborationism, and when he chastised one of them it was for seeming to waver in his commitment to the new fascist order. In August 1941, he addressed himself to Robert Brasillach's account of life in prewar France, *Notre avant-guerre.* A wide-eyed rhapsodist, who has been called "a sort of fascist Rupert Brooke," Brasillach was the militantly pro-German editor of *Je suis partout,* a weekly that presented the major literary talents of the collaboration. In his review of *Notre avant-guerre,* de Man took note of Brasillach's accomplishments, his "excellent pages filled with poetry and freshness." At the same time, de Man upbraided Brasillach for his romantic individualism. What was needed, in de Man's view, was discipline and order, not the "apolitical" pleasures of the aesthete. In particular, he criticized the chapter in *Notre avant-guerre* in which Brasillach evokes the Nazi Party Congress he had witnessed in Nuremberg in 1937. Brasillach's reaction to the spectacle, showing "some fright when faced with the 'strange' nature of the demonstration," was that of a man "for whom this sudden importance of the political in the life of a people is an inexplicable phenomenon." In sum, Brasillach was not sufficiently political, sufficiently tough-minded, sufficiently committed to the fascist future. The clear implication is that de Man practices a purer, more serious form of fascism than even Robert Brasillach—a man famous for prophesying the emergence of a new twentieth-century hero, *homo fascista.* Fascism was "a kind of poetry" for Brasillach. "I tell myself that it cannot die," he wrote in prison in 1945. "I shall never forget the radiance of the fascism of my youth."

Wolfgang Holdheim, the Cornell professor who succeeded Paul de Man as chairman of that university's comparative literature department, was in a unique position to judge the seriousness of what de Man had written during the war. In the early days of the controversy, when attempts were made to minimize the ideological character of de Man's wartime journalism, Holdheim spoke out. He drew upon the authority of his "own historical experience, which was unfortunately quite concrete." The half-Jewish Holdheim spent the war years in Holland, which had the same Nazi nightmare to endure as its neighboring Belgium; he saw his father, a Jew, carted off by the Nazis to be murdered. Holdheim characterized de Man's articles for *Le Soir* as, collectively, "common Nazi hack work, excruciatingly dull and totally unoriginal, embarrassing to read in their mediocrity." He went on:

> How could one view the publication of articles such as de Man's, written by a Belgian, in occupied Belgium in 1941 and 1942? Only as an act of unspeakable moral shabbiness. And what must have been the status of such an author in 1945? Nothing less than that of a moral, political and probably social outcast. This may be hard to understand for a generation safely shielded from that period by temporal distance, and often by a chronic lack of historical insight. We can be certain, though, that it was fully understood by de Man. In the light of the atrocious revelations that flooded us in 1945, he may even have reconsidered that praise of the Germans as exquisitely civilized occupiers which he had found it necessary to insert into a literary article at the time of his country's humiliation. He must have been permanently traumatized by events.

Holdheim spoke sternly, knowing that de Man remained "the object of a personality cult" and fearing that "students continue to be ideologically indoctrinated with his very particular idiosyncrasies."

It has been said in de Man's defense that he was a very young man and that young men make mistakes. His relative youth may explain why a military tribunal in Antwerp, after questioning de Man, released him without charges in 1945. It is important, too, to recall the distinction between Belgian national fascism and the particular ideology of the Nazi party. It is a distinction that would not have been lost in the courts of postwar Europe: a Belgian nationalist—even if he espoused the politics of fascism—would be spared the punishment meted out to an active collaborator. The difference between Belgian fascism and Nazism was at least as wide as that between the varieties of European anti-Semitism. There was the old-fashioned kind of anti-Semitism (based, in the words of one Belgian commentator, on "the fear of economic competition" and "the Christian myth that they [Jews] were the people who had killed God"). And then there was the racial anti-Semitism of the Nazis—the insistence that Jews were a polluting force, a people of contaminated blood. The anti-Semitism that de Man expressed in *Le Soir* was, as we shall see, far closer to the traditional kind than to the Nazi dream of state-sponsored genocide. The leniency of the military tribunal strengthens the view that de Man was primarily a Belgian nationalist who envisaged a fascist Belgium having a degree of autonomy and independence from direct German rule. But too much stress should not be placed on the court's deliberations. Though Belgium was tougher on suspected collaborators than its neighbors were, the system had plenty of loopholes. In Wolfgang Holdheim's words, "Postwar Belgian justice with regard to collaborators was notoriously hit-or-miss—sometimes very severe, sometimes very lenient—and de Man was really a very small fish."

Others certainly did worse. De Man was a free-lancer at *Le Soir* and not part of its regular full-time staff. He continued to maintain good relations with writers who opposed the Nazis, and his personal conduct toward Jewish acquaintances was evidently blameless. De Man was capable of offering the shelter of his home for several nights to a Jewish couple who found themselves on the streets of Brussels— accidentally locked out of the flat where they had been staying—after curfew. It is possible that de Man, for all his intellectual precocity, was basically a man of shallow character. This was the opinion of Georges Goriely, a Jewish friend of de Man in Brussels during the war years. Goriely felt he could speak freely about his "clandestine activities" to de Man; de Man was personally not threatening, because his affirmation of the German "new order" reflected "primarily his opportunism" and "his profound lack of moral conscience rather than any ideological choice." The fact that de Man wrote before the war for the student publication *Cahiers du Libre Examen,* which had a socialist tilt, complicates our sense of de Man only somewhat. Historians of socialism, charting its wayward course, keep reminding us that the road to fascism was paved by ex-socialists: Mussolini had begun his political life as a socialist, and Hitler's party called itself "national socialism." But in de Man's case, the gravitation from *Cahiers du Libre Examen* to *Le Soir volé* seems merely to confirm the opportunistic character of his early journalistic career.

If excuses can be made for a young man's erratic behavior, there are also reasons to resist the impulse. A good reason is that the practical effect of de Man's wartime journalism was far from negligible. On the contrary: it was substantial enough to make the Resistance take note. On the sixth of September 1944, days after the liberation of Brussels, the journal *Debout* denounced de Man in contemptuous terms—going so far as to liken his personal appearance to that of the Führer. For "the self-proclaimed *Le Soir*," the journal reported, de Man "dissects novels and essays" in literary chronicles "as unreadable as those he wrote in the *Cahiers du Libre Examen*." True, his activities at *Le Soir* ended by December 1942—or, as *Debout* explained, "After a while, he senses that things are taking a bad turn and he beats a very prudent retreat. His name no longer appears in the columns of the self-proclaimed *Soir*. The poor little carcass of this little man, blond and frail, with his lock of hair à la Hitler, deserts the Place de Louvain." The Place de Louvain was where *Le Soir* had its offices in Brussels.

The timing of de Man's actions puts them in a decidedly unfavorable light. De Man began his association with *Le Soir* at a moment of supreme moral crisis—a moment when Europeans had to decide whether to resist the Nazis or to yield to them as to an inevitable fate. Seven months had gone by since the fall of Belgium, and six months since the fall of France, when de Man began writing for *Le Soir* in December 1940. It was, for many in the West, the darkest winter of the war. Stalin was still in league with Hitler, the United States remained isolationist, and the British had narrowly escaped the annihilation of their army at Dunkirk. All that stood between civilization and the Nazis, it sometimes seemed, was Winston Churchill's radio voice. To have chosen such a moment to write for the Nazi-controlled press was not something a man could look back on with pride. At the very least it meant he had participated in—and was prepared to profit from—the ignominy of Hitler's conquest of Belgium. The surfacing of de Man's *Le Soir* articles in 1988 made this much clear. It was a bitter blow to those for whom de Man once "seemed to exemplify an intellectual seriousness that also felt like moral seriousness." The phrase is from an article on the de Man controversy by William Flesch, a

Brandeis professor. De Man's *Le Soir* career, Flesch wrote, is "unforgivable," and for this reason: "As a public act it is deeply collaborationist. There is no question that collaborationism can often be defended as the lesser of two evils. Historians frequently and rightly distinguish between collaborators and collaborationists, the former out simply for a share of the Nazi's spoils, the latter seeking an alliance which would spare their countries from the utter destruction reserved for less pliant victims of Nazi aggression. In specific cases the distinction is almost always blurred, and so it seems to be with de Man."

It was always more comforting to attribute de Man's wartime journalism to expediency and opportunism rather than conviction. To write for *Le Soir,* the newspaper with the widest circulation in Belgium, could be construed as an opportunity that many ambitious young critics would find tempting, even if it meant subscribing to Nazi propaganda. "His was not a political mind," reports Georges Goriely. "It was simply that an occasion presented itself for a young man of about twenty to become the literary critic for a newspaper with a large circulation and which certainly paid its contributors well." Not everyone will concede the point. But in any case it leaves de Man's defenders in a quandary. For how, then, can one assert that it was principle that drove de Man to quit *Le Soir* at the end of November 1942? It would appear that de Man threw in the towel as a cultural correspondent at just the moment when the Nazis had given up as lost their propaganda campaign to win over the Belgian populace to the glories of German *Kultur.* In October 1943, eleven months after de Man's last *Le Soir* column, Anne Somerhausen noted in her journal that "No Belgian patriot can possibly attend a German lecture during the Occupation. The Germans have, in fact, so well realized the failure of their Kultur campaign that for a year past they have sent no apostles of art or intellect to Belgium." By November 29, 1942, the date on de Man's last dispatch for *Le Soir,* the course of the war had significantly changed. With the Americans and Russians as desperate allies, the hope of Hitler's eventual defeat had become credible. Though there were not yet two fronts in Europe, the British had just prevailed at El Alamein. The Americans had successfully launched "Operation Torch," thus gaining a foothold in Africa. At Stalingrad, where the Germans would suffer a devastating loss, the battle had taken a decisive Russian turn. Reporting on these military developments for the BBC, George Orwell declared on November 28, 1942, that "the final death blow to the New Order" had been delivered. During the previous week, French West Africa had defected to the Allies. The behavior of the Vichy turncoats meant that they, with their inside knowledge of developments in Europe, had decided that the Nazi ship was going to go down. "Any chance of French collaboration with the Nazis has now gone for good," Orwell said. Getting out of Le Soir just then would have been a shrewd career move even if de Man hadn't had a more palpable reason to quit: he knew he had earned the enmity of the Resistance, and it took little imagination to speculate where that might lead. The fate of Louis Fonsny took the matter out of the realm of conjecture. Fonsny had been de Man's colleague at Le Soir; the two men had in fact patrolled the same literary-cultural beat during the Nazi occupation. In January 1943, Fonsny was assassinated by the Resistance at a Brussels tram stop. It could just as easily have been Paul de Man.

Reading de Man's wartime journalism is an unsettling experience made even more disquieting by the company he kept in the pages of Le Soir and Het Vlaamsche Land. The latter's editorial policy was straightforward. The war was blamed on the Jews—Jewish Bolsheviks in league with Jewish capitalists. The Nazi "revolution" would put an end to that. It would vouchsafe the survival of "Western Christian civilization" in its struggle with "the godless barbarians" of socialism. Perhaps, indeed, the Nazis should annex Flanders—the editors of Het Vlaamsche Land could see the advantages of that. The Third Reich's Propaganda Abteilung was well pleased with such sentiments. The paper was "an extremely useful instrument for propaganda purposes," the ministry reported in March 1941. As for Le Soir, suffice it to say that its wartime editor-in-chief was a figure of infamy in postwar Belgium. Convicted of war crimes in Brussels in 1946, Raymond de Becker was sentenced to death. (The sentence was later commuted.) Among the French collaborators reviewed by de Man, Robert Brasillach was executed in Paris in 1945. Later that year, Pierre Drieu la Rochelle committed suicide rather than stand trial.

What de Man had written in these two newspapers earned him no reprimand in the courts of postwar Belgium. But the judgment that a Resistance newspaper passed on him in 1943 was severe enough. That fall, de Man was one of forty-four Le Soir contributors to be denounced in a pamphlet entitled *Galerie des Traitres*—"the Traitors' Gallery." There is a photograph of de Man and next to it he is described as one "who knows whom to stick with"—or, as we would say, one who knows which way the wind blows. He took advantage of connections to land at *Le Soir,* the pamphlet reported, but succeeded in staying there "thanks to his energetic propaganda."

The most notorious of de Man's *Le Soir* articles—the one that caused the greatest pain and outrage when its contents were revealed in 1987—was entitled "The Jews and Contemporary Literature" ("Les Juifs dans la littérature actuelle") and dated March 4, 1941. It appeared in *Le Soir* in the thick of the Nazis' most concerted hate campaign against the Jews in Belgium. A month later, when hooligans vandalized synagogues in Antwerp, Belgium had its own version of Kristallnacht. "The Jews and Contemporary Literature" was surrounded by virulent articles on the same racial theme; *Le Soir*'s editors had decided to devote a special afternoon edition to the cause of anti-Semitism, which they defined in an editorial headnote. "The Jews have committed numerous social wrongs," wrote the editors. "With their trickery and tenacity, they have seized control of politics, the economy, the press; they have profited from their privileged status, getting rich at the expense of their host nations and luring them into catastrophes that can only lead to war." The anti-Semitism of *Le Soir* went beyond "social grounds," however. It went beyond the old-fashioned anti-Semite's bogey to propound the Nazi line that Jews were inferior as a race. The distinction was important: if the fault was biological rather than religious, cultural, or ethnic, then the most dire measures would be justified. "Our anti-Semitism is of a racial order," the editors of *Le Soir* proclaimed. The Jewish "type" must be combatted, expelled: "We are determined to forbid ourselves any cross-breeding with them and to liberate ourselves spiritually from their demoralizing influence in the realm of thought, literature, and the arts."

De Man's article in *Le Soir* that day was less extreme in tone but unmistakable in its drift.* The writer begins by treating the question of "vulgar anti-Semitism," which portrays Europe as "degenerate and decadent because Judaizied [in French, the pejorative *enjuivé*]." He rejects this argument on the grounds that European culture was healthy

---

*A translation of "The Jews in Contemporary Literature" is included as an appendix to this book.

enough to resist the nefarious Jewish influence. Jewish writers are invariably of "the second rank," he writes. Thus, he concludes, "a solution to the Jewish problem" entailing "the creation of a Jewish colony isolated from Europe" need not have "regrettable consequences for the literary life of the West." Europe stood to lose, at most, "some personalities of mediocre worth." A quote box below de Man's byline contains an anti-Semitic slur that Le Soir ascribed falsely to Benjamin Franklin. It's worth quoting to make plain what sort of newspaper this was: "A leopard cannot change its spots. Jews are Asiatics; they are a menace to the nation that admits them, and they should be excluded by the Constitution."

It is reasonable to ask what de Man knew, and when he knew it, at the time he was writing for Le Soir. In March 1941, when de Man pondered the merits of deportation as a possible "solution to the Jewish problem," the Nazis had not yet identified deportation with murder. The "Final Solution"—that grim euphemism for the extermination of a people—was not introduced until the Wannsee conference in January 1942. When de Man wrote of "the creation of a Jewish colony isolated from Europe," he may have had in mind the so-called Madagascar plan that several Nazi officials, Himmler and Heydrich among them, had briefly considered in 1940 pending the outcome of the Battle of Britain. The Madagascar plan called for the forced relocation of four million European Jews to that African island, then a French colony. The problem with this "solution" was that it would have required the active collaboration of both the British and the French. That was no longer a serious possibility in the fall of 1940, after British Spitfires and Hurricanes beat back the enemy's Messerschmitts in their epochal battles in the air. On September 17, the tenacity of the R.A.F. forced Hitler to abandon Operation Sea Lion, his plan for the invasion of England. With Britain in no mood to capitulate, the Madagascar option was killed.

It is only fair to assume that de Man wrote as he did in complete ignorance of the Nazis' genocidal aims. But the systematic persecution of the Jews was as clearly evident in Belgium as in the rest of Nazi Europe when he wrote for Le Soir. Jews in Belgium were banned from the civil service, the press, the practice of law, and the teaching profession by a decree issued in October 1940 that went into effect at the end of that year. The expulsion of several hundred Jewish aliens from Antwerp to northern Belgium in November 1940 caused a panic among Belgium's Jewish citizenry. Many tried to emigrate, but in February 1941 the Germans stopped issuing exit permits to Jews. On January 30, Hitler stood before the Reichstag and repeated his vow that the war would result in "the annihilation of the Jewish race in Europe." Apocalyptic threats could be heard closer to home as well. "The last Jew must be driven out of Flanders and the Walloons," the leader of the rabidly anti-Semitic *Volksverwering* ("the People's Defense") told an audience in Antwerp that March.

In the words of the Holocaust historian Michael Marrus, "One would have had to live in a plastic bubble to be oblivious to the massive, open, intense persecution of the Jews then under way, and which was perfectly evident to someone in de Man's position." Yet none of it modified de Man's stance toward "Hitlerism" and "the present revolution." A curfew on Jews was imposed in September 1941; Jewish businesses had been seized earlier that summer. The following June, Belgium's Jews were forced to wear the yellow star. On August 20 of that year, de Man published an article in *Het Vlaamsche Land* arguing that Jews were responsible for an "aberrant" strain in modern literature, "a forced, caricatured representation of reality." That was the month when the Nazis commenced transporting Belgian Jews to Auschwitz. Rumors of the death camps surfaced in Brussels early in the month. Anne Somerhausen reported on "fantastic" tales "of Jews shipped in hermetically sealed cars to Berlin, killed with poison gas on the way, and thrown into a canal on arrival." Though the rumors may have seemed incredible at first, their very currency made de Man's derogation of the Jews seem a calculated blow. By the most conservative estimate, at least twenty-five thousand Belgian Jews were deported to their deaths by the end of the war. And they had been de Man's neighbors: the Jews of Belgium were most heavily concentrated in Antwerp, where de Man was born and raised, and in Brussels, where he wrote for *Le Soir*.

And that brings us to another inescapable irony. A high proportion of de Man's closest friends and colleagues, at Yale and elsewhere, were Jewish. He had given none of them reason to suspect that he had an anti-Semitic past. It was they who, though they may have felt personally betrayed, also felt obliged to ask themselves the questions that de Man had managed to evade. Geoffrey Hartman, who had helped bring de Man to Yale, was in a particularly poignant position. Besides being a "Yale School" eminence, Hartman was a founder of

Yale's Judaic studies program and an organizer of the university's video archive for Holocaust testimony. As a boy growing up in Germany in the 1930s, Hartman had himself narrowly eluded the clutches of exterminating Nazis. At the age of nine he was separated from his mother, not to see her again until seven years had passed and she had become "a stranger"; Hartman's wife, Renee, is a death-camp survivor. "There is nothing explanatory that relieves very much the shock I feel when there is an anti-Semitic act," Hartman said with evident anguish after the *Le Soir* papers surfaced. "In the man I personally knew there was not a trace of anti-Semitism." A veteran of graduate studies at Yale made the irony more plain. Asked to characterize de Man as a teacher and a presence, the former student (now a professor elsewhere) replied without hesitation, "He was *haimish*"—a Yiddish word meaning friendly, unpretentious, the opposite of snobbish and supercilious. Leo Rosten, who supplies such definitions in *The Joys of Yiddish,* adds that "Jews put a high value on being *haimish.*" Jews had put a high value on Paul de Man as a teacher and colleague. Ted Weiss, who helped arrange de Man's first academic appointment at Bard College, remembers visiting de Man in Boston in the early 1950s. De Man was then teaching French at a Berlitz school. "We were dismayed," Weiss recalls. "We goaded him to overcome his passivity and to look into Harvard for some work. I wrote to [Harry] Levin [then director of the Harvard Society of Fellows], whom I knew well. Paul saw him, and despite his age became a Junior Fellow; the rest is history. So his path was strewn with helpful Jews!" Or, as Harry Levin put it, "some of his best friends were non-Aryan."

By not owning up to what he had done, de Man left his friends and former associates with the responsibility, after his death, to make his explanations for him. Because they had been his academic allies, they felt they would have to get on the witness stand in place of de Man himself—and answer questions on the basis of incomplete information, the fragmentary traces of their colleague's repressed past. But everyone who was anyone in literary criticism was determined to have his or her say about the de Man disclosures. Here was a story full of pathos and irony, revelation and reversal, controversy and conflict. Here, too, was a pattern of voluble discourse and mysterious silence— and wasn't that what deconstruction is all about? Like a rich scholarly find, the *Le Soir* papers offered an unexpected convergence of two realms usually kept in separate compartments: the realm of literary theory and the realm of historical actuality.

It was never very difficult to understand what made the de Man disclosures so incendiary—or why every last article on the subject seemed to fan the flames of the scandal, even (or especially) those articles that sought to lay it to rest. The enmity between deconstructionists and their rivals is only part of the story. The other part is history—the singular history of Europe in the years of the Third Reich. In the end, what was hard to swallow was not that de Man, of all men, had an unsavory past but that he'd had precisely the one of a Nazi apologist. Among American intellectuals, there is no horror quite equal to that of the specter of fascism—the Nazi variety, above all. A grim joke making the rounds inevitably found its way into journalistic accounts of the scandal. Why didn't de Man acknowledge his guilt? He couldn't remember, went the bitter punch line, because he had a severe case of "Waldheimer's Disease."

CHAPTER 8

LIKE UNCLE,

LIKE SON

This sudden reflux of a past presented in such a light, when I had devoted the last seven years of my life to building an existence entirely separated from former painful experiences, leaves me weary and exhausted.

—*Paul de Man, Letter to Professor Renato Poggioli, Harvard University, January 26, 1955*

I am not given to retrospective self-examination and mercifully forget what I have written with the same alacrity I forget bad movies— although, as with bad movies, certain scenes or phrases return at times to embarrass and haunt me like a guilty conscience.

—*Paul de Man, January 1983*

When a man without a past acquires one after his death, and the man is an intellectual celebrity and his secret past involves the Nazis, the journalistic community gets busy in a hurry. The search for more information begins with the anticipation that there's more to be had;

a long-repressed, carefully concealed past doesn't emerge into the light all at once, but in stages. It is easy to understand the public's craving for the juicy details. John Updike recently observed that the Second World War, "at least for Europeans and North Americans, has become the century's central myth, a vast imaging of a primal time when good and evil contended for the planet, a tale of Troy whose angles are infinite and whose central figures never fail to amaze us with their size, their theatricality, their sweep." The traumas of World War II are never far below the surface of our conscious fears and anxieties about our global destiny; the horrors wrought by the Nazis, so singular in their cruelty and so unprecedented in their scope, still defy comprehension even as they demand to be understood. They serve, for many of us, as the reference point in any discussion of absolute evil, and we are vexed and haunted—and sometimes vexed and outraged—by revelations that this or that upstanding citizen may have been implicated, to whatever extent, in the Nazi horror. How, we wonder, could this have happened? There is, besides, a special fascination in a posthumous shock, a buried secret, something learned too late, something that alters our whole sense of a person's life—like the "extra" chapter in some murder mysteries, a coda in which the detective explodes the ingenious solution he had himself proposed a chapter earlier.

The sudden reflux of his past made Paul de Man's life resemble a false-bottomed narrative. His case did funny things with time. His past was *presented,* in every sense, after his death. Things he had written in his youth came to seem like a commentary on his mature writings, or a caveat about them; what he wrote during World War II preceded his American career but—surfacing when it did—seemed like a postscript to that career. In one of his celebrated essays, de Man argued that the dominant rhetorical figure in autobiographical writing is "the prosopopeia, the fiction of the voice-from-beyond-the-grave." To the extent that the body of de Man's critical writing, impersonal and abstract though it was, could be seen to constitute a kind of oblique autobiography, the precociously authoritative voice that spoke in *Le Soir* during World War II was "the voice-from-beyond-the-grave"— the voice that his American readers heard for the first time four years after his death.

As if the Nazi connection weren't enough of a shock to the liberal American academic community, de Man left other posthumous surprises that sprang from their jack-in-the-box lair in 1988. A chain of unsavory revelations made it fruitful for reporters on the cultural beat to cover academic conferences as if they were political conventions. In a year when candidates for high office were revealed as philanderers or plagiarists by aggressive newshounds, de Man's character—which had once seemed thoroughly above reproach—took a regular beating. His early life, as journalists began piecing it together, was the stuff of gothic melodrama, with turns as wild as one finds in a Dostoevski novel and with a textbook example of an unreliable narrator. In the light of his wartime activities, the very fact that so few of de Man's American readers knew anything about his European years began to take on an eerie significance. Who was this reticent man, and what, in retrospect, did his reticence betoken? Might it be that de Man's intellectual skepticism about history was the expression of a wished-for amnesia about his own disquieting past? "We try to give ourselves a new past from which we should have liked to descend instead of the past from which we actually descended," wrote Nietzsche in a passage that de Man quoted in *Blindness and Insight*.

The young de Man, we learned, had gone from journalism into business, and "shady" was the adjective of choice when his former associates were asked to describe his business dealings. In 1943, some months after his departure from *Le Soir*, de Man left Brussels for his native Antwerp, where he sat out the remaining years of the war. He lived quietly; among the tasks he set for himself was the translation into Flemish of *Moby Dick*. The translation, which was published in 1945, marked the first time Melville's masterpiece had been rendered in Flemish. A year later, de Man set up a publishing house, Editions Hermès, devoted to fine-art books; he borrowed heavily from his father to finance the venture. The business failed. When the twenty-eight-year-old de Man embarked for the United States in 1948, he left behind a crowd of angry creditors and the prospect of a lawsuit. He had ruined his father and had earned himself a local reputation for dishonesty. Ortwin de Graef noted that Editions Hermès was "appropriately" named—Hermes being the patron of thieves in Greek mythology. The Belgian sociologist Georges Goriely recalled de Man, the friend of his youth, for conferencegoers at the University of Antwerp in June 1988. "A charming, humorous, modest, highly cultured man," said Goriely. But a scoundrel. "Swindling, forging, lying were, at least at the time, second nature to him."

There was more, there was worse. There were the curious, disturbing revelations about de Man's *other* family, his first family. In 1939, while still a student at the Free University of Brussels (Université Libre de Bruxelles, or ULB), de Man had become friendly with a young married couple who traveled in the same cultural-political circles as he did. The man's name was Gilbert Jaeger; his wife was a Roumanian expatriate named Anaide Baraghian. At some point in the following year, de Man replaced Jaeger as Anaide's common-law husband—though the three of them continued to share an apartment. "It was like a *Jules and Jim* situation," said Marc de Man, the third of three sons born to Anaide and Paul. The Nazi blitzkrieg in May 1940 changed the relationship. In that month Holland fell, Belgium fell, and by June the Nazis were marching down the Champs-Elysées. Paul de Man and Anaide fled Belgium together; Jaeger stayed behind.

De Man and Anaide joined a mass exodus of civilian refugees on the roads of Belgium and France. The lightning-quick Nazi conquest—it took eighteen days for the Germans to conquer Belgium—had triggered a panic. The people were reacting to the colossal nature of the defeat; it happened so fast that there hadn't been time to organize a proper departure, only the certitude that departure under any conditions was preferable to living under the swastika. People took to the roads with only the vague sense of a destination—westward, to the parts of France not yet under Nazi rule. The panic accelerated as the Germans advanced on Paris. The roads were choked with refugees; they fled on cars or on foot, piling their possessions in carts, bicycles, and barrows. In Alistair Horne's description:

> At one point it was estimated that as many as 2 million Dutch and Belgians and nearly 8 million French refugees were on the roads; some nine-tenths of the population of a city like Lille departed. During the first five days of the battle, the French kept the Belgian frontier closed. Then the human flood burst into northern France, resembling more one of the great migrations fleeing before the Barbarian in times of yore than any event hitherto seen in modern Europe. The number plates on the cars of the refugees, telling the truth the censors were trying to hide, in turn set more and more in motion as they realised the speed at which the Barbarian was approaching.

Paul de Man and Anaide Baraghian joined the exodus, getting as far as the French border with Spain before returning to Brussels in August. For the rest of the year they continued to share their household with Jaeger. In January 1941 Hendrik, their first son, was born. Shortly afterward, they moved to a place of their own.

One can only speculate about why de Man and his pregnant mistress left Belgium in the early summer and returned in August. It is reasonable to assume that the couple fled from Brussels for the same reason that so many of their compatriots did—out of fear of the barbarian. Unable to cross into Spain, they had no other place to turn but home, though home was in shambles; all their escape routes had been cut off. And perhaps by that August it became clear to Paul de Man that such a man as he, with his connections and his background, needn't suffer under the Nazi occupation. There might even be a place for him within the New Order. The fact that he and Anaide were turned back at the Franco-Spanish border was, in retrospect, another of the case's painful ironies—given Paul de Man's scholarly devotions, in the last years of his life, to Walter Benjamin, the great German-Jewish writer who met his end at that same border in that same summer of 1940. Many of de Man's followers have emphasized the increasingly vital influence that Benjamin exerted on de Man's late work. The project on which de Man was working when he died was a critique of "aesthetic ideology," a term derived from Benjamin's essay "The Work of Art in an Age of Mechanical Reproduction." The last public lecture de Man delivered was devoted to another of Benjamin's essays, "The Task of the Translator." Yet, despite his admiration for Benjamin, de Man never adverted to the crossing of their destinies in the summer of 1940.

Like de Man, Walter Benjamin could not cross into Spain—the border officials refused to honor his visa. But unlike de Man, Benjamin had nowhere else to go. Benjamin's status as a German Jew had made it imperative for him to escape Nazi Europe. On September 26, 1940, Benjamin reached the border and was turned away. Faced with the prospect of a hike across mountain paths to elude the Gestapo-conscious French border patrol, the forty-eight-year-old Benjamin, exhausted and suffering from a cardiac condition, ended his life in despair. It was a heartbreaking story. The day before he arrived, the border was still open; had he set out on the journey a day later, he'd have been forewarned in Marseilles that the border was closed. "Only on that particular day was the catastrophe possible," Hannah Arendt grimly noted. The suicide caused the border officials to show mercy to the band of refugees with whom Benjamin had arrived; they were permitted to proceed to Portugal. And within a few weeks the embargo on visas was lifted. The story of the catastrophe that could only have taken place "on that particular day" was well-known in de Man's circle. Hannah Arendt told it in her introduction to Benjamin's *Illuminations*—his most widely read book in the United States. In omitting any reference to the historical circumstances of Benjamin's death—and to the near-intersection of his own path with Benjamin's—de Man was, perhaps, just being consistent in refusing to introduce pathos, biography, and social history into his disclosure. But what a glaring omission—and how one wishes one could have put the question to de Man, had he not died before his past was recovered.

Anaide Baraghian bore Paul de Man three sons in all. The family remained together until 1948. It was then that de Man, discredited and bankrupt, decided to emigrate to America. He came to the United States on a tourist visa; his wife and sons, denied visas on the grounds of questionable means of support, sailed to Argentina, where Anaide's parents had resettled. "The idea," said Marc de Man, now an attorney in Montreal, "was that we would join him later after he got organized. My parents felt it would be too difficult to come as immigrants to the United States if my father were encumbered by three children and a wife." But rather than send for his family as planned, de Man wedded his student Patricia Kelley during his teaching stint at Bard College between 1949 and 1951. Having an American wife would prove useful to de Man. It guaranteed him the right to live and work in the United States, and it made it easier for him to obtain the exit and entrance visas needed to visit Europe for extended periods of study. The hitch was that he was still married to Baraghian—assuming that the two *were* legally married—at the time he took his second wife. The scandalous revelation cast the legitimacy of one or another of de Man's families in doubt. *Bigamy!* It was like a tabloid truth in the middle of an abstract intellectual debate. "He was very private," de Man's American daughter Patricia told a reporter. "I did finally find out that he had another family."

One of the more remarkable aspects of de Man's American career was his success at keeping past and present in separate compartments.

Marc de Man reports that he saw his father "only two days in my life" after 1948, when the boy was two years old. In Argentina, de Man's first family "never had any news from him, never a Christmas card. He sent very little money—$50 a month for a few months, and then nothing at all." Marc de Man remembered the shock he was in for when he met his father for the first time in his adult life. It happened in Zurich in the late 1960s. When introduced to his American half-brother and half-sister, Marc realized that they hadn't the slightest idea who he was. In fact, they had never heard of him. "And there was another shocking thing," said Marc de Man. "My father didn't leave us anything, not a memento, not a manuscript. He totally disinherited the three sons. He left us nothing whatsoever. And," he added wistfully, "we were very interested in him."

From 1948 until his death thirty-five years later, Paul de Man contrived to keep his pre-American days, and the living evidence thereof, at a safe distance. His private nature discouraged questions, and he volunteered little about his past. He never corrected the vague impression that he'd been in the Resistance during the war. On the contrary, he obliquely encouraged this misrepresentation—as when, in a letter to Harry Levin in 1955, he described himself casually as one who had "come from the left and from the happy days of the Front populaire." No double agent was more suave at disarming an inquisitive acquaintance—with an ambiguous and vague reply. It was as if in coming to America de Man had decided not only to abandon a family, but an identity and a history as well: a failed business, a bankrupted father, an unfortunate political past. In the time-honored tradition of the American dream, he would escape from the circumstances of his youth and his family history. Like a character in an American novel—like Ishmael in *Moby Dick* and Gatsby in *The Great Gatsby*—he would explore the possibility of a fresh start, a clean slate. He would invent himself anew.

In de Man's former life there was one man in particular about whom questions could be dangerous and answers imprudent. The time de Man came closest to blowing his cover was when, in response to an anonymous denunciation at Harvard in January 1955, he invoked the name of this man. Hendrik de Man (also known as Henri de Man) was Paul's uncle. One of the more celebrated European political thinkers of his time, he was famous most of all as the quisling who welcomed the Nazi conquest of Belgium. In the painful chapter of

European intellectual history dealing with socialists who became fascists, this man would play a fateful part.

Born in Antwerp in 1885, Hendrik de Man came from a well-to-do family of high social standing. He was the son of a business executive with aristocratic pretentions, and the grandson of a leader of the Flemish cultural movement, the poet Jan van Beers. Like his nephew after him, Hendrik de Man spoke and wrote four languages with cosmopolitan ease—Dutch, German, English, and French. He felt he had, as he once remarked, "as many homelands as languages." In 1941, Hendrik was fifty-six and Paul twenty-two. Paul had come under his uncle's wing several years earlier; the deaths of Paul's mother and his older brother had left Paul's father so distraught that he asked Hendrik to take the young man in his charge. One way to make sense of what Paul de Man did during World War II is to understand his uncle's influence upon him—influence in a double sense, since the nephew was not only profoundly affected by the uncle's ideas, but had also gained his entrée into fascist circles thanks to his uncle's influential connections.

Hendrik de Man was a regular at the home of Edouard and Lucienne Didier, which served as a gathering place for Belgian intellectuals of the fascist persuasion. Otto Abetz, Nazi Germany's ambassador to France, frequented the Didier salon. So did, among other well-known collaborationist writers, Robert Brasillach and Alfred Fabre-Luce. The Didiers had set up their salon before the outbreak of World War II and it functioned as a collaborationist center during the occupation. In all likelihood it was here that Paul, sponsored by his uncle, met and was recruited by Raymond de Becker, the pro-Nazi editor-in-chief of *Le Soir*. De Becker became editor-in-chief on December 5, 1940. Paul de Man's first byline appeared nineteen days later. The Didiers themselves, together with de Becker and another man, set up a publishing house in March 1941. *La Toison d'Or* (the Golden Fleece) was subsidized and controlled by von Ribbentrop, Nazi Germany's foreign minister. The firm published the works of the leading collaborationists of the day. These were the very authors and in many cases the very books that Paul de Man praised in *Le Soir*.

Hendrik de Man began his intellectual career as a socialist theoretician, the author of *The Psychology of Socialism* (1926) and other books that made his a prominent voice in the political debates of the

1920s and 1930s in Europe.* While he began with a straightforward Marxist perspective, Hendrik de Man's experience as a soldier in World War I, coupled with his exposure as a young man to life in England, had convinced him that Marx was in need of a major overhaul. Marx's concept of the superstructure, for example, was seriously flawed. Marx held that ideas and ideologies merely reflect economic self-interest. He was wrong, in de Man's view, and the reason he was wrong was that he left out psychology: the importance of willpower, for one thing; the psychology of mass-behavior, for another. A worker's self-esteem was as important as his material well-being, and it could be elevated through ideals—through, as Hendrik de Man's theories evolved, the fascist ideals of sacrifice, duty, and the subordination of the individual to the state.

In time, Hendrik de Man would reject the institutions of parliamentary democracy in favor of authoritarianism. His revision of Marx and his simultaneous embrace of nationalism provided a theoretical footing for fascism—though he considered himself a socialist to the last. Already in 1930 he was corresponding on friendly terms with Mussolini, another fascist authoritarian with socialist origins. By the time the *Wehrmacht* marched into Belgium, de Man was calling Nazism "the German form of socialism." He stated his political creed at a conference in Brussels on February 16, 1941. "I am not a German nationalist, but a Belgian socialist, or, if you prefer, a national-socialist Belgian," said Hendrik de Man. He envisaged "a social order in which labor is able to rule and in which the right to work can have value for everyone," but added that such a social order would not be possible "without an authoritarian state." Only authoritarianism was capable of ending the ruinous rule of money, which had corrupted every sector of society. The parliamentary system was just a bourgeois form of democracy, an instrument of capitalist corruption, and its time had passed. "The State must take on a new form," Hendrik de Man asserted. "That form can only be authoritarian since that characteristic goes hand in hand with revolution."

Not every theorist has the chance to translate his ideas into revolutionary action. Hendrik de Man did. His formulation of "Le

Zur Psychologie des Sozialismus was translated into French as *Au delà du marxisme—Beyond Marxism—*and into English as *The Psychology of Socialism.*

Plan du Travail"—"the de Man plan" or simply "the plan" as it came to be known—made him the chief theoretician of Belgium's Socialist Party, the *Parti Ouvrier Belge* (POB), in the 1930s.* Nominally a socialist program, "Le Plan" called for the elimination of unemployment through the means of a planned economy. It was enthusiastically adopted by the POB in 1933; de Man became the party's vice-president that same year. Neither event arrested his evolution from Marxist revisionist to fascist ideologue. "One can no longer achieve power through revolution, but one can achieve a revolution through the exercise of power," he declared in 1934. Bourgeois democracy was obsolete. Fascism, the cult of power, was the answer. "In the future," he said in 1938, "one will have to be more bold in establishing a socialist order while setting up an authoritarian state—the one being conditional on the other." In May 1939 Hendrik de Man succeeded to the presidency of the POB. When Belgium fell, he heralded the Nazi invaders and the new order they represented. Then he declared the dissolution of his political party and the establishment of a new union with a policy of "national revival"—a union that the German authorities endorsed.

Throughout the 1930s, Hendrik de Man was a strong advocate of strict Belgian neutrality—the policy of refusing to choose sides between the Allies and the Axis. "Peace with Hitler is worth more than any war whatsoever," he argued in 1934. Neutrality was still officially Belgium's foreign policy, and de Man still its champion, when World War II began. He was appointed minister without portfolio in the unity government that was formed in Belgium on September 3, 1939—the day France and Britain declared war on Germany, two days after Germany's invasion of Poland. But Hendrik de Man's influence went further. He had become an intimate of King Leopold III, and in January 1940 he resigned from the government in favor of a military appointment attaching him directly to the king's service. When the Nazis invaded Belgium on May 10, Hendrik de Man was King Leopold's closest political confidant. Alone among the king's advisers, Hendrik de Man supported Leopold's decision to surrender to the Germans on May 28. When the time came to explain the capitulation, de Man helped draft the letters that Leopold sent to the

*The *Parti Ouvrier Belge* has been rendered variously as the Belgian Workers Party, Labor Party, and Socialist Party.

king of England, the pope, and the president of the United States. Had the Nazis permitted Leopold to form a new government under the occupation, his choice to head that government—the Belgian Vichy that never came to pass—would have been Hendrik de Man.

As Leopold's chief counselor, Hendrik de Man propounded the rationale for the king's decision to remain in Belgium under Nazi rule rather than join the government-in-exile. De Man made it plain that it was a choice of collaborationism over resistance. So plain, indeed, that when the war was over, Leopold's association with de Man was high on the list of charges leveled at the king by those parliamentarians and others who felt that their monarch had forfeited his right to rule. The central document in de Man's wartime portfolio was the infamous "Manifesto to the Members of the Parti Ouvrier Belge" with which he welcomed the Nazis into Belgium in July 1940. He spoke in his capacity as head of the Socialist Party—and made the proper fascist noises about the role of the leader. "The role of a leader is not to follow his troops, but to lead them by showing them the way," he said. Then he urged his troops to give up the battle as lost. "Do not believe that it is necessary to resist the Occupying Power; accept the fact of his victory and try rather to draw lessons therefrom." The manifesto's hostility to parliamentary institutions and democratic ideals is remarkable:

> The war has led to the debacle of the parliamentary regime and of the capitalist plutocracy in the so-called democracies.
>
> For the working classes and for socialism, this collapse of a decrepit world, far from being a disaster, is a deliverance.

And:

> For years the double-talk of the war-mongers had concealed from you that this regime [i.e., Nazi authoritarianism], despite everything in it that strikes our mentality as foreign, has lessened class differences much more efficaciously than the self-styled democracies, where Capital continued to lay down the law.
>
> Since then everyone has been able to see that the superior morale of the German army is due in large part to the

greater social unity of the nation and to the resulting prestige of its authorities.

The manifesto ends with the code words of fascism: the call for "a
movement of national resurrection, which will include all the vital
forces of the nation, of its youth, of its veterans, in a single party."
When, following the liberation of Belgium, a military tribunal convicted Hendrik de Man in absentia, the charge was treason. He had
"knowingly and maliciously served the design of the enemy," and the
documentary evidence began with the manifesto. It initially appeared
in a provincial newspaper, the *Gazette de Charleroi*, on July 3, 1940.
On July 6 it addressed a national readership in the pages of the
newspaper to which his nephew would later contribute, *Le Soir*.

It is instructive to compare the public statements of Hendrik de
Man and his nephew during the Nazi occupation of Belgium. In *Le
Soir* on March 4, 1941, Paul de Man dismissed Jewish writers as
mediocrities whose banishment from Europe would not injure Western culture. Two days later, his uncle took a moment to make his
stance on collaborationism perfectly plain. France, he told an interviewer, was luckier than Belgium since the French "have a government that has allowed them to enter into a policy of collaboration with
Germany." On October 25, Hendrik de Man declared: "Henceforth,
democracy and socialism will be authoritarian or they will not exist
at all." On October 28, his nephew wrote in *Le Soir* that "Hitlerism"
promised the "definitive emancipation" of the German people, whose
destiny it was to rule over Europe.

There is every reason to suppose that uncle and nephew were
close—not only politically, but on the deeper level of what Freud called
the family romance. Necessity had made their relationship a special one,
rather like father and son. Hendrik had, in fact, acted as Paul's surrogate
father at a crucial point in the young man's development. And there was
a second complication: the two men were linked by a crisscross pattern
between two generations—the sort of narrative pattern one finds in
folklore. It is the story of two pairs of brothers in succeeding generations. Hendrik de Man, the older of two brothers, was favored by this
circumstance as a child. Great things were expected of him; his father
projected his aristocratic aspirations onto the boy's education. Hendrik's
younger brother Robert was, in sharp contrast, the expendable child—
Hendrik de Man's biographer tells us that Robert "was actually surren-

dered to a maternal aunt after she had tragically lost her own children."

The fraternal roles were reversed in the next generation. Robert de Man had two sons, Hendrik and Paul. It was Paul, the younger brother, in whom his family's hopes came to be invested—out of necessity. For in the family history of Paul de Man, two traumatic events followed one another in a terrifying sequence as he entered his late adolescence. On June 20, 1936, Paul's brother Hendrik was killed when his bicycle crashed at a railroad junction. Exactly one year to the day later, Paul's mother hanged herself. It was Paul, still months shy of his seventeenth birthday, who discovered the body. Robert de Man, overwhelmed with grief, entrusted Paul to his uncle's supervision at this time. The destinies of uncle and nephew, of older brother and younger brother once removed, were now intertwined. Paul would take the place of his famous uncle's deceased namesake. He would be the bearer of the birthright if not of the name. The relationship that resulted between uncle and nephew has its analogue—as Paul de Man, master analyst of rhetoric, must surely have recognized—in the rhetorical figure of the chiasmus. The crisscross pattern linking this uncle and this nephew has the symbolic significance of the biblical Jacob crossing his hands when blessing the heads of Joseph's sons, so that his right hand would favor the younger brother.

The Nazis grew disenchanted with Hendrik de Man, and by 1943 he was spending his days in lonely retreat in the French Alps. In 1944 he escaped to Switzerland with the French underground in pursuit. Following the war, he managed to elude extradition to Belgium and lived out his remaining years in bitter exile, writing and revising his memoirs. The end of his narrative underscores just how important the sense of a collective family tragedy was to Hendrik de Man. On June 20, 1953, the sixteenth anniversary of his sister-in-law's suicide, Hendrik de Man took his own life. He chose the same day, the same circumstances, and the same means of death as his oldest nephew and namesake: he drove his car into the path of a train. He extended a traumatic sequence, as though his own suicide could somehow serve as a kind of memorial to the deaths of his sister-in-law and nephew before him. For the surviving nephew, he left a complicated legacy. One wonders what thoughts ran through Paul de Man's mind each year on the twentieth of June.

· · ·

A year after his uncle's death, Paul de Man was appointed to his three-year term in residence as a Junior Fellow of Harvard University's Society of Fellows. It was a much-coveted appointment. Besides the prestige it conferred upon the holder, it had substantial practical value. Junior Fellows were given a stipend, exempted from tuition charges, and spared from onerous teaching assignments. Paul de Man was popular with the other Fellows. His personal charm took the edge off his ferocity in debate. "He was," remembers Donald Hall, "a tiger, but he always smiled." It was no secret that Paul's uncle had been a Belgian collaborator, but Paul himself was understood to be a man "from the left." He let on that he had been in the Resistance, though he was not forthcoming with details. His friends respected his reticence.

At Harvard, Paul de Man had a special knack for skewering an inflated intellectual reputation. In Donald Hall's account, "he knew Camus, and Camus (tilt of the head, a confidential look of disparagement) 'was a phoney.' " De Man's own claims to genuineness were challenged that winter—though, thanks to the discretion of the Society's Senior Fellows, the word didn't get out. In January 1955 de Man, planning a trip to Europe, applied for a new Belgian passport. De Man believed it to be in consequence of this application that he was denounced, anonymously, to the Society of Fellows. While the Society has no record of the denunciation on file, we may infer from the letter that de Man wrote in his own defense that he stood accused of wartime collaboration with the Nazis; his emigration status was questioned, moreover, and his allegedly dishonest activities at Editions Hermès had come to light. On January 26, 1955, de Man wrote to Harvard's Renato Poggioli, co-director of the Society of Fellows. It was the only time in his American career that de Man addressed himself to the issue of his past. But it is difficult to credit the claim—made by Jacques Derrida, among others—that the letter constituted "a public act" on Paul de Man's part. It was in fact anything but a public statement. Written in great confidentiality, it was treated with such discretion at Harvard that its existence was entirely clandestine until the *Le Soir* scandal broke in late 1987. The simple truth is that de Man never made public acknowledgment of his wartime behavior.

The letter that de Man sent to Harvard is, in any event, remarkable for its combination of evasiveness and self-righteous indignation. "I could not possibly have come to this country two times, with proper passport and visa, if there had been the slightest reproach against me," de Man wrote. A minor portion of his very long letter addresses de Man's "political past, particularly under the German occupation." The defense is cleverly constructed—it is predicated on several small lies, one big one, and the calculated risk that the readers of the letter, trusting the writer's good faith, would not seek out the actual articles in *Le Soir*. This is what de Man wrote:

> My father, Hendrik de Man, former Belgian Minister and Chairman of the social-democrat party, is a highly controversial political figure. Because of his attitude under the German occupation, he was sentenced in absentia after the war and died in exile in Switzerland last year. He remains an extremely debatable case and, for reasons that go to the roots of internal Belgian political problems, his name arouses extremely strong feelings at least in some Belgians, apparently still to-day.
>
> I certainly am in no position to pass judgment on him, but I know that his mistakes were made out of a lack of machiavellism and not out of lack of devotion to his ideals. He did what he thought best for his country and his beliefs, and the final evaluation of his acts is a matter of history. One can find his own justification stated in the last two chapters of his autobiography, published last year in Germany under the title *Gegen den Strom*.
>
> I hear now that I myself am being accused of collaboration. In 1940 and 1941 I wrote some literary articles in the newspaper "le Soir" and, like most of the other contributors, I stopped doing so when nazi thought-control did no longer allow freedom of statement. During the rest of the occupation, I did what was the duty of any decent person. After the war, everyone was subjected to a very severe examination of his political behavior, and my name was not a favorable recommendation. In order to obtain a passport, one had not merely to produce a certificate of good conduct, but also a so-called "certificat de civisme," which stated that one was cleared of any collaboration. I could not possibly have come to this country two times, with proper passport and visa, if there had been the slightest reproach

against me. To accuse me now, behind my back, of collaboration, and this to persons of a different nation who can not possibly verify and appreciate the facts, is a slanderous attack which leaves me helpless.

The statement contains a number of mistruths and half-truths. De Man characterized his wartime journalism as "some literary articles" when in fact many were overtly political. He made no mention of his anti-Semitic articles or his praise of "Hitlerism." He limited the years to "1940 and 1941" when in fact he wrote for *Le Soir* until the end of November 1942. He misrepresented the situation at the newspaper. He stopped writing for it, he said, "when nazi thought-control did no longer allow freedom of statement." At first this seems like a simple falsehood, since it is hard to credit the notion that "freedom of statement" was ever allowed at *Le Soir volé*. But like many lies, this one reveals more than it is intended to. It raises the question of Paul de Man's sense of chronology. Perhaps in his mind there was a valid distinction between *Le Soir* in December 1940 and the same newspaper two years later. Perhaps he felt that he could "no longer" write honestly in late 1942. The implication is that what he wrote in the war years was heartfelt, the product of his own volition, and not cleared for publication by a Nazi censor. The whole thing was a gamble de Man may not have taken if he felt there was the slightest chance that the articles in question might turn up.

The biggest lie in the statement was de Man's claim—curiously self-aggrandizing and self-incriminating at once—that he was the son of Hendrik de Man. At first glance this appears enigmatic. Why would he want to link himself more closely with his uncle? Wouldn't he wish, on the contrary, to dissociate his name from that of the convicted collaborator? But that is to underestimate de Man's subtlety. Only upon reflection does one realize what he has to gain by claiming paternity for his uncle. For if one's father has embraced a cause, it is perhaps understandable that the son would follow suit; there is more pressure on a son than on a mere nephew to toe the parental line.

The irony, so plain it smarts, is that in one sense Paul wasn't lying when he called his uncle his father—in one sense Paul de Man *was* Hendrik's chosen son. By 1972, however, Paul had conveniently developed amnesia about his youthful complicity in his uncle's collaborationist career. That year, a critical essay by Richard Klein, a student

of de Man who made no secret of his filial attachment to him, appeared
in *Diacritics*. Klein's article discusses the relationship of Paul de Man
to Hendrik—only Klein mistakenly assumes that Hendrik *was* Paul's
father. Klein's theme is oedipal. He examines Paul's "moralistic nihilism," his avoidance of psychology, his seemingly systematic "repression of Freud." He concludes that Paul was not so much repudiating
his "father" as conducting his oedipal rebellion against him. Hendrik
de Man was, after all, "the first serious Marxist thinker to apply
explicitly Freudian categories to the analysis of alienation." Yet Freud
never turns up in Paul de Man's literary work. In a postscript to the
Diacritics essay, Klein admitted his mistake. He had been, he writes,
corrected by Paul de Man. "My scepticism doesn't spring from the
fact that Henri de Man is my uncle and not my father," de Man coolly
informed him. Never dreaming that the error in paternity was one that
Paul de Man had himself perpetrated when it suited him to do so, Klein
retreated to the position that an oedipal relation could occur on a
symbolic level, with a father by another name. Klein asked: "What,
after all, is an uncle?"

In truth, it wasn't an avuncular influence that Paul de Man was
trying to evade when he skirted clear of Freud and Marx, psychology
and the philosophy of history; it was something more immediate,
something like the paternal legacy of a past. He would try to overcome
it by rejecting the very categories that seek to render the past available—politics, history, and biography. By fiat de Man would declare
an irrevocable rupture between the world of literature and the world
of empirical facts. As for the facts of his personal past, he evaded them
with silence, exile, and cunning. And in retrospect, it was his silence
about his wartime past as much as that past itself that vexed and teased
the ranks of his admirers. Shoshana Felman, a colleague of de Man in
Yale's comparative literature department, was one of those who tried
to vindicate the fallen leader by portraying his silence in the most
flattering possible light. Felman goes through extraordinary contor-
tions to arrive at the quite incredible assertion that "History as Holocaust is mutely omnipresent in the theoretical endeavor of de Man's
mature work." De Man kept silent about the part he played in the
Second World War "not (as some would have it) as a cover-up or
a dissimulation of the past, but as an ongoing active *transformation of
the very act of bearing witness*" [Felman's emphasis]. In her brief for de
Man, Felman audaciously quotes from the writings of Primo Levi,

who was deported to Auschwitz from his native Italy in 1944. Levi wrote that the "true witnesses" of the Holocaust were those victims who "have not returned to tell about it or have returned mute," and Felman cites the passage as though it somehow applied to the young, well-connected Belgian journalist who faced none of the deprivations and perils of a death camp inmate. How de Man could bear witness "to the complexity and ambiguity of history as Holocaust"—when in fact he never wrote about either the Holocaust or his career as a quisling pundit—is just another of those deconstructive mysteries that readers are asked to take on faith. But that the author of anti-Semitic articles could, by concealing them from view, serve as an honorable witness of "history as Holocaust"—well, one wonders which is worse: the desecration of the Holocaust or the ignobility of a theory that invites a scholar to play so fast and loose with such grave historical matters. No wonder so many "nonaligned" individuals were taken aback by the deconstructionist response to the Paul de Man case. In the Holocaust, after all, human beings perished by the millions; it was not, for them, a linguistic predicament.

As Shoshana Felman sees it, "de Man's entire writing effort is a silent trace of the reality of an event whose very historicity, borne out by the author's own catastrophic experience, has occurred precisely as the event of the preclusion—the event of the impossibility—of its own witnessing." Translation (approximate): de Man kept silent about his past "precisely" because history made it impossible for him to do otherwise. Notice the tricks Felman plays. She paints de Man's collaborationist career as his "own catastrophic experience," as if he were the victim of the "events" in question. Though her syntax confuses the issue, she also seems to be saying that a person cannot act and witness himself acting at the same time. De Man's failure to own up to his past somehow becomes mute eloquence; more than that, his silence is seen as perfectly consonant with the tenets of deconstruction. It is not difficult to punch holes in Felman's argument. There are, perhaps, times when a witness exercising his constitutional right against self-incrimination is giving "mute" testimony. De Man, however, didn't take the Fifth when confronted with his past; he actively dissembled. The real moral issue is stated not in the Fifth Amendment but in the Ninth Commandment—the injunction against bearing false witness.

Andrzej Warminski, another of de Man's avid defenders, waxes indignant over the prominence given to the theme of de Man's silence in journalistic coverage of the case: "Why didn't he confess?" "Why did he keep it a secret?" Warminski answers these pertinent questions with a haughty one of his own: "What do they want de Man to have done? To have sent out a press release, held a news conference?" Warminski gives the back of his hand to those who wondered what it said about de Man and his theories that he tried to bury his disreputable past. In Warminski's words, "Only the trivially guilt-ridden pathology of bitter academics who have always resented de Man's intellectual, i.e., critical, power would want de Man to have inscribed himself in a conversion narrative!" It does not seem to have occurred to Warminski that something other than a "conversion narrative"—or a "press release"—might have been more appropriate than silence for an honorable man, particularly one of de Man's critical powers and stature. What was startling was not so much that de Man didn't "confess" as that he shrouded his past in secrecy; he simply ignored his firsthand experience when discussing books and issues to which that experience was relevant. Perhaps it is not so unreasonable to expect a greater amount of candid self-examination from a scholar praised for his "intellectual honesty."

It is a characteristic of deconstructive criticism that its practitioners often advance their arguments not by logical exposition but by a triple threat of paradox, jargon, and literary analogy. True to form, Shoshana Felman makes her case for de Man through the agency of a literary parallel. Felman fastens on the fact that de Man translated *Moby Dick* into Flemish after his career at *Le Soir* was over. The choice of *Moby Dick,* she observes, "prefigures not merely de Man's future choice of America as a physical and cultural destination but the radical nature of the departure, which will create an absolute break with what preceded, as he leaves behind everything connected to the Belgian past, including his own family, wife and children." Captain Ahab and the narrator Ishmael, the protagonists of *Moby Dick,* have made a similarly "radical departure" in going to sea. Ahab leaves behind wife and children to pursue his grudge match with the white whale, Felman writes, while Ishmael goes to sea "as a substitute for committing suicide." It will be recalled that Ahab dies in his battle with the whale while Ishmael survives the shipwreck by floating on a coffin. To Felman, the postwar Paul de Man combined the destinies of both Ahab and Ishmael. According to her allegorical reading, Ahab's fanatic hunt for the whale seems to correspond to "Nazi ideology." The Ahab side of de Man has died at sea; he survives as Ishmael, whose mission it is to tell the tale. One wonders that Felman didn't clinch her case by pointing out that Melville was born in 1819—exactly one hundred years before de Man's birth—and that he went to sea on a whaling-ship in 1841—one hundred years before de Man confronted the Leviathan in the offices of *Le Soir*.

What Felman neglects to explain—and what undermines her argument—is the sharp discrepancy between Ishmael's postshipwreck behavior in *Moby Dick* and de Man's postwar sojourn in America. You simply cannot double-talk this out of existence: *where Ishmael narrates his tale, de Man kept silent about his.* Far from explaining or helping to exonerate his silence, the analogy with *Moby Dick* throws it into relief. Felman reminds her readers that Melville quotes the book of *Job* in the epilogue to Ishmael's narrative: "And I only am escaped alone to tell thee." But unlike Ishmael, de Man wasn't the sole survivor of the catastrophe. And unlike Ishmael, he told nobody—unless you somehow equate, as Felman does, de Man's silence with its opposite, testimony.

I have picked on Shoshana Felman's analogy with *Moby Dick* not because I disapprove of literary allegories but because I think her reading is so wrongheaded. It showcases the dangers of a method that invariably interprets texts as internally self-contradictory—a method that would reduce historical complexities to binary oppositions to be gleefully reversed. Somehow Ishmael's narration of the doomed voyage of the *Pequod* equals de Man's intransigent silence—the world is simply turned upside down to fit not the facts but a theory. Felman demonstrates a species of logic that would verify its wildest suppositions not by reasoning but by metaphors—metaphors that don't necessarily add up or ring true. Still, literary examples can help us understand the life of an enigmatic protagonist who can't himself be reached for comment, and I rather like the idea that the author of *Allegories of Reading* may have led an allegorical textual life. Felman's reading of *Moby Dick* as an anticipatory allegory of the career of Paul de Man inspires me to propose three other textual parallels, two from literature and one from the movies, that could be called unconscious treatments of Paul de Man's predicament in America.

The first and least substantial of these fictional treatments is suggested by a sentence that Paul de Man wrote in the foreword to one of his books. "I am not given to retrospective self-examination," he observed in 1983, "and mercifully forget what I have written with the same alacrity I forget bad movies—although, as with bad movies, certain scenes or phrases return at times to embarrass and haunt me like a guilty conscience." The association of a guilty conscience with scenes from bad movies authorizes one to imagine the Hollywood version of de Man's drama—luridly melodramatic and easy to forget, though capable of haunting and embarrassing the forgetful one. I propose Orson Welles's 1946 movie, *The Stranger*. Welles directed it and played the lead; the supporting cast included Loretta Young (radiating goodness as the sweet, innocent young woman he marries) and Edward G. Robinson (the FBI man on the trail of the notorious Nazi war criminal). Welles plays the Nazi bigwig (Franz Kindler) who escaped from Germany in the ruins of 1945 and has somehow lost his German accent and acquired a cover of utter respectability in a serene, picture-postcard New England village. Kindler is now Professor Charles Rankin and teaches at a venerable boys' school in Connecticut. It's not quite Yale, but almost: the fictional Harper School for Boys, founded in 1827, educates the "sons of America's first families," Welles says. To seal his subversive assimilation into American life, he has managed to woo and wed the daughter of a United States Supreme Court justice, a famous liberal at that. "The girl is even good to look at," Welles confides. The analogy with de Man, exaggerated to begin with, soon falls apart entirely, and I wouldn't raise it at all except in an effort to verify the notion that a guilty conscience can act upon one like a melodramatic movie, with nightmare logic. The last time I saw *The Stranger* I was struck by the scene in which Welles, making a telephone call in the drugstore phone booth, doodles on a pad in strong vertical and horizontal lines. A swastika emerges—as if drawing one were the most natural thing in the world for the doodler, who then prudently links the lines into a square. I thought of de Man's interest in "deface-ment" and "disfigurement" as figurative terms for what texts do to themselves. It would be interesting, I thought, to subject this scene in *The Stranger* to a de Manian rhetorical reading, in which the "text" is seen to enact a "movement of effacing and of forgetting."

The second textual analogy I propose is to Joseph Conrad's *Heart of Darkness*. Here there are several outstanding coincidences. Marlow, the narrator of Conrad's tale, begins his journey in "a city that always makes me think of a whited sepulchre"—Brussels, the city where de Man began his literary career. Marlow's journey will take him to the

Belgian Congo and primeval darkness. And the culmination of the journey is his encounter with Kurtz, the "universal genius." Kurtz is greatly esteemed by his employers not only for his constant supply of treasure but for his purportedly civilizing influence on the natives. In reality, Kurtz's "method is unsound," as one company man puts it: there are heads on stakes that tell how Kurtz has worked his will in Africa. "All Europe contributed to the making of Kurtz," Conrad tells us. In my deconstructive allegory of *Heart of Darkness,* I see de Man not as Kurtz but as Marlow—de Man was not the perpetrator of atrocities but a witness who was somehow implicated in what he beheld and reported (or failed to report). But of de Man, too, it could be said that all Europe went into his making. Like his uncle Hendrik, he was fluent at an early age in four languages; he was intimately familiar with the masterworks of European philosophy and literature. His accent alone, which sounded neither German nor French but included traces of both, served to identify him broadly as European— as indeed an emissary of European culture in the United States. Friends fondly recalled how *the truth* came out in de Man's accent: *de Trut.* But the most important point of coincidence between the text of de Man's life and *Heart of Darkness* is not "de Trut" but a lie. Marlow's tale concludes with his account of a deliberate falsehood—the lie that he told Kurtz's intended rather than disabuse her of her cherished illusions about the man she had expected to marry. Kurtz's famous last words were "The horror! The horror!" But Marlow, pressed by Kurtz's intended, tells her that he died pronouncing . . . her name. Marlow's lie is a brilliantly enigmatic stroke on Conrad's part, and one to which commentators keep returning. A consequence of Marlow's lie is that it renders problematic all that he has told us before. If he could lie to Kurtz's fiancée, what makes us so sure that he isn't lying to us? What assurance do we have that his version of events is the true one? De Man's steadfast silence about his wartime past is equally enigmatic and similarly undermines his credibility. At the very least, it calls into question the motives, conscious or unconscious, behind his literary theories. Were those theories, as Shoshana Felman supposes, founded on an omission? Was a dark memory "mutely omnipresent" in them? And if so, if they were so much the function of one man's historical experience and one man's psychological idiosyncrasies, doesn't that dash their claims of universal validity?

My third textual analogy is based on a sentence in *The Great*

Gatsby that extends to de Man and allegorizes his American career in the process. Gatsby, wrote Scott Fitzgerald, "sprang from his Platonic conception of himself." Was this not true of Paul de Man? Did he not fashion an entirely new identity for himself, retaining his name (as Jay Gatsby, born James Gatz, did not) but jettisoning all other links to his past? De Man's triumphant American career seems either to dramatize something about our national capacity for amnesia or to illustrate the idea of America as a haven for those who want to bury the past. Scott Fitzgerald once remarked that there are "no second acts in American lives." Of course we know that's wrong: as a nation we are generous to a fault with second and third chances. One thinks of the corrupt official, convicted and sentenced, who surfaces a few years later as a talk-show guest hawking his latest inside-the-beltway potboiler. And surely it is to the glory of our nation's heritage that we have offered a fresh start, few questions asked, to the refugees of war and revolution and disaster abroad. It speaks to our trust and our faith in democratic ideals; America is still naive enough and confident enough to take people at their word. It is, nevertheless, a virtue that suggests a failing. Since the American spirit is one of rebellion—breaking with traditions, starting all over, seeking new origins—we tend to erase our own traditions, and we forget our own history, hoping for the best. To say that Paul de Man resembled Gatsby is simply to point to de Man's extraordinary success at inventing himself—in creating an American career of "greatness" that depended, to a large extent, on the erasure (or *rature*) of the past, as if, because it happened far away, it never happened at all.

For textual scholars of Scott Fitzgerald, the tripartite structure of *The Great Gatsby* long presented a vexing riddle. That structure appears to have been adapted from Spengler's seminal book, *The Decline of the West*. Fitzgerald wrote a letter to his editor, Maxwell Perkins, granting as much; Fitzgerald acknowledged reading Spengler the same summer he was writing *The Great Gatsby*. But how, scholars wondered, could this be? Fitzgerald wrote *The Great Gatsby* in the summer of 1924. He knew no German and an English translation of *The Decline of the West* didn't appear until two years later. Some Fitzgerald experts scoffed at the author's reference to Spengler. But the most persuasive solution to the mystery was given by a scholar named Barry Gross in 1967. Gross adduced that Fitzgerald learned all the Spengler he needed to know from the July 1924 issue of the *Yale*

Review. The issue came out at just the time he was working on *Gatsby,* and the *Yale Review* was the sort of magazine he liked to read. The fact that Fitzgerald went out of his way to obtain a copy of a book reviewed in that issue suggests his familiarity with its contents. And it was in that issue that he would have come across a cogent summary of Spengler's theory of the cycles of history. The article was titled "Germany's New Prophets." The author was Hendrik de Man.

CHAPTER 9

A SCANDAL

IN ACADEME

It is always possible to face up to any experience (to excuse any guilt), because the experience always exists simultaneously as fictional discourse and as empirical event and it is never possible to decide which one of the two possibilities is the right one. The indecision makes it possible to excuse the bleakest of crimes because, as a fiction, it escapes from the constraints of guilt and innocence.

—*Paul de Man*, ALLEGORIES OF READING
(1979)

De Man's wartime journalism was collected and published in 1989 by the University of Nebraska Press. The articles written in French were left untranslated—and were in fact photocopied from the original newspaper rather than set into type; English translations were provided for the ten articles de Man wrote in Flemish for *Het Vlaamsche Land*. A useful appendix reproduces the page from *Le Soir* on which de Man's anti-Semitic article appeared on March 4, 1941. The reader can see that pieces by other hands on Jewish painting and on Freudian psychology ("a Jewish doctrine") accompanied de Man's critique of the Jewish influence in literature. Taken together, the articles represented a concerted campaign to vilify the Jews as agents of cultural decadence. It seems fair to say that the surrounding articles and the paper's editorial were far more viciously anti-Semitic than "The Jews in Contemporary Literature." That was, at any rate, a judgment some of de Man's defenders used to relativize his guilt. His complicity in the anti-Semitic campaign was, they contended, more nearly passive than that of others in the quisling press. But in the trial of Paul de Man—a trial conducted in intellectual journals for the better part of two years—it was not at all clear that this "contextualizing" of de Man's efforts worked in his favor. The page in *Le Soir,* when you see it, delivers quite a shock; de Man's participation becomes more rather than less disturbing when you consider, in its full intensity, the hate-filled project to which he lent his name.

De Man's articles for *Le Soir* were widely read, quoted, and argued over well before the publication of *Wartime Journalism, 1940–42.* The photocopying machine made them the common property of numerous professors and journalists, in the United States and abroad, in the months after Ortwin de Graef's initial discovery in the summer of 1987. This curious method of dissemination was one more aspect of the de Man affair that made it seem somehow paradigmatic of the academic situation today.

It has been suggested that the photocopying machine has helped transform the practice of literary criticism into a nomadic sideshow: a world of academic conferences in far-flung places where the superstars of the lit-crit biz, armed with photocopies of one another's papers, enter into combat. The combat metaphor is taken from David Lodge's *Small World:* the novel is a parody of an Arthurian romance, with the Modern Language Association's annual convention serving as the ultimate tournament for jousting profs. The character whom Lodge calls Morris Zapp, who teaches at "Euphoric State" and aspires to become "the highest paid Professor of English in the world," is notable for his grasp of the changing sociology of academe. At one point Zapp explains why the era of the individual college campus is over. "It belongs to an obsolete technology—railways and the printing press," he says with the confidence of one who has mastered Marshall McLuhan. "There are," Zapp adds, "three things which have revolutionized academic life in the last twenty years, though very few people have woken up to the fact: jet travel, direct-dialling telephones and the

Xerox machine. Scholars don't have to work in the same institution to interact, nowadays: they call each other up, or they meet at international conferences. And they don't have to grub about in library stacks for data: any book or article that sounds interesting they have Xeroxed and read it at home. Or on the plane going to the next conference." The result, according to the flamboyant Zapp, is "a global campus," in which "the American Express card has replaced the library pass."

The circulation of de Man's *Le Soir* articles seemed to bear out Morris Zapp's take on things. The news of Paul de Man's wartime career traveled by telephone, spread by photocopy, and supplied the reading material on jet planes conducting scholars to their next academic conference. The process began when Ortwin de Graef, through an intermediary, approached Jacques Derrida for advice in August 1987. As a result of that phone call, de Graef shipped copies of twenty-five of de Man's *Le Soir* articles to Derrida. A perusal of these prompted the latter to suggest that copies be circulated in advance of an October gathering of deconstructionists at the University of Alabama in Tuscaloosa. A number of de Man's former students and associates made the trip, photocopies in hand. They listened to an anguished statement from Derrida, who spoke of his "bereaved friendship" and warned against organizing "a trial of Paul de Man." But at the same time he seemed to present a brief for the deceased. De Man, he speculated, "must have lived a real agony." He then misrepresented de Man's Harvard letter of 1955, pronouncing it "a public act," which absolved de Man of the charge that he had never acknowledged his damaging political past. Admitting that "we are not obliged to give credence to this presentation of the thing, his version of the facts, in this letter," Derrida nevertheless cited it as evidence that de Man "wished in 1955 never to have done anything that could be suspected of Nazism or collaboration." While it is highly likely that de Man wished in 1955 that he had not "done anything that could be suspected of Nazism or collaboration," that wish may as easily have followed from abject fear as from anguished regret. Yet Derrida attributes an honorable intent to this letter, a text remarkable for its falsehoods, denials, and evasions. Thus Derrida, even while denouncing "the jubilation with which some may hasten to play that game," had in effect already begun the trial proceedings by launching a preemptive and highly tendentious defense of de Man.

To his credit Derrida insisted that the damning documents be made public. "It is urgent," he said, "that some of us hasten to take their responsibilities as regards these texts, to be the first to show that there is no question of dissimulating them or of participating in any kind of camouflage operation." Accordingly, the Tuscaloosa group decided to return to the photocopying machine. Three professors were entrusted with the task of collecting de Man's *Le Soir* articles and mailing copies to various other professors of note in the lit-crit hierarchy. It was announced that an issue of the *Oxford Literary Review* would reprint the articles along with "responses" by assorted theorists. In the meanwhile, reporters had no trouble obtaining *their* copies from compliant professors—it would be interesting to calculate what the photocopying budget of all this activity must have been. Word of mouth works fast in the academic community. A session of the Modern Language Association's annual convention—the big daddy of academic conferences, held, that December, in San Francisco—was converted into a more-or-less impromptu discussion of what de Man had done in the war.

Once the cat was let out of the bag—after the *New York Times,* the *Nation,* and *Newsweek* reported the story—the traffic in photocopies accelerated. From one quarter, expressions of shock and dismay could be heard; from another, the distinctive note of *Schadenfreude;* and these reponses quickly gave way to a more incendiary level of discussion as the *Le Soir* articles reached the desks of professors in campuses near and remote. At issue was not only de Man's reputation for personal integrity but the prestige of the entire critical movement he had championed. At subsequent conferences and in the pages of highbrow literary supplements, de Man's detractors and defenders went at each other with a venom remarkable even by the usual acrimonious standards of intellectual disputation. The scandal left an unmistakably acrid taste in a number of big academic mouths. Professors venting their ire over de Man's secret life didn't hesitate to propose links between de Man then and deconstruction now. "The real problem of the de Manians is hero worship—the spectacle of grown men and women idolizing another person," said Frank Lentricchia, the Duke University professor who had once labeled de Man the "godfather" of the Yale "Mafia." "It's very bad to communicate this hero worship to students," Lentricchia told the *Nation.* "It's politically ugly. Students need independence, scrutiny, self-reliance." "There's no doubt that de Man was a gung-ho collaborator," Jeffrey Mehlman told

Newsweek. Mehlman, a Boston University professor of French, had done a considerable amount of research on the behavior of fascist intellectuals in the 1930s. In the face of de Man's lack of candor about his past, Mehlman speculated that there might even be "grounds for viewing the whole of deconstruction as a vast amnesty project for the politics of collaboration in France during World War II." It was a rather spectacular charge, and doubtless an exaggeration, but it was not made in a know-nothing spirit. Mehlman spoke "as one of the people who introduced Derrida to this country." He had long since aired his doubts about the political implications of deconstruction.

It became widely known that one of de Man's *Le Soir* articles "engaged with the ideology of anti-Semitism," to use the locution the professors seemed to favor. It also became known that the deconstruction elite were preparing a hefty tome of "responses" to be published alongside the volume of de Man's articles themselves. (The project, outgrowing the resources of the *Oxford Literary Review,* eventually filled two oversize books rather than one scholarly magazine. The volume of *Responses* comes out to 477 double-column pages, and the volume of *Wartime Journalism* to some 399 photocopied sheets.) What was planned, in effect, was a major symposium on de Man's wartime writings—a kind of free-floating academic conference; each prospective contributor was sent a packet of the photocopied articles and was asked for cogent and informed commentary. This development itself outraged some in the academic community. "I am shocked that there is to be a symposium," a critic described as "very close to de Man" told Jon Wiener of the *Nation.* "Paul must have known the Jews of Belgium were being carted away. We are discussing the butchery of the Belgian Jewish community, down to the babies. To treat this as one more item about which to have a symposium is outrageous. The people who are organizing this have lost all moral perspective; they are so much under the sway of the man they cannot bear to consider what they are doing." In lit-crit circles, the identity of the speaker was never in doubt: everyone assumed it was Harold Bloom. Because of Bloom's stature and because he had been one of de Man's closest friends on the Yale faculty, the comment drew blood; in the months ahead, more than one deconstructionist critic cited it with anger in the pages of literary periodicals. "When someone asking 'not to be identified' sees himself quoted by an unscrupulous professor-journalist, when he says he is 'shocked' by the fact that certain people are gathering, if only in order to *discuss* these problems (he would thus like to forbid the rights to assembly and discussion? What does that remind you of?), and when he says he is 'shocked' in the name of a 'moral perspective,' you can see why I am indignant and worried," wrote Jacques Derrida. Derrida's indignation and worry came through, though his logic left something to be desired; to express outrage over a symposium is scarcely "to forbid the rights to assembly and discussion."

The protest against the symposium was not the only statement in the article in the *Nation* that enraged deconstructionists from Derrida on down. Jon Wiener's piece was, they claimed, "rife with distortions and insinuations." They took issue with Frank Lentricchia's charge of "hero worship"—and the implicit analogy between the veneration of de Man and the fascist cult of the leader; de Man's former colleagues insisted that his charisma had been benign, characterized by monastic rigor rather than by dictatorial flamboyance. What irked the deconstructionists above all was the accusation, which Wiener reported, that the Tuscaloosa conference had been convened as a preemptive strike—"an exercise in 'damage control.' " The deconstructionists could defend themselves plausibly on this count. The three professors entrusted with the task of assembling de Man's wartime writings did so with a scrupulous attention to detail. And the companion volume of "responses" contains much that is valuable—the text of de Man's letter to Harvard, a good chronology of his early years, a number of highly intelligent essays—along with the special pleading that one expected to find in such a massive volume. It was, in any event, surely understandable that the deconstructionists would take umbrage at the imputation of a cover-up. It was understandable, too, that they would react in self-defense against the inflammatory statements made by Lentricchia, Mehlman, and various others, identified or not, in the *Nation* and in *Newsweek*.

Yet the embattled posture of the deconstructionists, and in particular their hostility toward journalists and journalism, far exceeded the logical cause. First Wiener, then others on the de Man beat were subjected to shrill abuse. For Jacques Derrida, criticism of de Man was held to be the figurative equivalent of "burning his books"—as if dissent were equivalent to censorship: "To judge, to condemn the work or the man on the basis of what was a brief episode, to call for closing, that is to say, at least figuratively, for censuring or burning his books is to reproduce the exterminating gesture which one accuses de Man of not having armed himself against sooner with the necessary vigilance." The recklessness of the charge was breathtaking, but it was not atypical. To some extent the deconstructionist defensiveness was anticipatory. As one who covered the story for *Newsweek,* I was often rebuffed in my efforts to speak with professors of the de Man party, and in the interviews I did manage to arrange, I felt as an attorney must with a hostile witness on the stand. That was as nothing next to the outcry that followed the appearance of articles in the popular press. *Newsweek* printed my three-column article, broken by advertisements, over the course of three magazine pages. On the top of one column appeared a photograph of Paul de Man in 1975; at the base of another column, on another page, the magazine ran a photograph of uniformed Nazis on the march. More than one deconstructionist or fellow traveler vociferously complained that the "juxtaposition" of the two photographs insinuated that deconstruction was a latter-day derivative of Nazism. One critic went so far as to liken the *Newsweek* layout to that of the page in *Le Soir* featuring de Man's article about the Jews. Another critic provided a full-blown rhetorical analysis: "Technically a catachresis, in its aberrant sequentiality with the picture of the amiable professor in his Yale office, the picture of the Nazis exaggerates the lack of any bridge between it and that face. The sequence is the allegory of the nonpicturability of the rhetorician's didactic effectiveness." To the deconstructionist faithful, the photograph of marching Nazis was unfair, irrelevant, even scary—though in its defense it could be said to dramatize exactly what was at stake in Europe when de Man wrote in praise of "the German revolution." In *Newsweek* I described de Man's *Le Soir* article about the Jews—the one in which he airily dismisses Jewish writers as mediocrities whose deportation en masse would not injure European culture. I labeled the article "blatantly anti-Semitic." A livid deconstructionist, insisting that I had it all wrong, demanded a retraction. My correspondent maintained that in the article in question de Man repudiates what he calls "vulgar anti-Semitism." He may, indeed, but what then did his article promote? Genteel anti-Semitism? If in the United States today a columnist were to recommend the mass deportation of blacks, would we hesitate to condemn this as virulent racism? I wondered whether my correspondent's reading of the *Le Soir* article was a fair example of deconstructionist text-interpretation at work. Not until a few months later, when Derrida's *Critical Inquiry* piece was published, did it become clear that the letter-writer was toeing a preordained party line: on the one side, to minimize what de Man had done; on the other, to vilify the journalists on the case.

Nothing quite prepared one for the virtual declaration of war on journalism that soon issued from deconstructionist quarters. Above all, the deconstructionists laced into "journalists who are also professors." Jacques Derrida, referring to Jon Wiener's article as "a stream of calumny," called for his head. "It is frightening to think that [Wiener] teaches history at a university," Derrida wrote, as if the dean were reading over his shoulder. J. Hillis Miller, taking his cue from the master, characterized "the violence of the reaction in the United States and in Europe to the discovery of Paul de Man's writings of 1941–42" as "a new moment in the collaboration between the university and the mass media." Presumably Miller understood the exact valence of the word *collaboration* in that sentence. Paul de Man is revealed to have been a collaborationist, and Miller can think of no better response than to insinuate a parallel between the Nazi-run *Le Soir* and the institutions of journalism in the United States and Europe today! (Miller included in his indictment the *New York Times,* the *Nation, Newsweek,* the *Los Angeles Times,* the *Village Voice,* the *Manchester Guardian,* and the *Frankfurter Allgemeine Zeitung*—a veritable international conspiracy.) Certainly it was noteworthy that Derrida and Miller condemned contemporary journalists and "professor-journalists" more straightforwardly, at greater length, and with less equivocation than either of them censured de Man's wartime journalism. Backfiring, this blame-the-messenger strategy managed to accomplish the opposite of what was intended: a "foregrounding"—to use the requisite jargon word—of deconstruction in the debate about Paul de Man.

When Jacques Derrida described his late friend's wartime journalism as "the literary and artistic column that a very young man wrote for a newspaper, almost a half century ago, for less than two years, in very singular private and political circumstances many of which remain unclear to us," it sounded very much like a case of special pleading. One sensed one was up against a deniability campaign when Jonathan Culler, Cornell University's premier deconstructionist, reduced de Man's offense to "one dismaying column," as if "The Jews in Contemporary Literature" were merely a lone, regrettable indiscretion. A shallow breath after charging that press accounts had "grossly misrepresented" de Man, Culler claimed—against the evidence—that de Man's other articles "occasionally praise the energy of the German 'renewal' and the tradition of German culture, but not Hitler, not the Nazi party, not the German government or its policies." Culler wrote in an even tone. Not so Andrzej Warminski, a de Man diehard, who complained that the reaction to the de Man revelations was evidence of "anti-intellectual hysteria" and a "frenzy of hatred." One had only to read the rest of his diatribe to realize that this was an inadvertent self-description. "If you are stupid enough to judge [de Man]," Warminski wrote in one characteristic passage, "you judge at your peril, for that judgment . . . judges only you." According to Warminski, the "academic journalists" on the case displayed "a dismaying ignorance," perpetrated "stupidities," and were "shrill, strident, violent, (male) hysterical." "What," he sputtered, "could make so many of these creatures crawl out from under the rocks of their pathologies?" In all this, Jeffrey Mehlman thought he could detect "the 'relativization' of Nazism" as "an item on the agenda of American 'deconstruction.' " He could already hear the preamble. As Mehlman put it, "So he was a Nazi . . . That is: so what!"

The seemingly orchestrated blame-the-media strategy made one wonder about the deconstructionists, who are supposed to be so alert to the ways and means of "mediated" expression. Could they have so fundamentally misunderstood the nature of literary journalism as to expect reporters to ignore, and writers to play down, a potentially fruitful academic controversy—fruitful because it may help to clarify the larger conflicts and crises in the academic enterprise? Deconstruction had cultivated controversy and prospered from the publicity it generated. Did its exponents really expect the press to turn its gaze away now that a major scandal had erupted? If the de Man revelations provoke a noted professor to air his misgivings about the "nihilistic" impulse in deconstruction or its "anti-historical" bias, the journalist has no choice but to present the quotation if he is to convey the terms of the debate and the intensity of the feelings aroused. The deconstructionists, challenging the use of such quotations, retreated to a position of mystification. They, and they alone, were qualified to discuss the matter; all others, keep out.

There were doubtless inaccuracies in the early coverage of the de Man affair; in journalism there always are. And deconstruction is a notoriously difficult concept to define in a column inch. But the essential facts were given straight, and the immediacy of the journalistic response was commendable—it meant that the reporters had very quickly grasped the disturbing implications of the affair and were striving to make recondite matters intelligible to a wide audience. Moreover, journalistic accounts of the case were far from one-sided. Even those of us who frankly expressed our suspicion of deconstruction took pains to present the other side. Finally, deconstruction itself did not lack for advocates in the press. It was, after all, in the guise of journalists that such defenders of de Man as J. Hillis Miller and Jonathan Culler wrote their articles for the *Times Literary Supplement* and the *Chronicle of Higher Education.* Yet these writers sweepingly condemned "journalism" and "journalists"—as if they and their allies were not subsumed under the rubric.

In the ferocity of the deconstructionist attack on the press, there was evidently an element of displacement. It was as if, in J. Hillis Miller's eyes, the "mass media" functioned as an extension of an academic faction—the retrograde professors who had it in for deconstruction in particular and critical theory in general. But Miller's condemnation of the press revealed—if you deconstructed it—a second agenda. If you vilified journalism, you could implicitly absolve de Man: not he, but journalism, stood trial for the *Le Soir* articles. Language speaks us—that old argument. And if making that argument under these circumstances implied a moral equivalence between what de Man wrote during the Nazi years and what journalists in 1988 wrote about de Man, that seems to have been Miller's point.

Above everything else, the deconstructionists objected to the journalistic inquiry into deconstruction itself—and the implication that "the trial of Paul de Man" would examine not only his behavior but his ideas, in the days of *Le Soir* and since. Deconstruction did become the real focus of the polemic generated by the de Man affair, but it is difficult to see how it could have gone otherwise. If a brilliant mathematician is revealed to have behaved disgracefully in a moment of historical crisis, we may alter our opinion of the man's character but we will readily agree that the new knowledge has no bearing on his mathematical formulas. But for a thinker whose lifework had to do with language and literature—and whose hard-core brand of deconstruction stressed the "indeterminacy" of texts—surely there was *some* relation between the texts he was intent on forgetting and the texts in which he campaigned to forget the "author," his "ideas," and his conscious "meaning." Deconstruction had long given people pause because it makes no provision for moral action and dismisses the historical dimension in literature. These omissions seemed all the more disquieting, and perhaps the more intelligible, in the light of the de Man disclosures. It was even possible to discern an oblique attempt at self-justification in some of de Man's flamboyant declarations. "The political destiny of man is structured like and derived from a linguistic model that exists independently of nature and independently of the subject," de Man wrote in *Allegories of Reading*. It follows from this radical assertion that, in de Man's words, "society and government" are neither natural nor ethical nor theological, "since language is not conceived as a transcendental principle but as the possibility of contingent error." Hence, de Man concluded, political activity is "a burden for man rather than an opportunity." The appeal of this position to a man with de Man's past needs no belaboring.

In the concluding chapter of *Allegories of Reading,* de Man treated at considerable length and in great detail an episode in Rousseau's *Confessions*—the episode in which Rousseau confesses that he stole a ribbon and falsely accused an innocent servant girl of the deed. Reviewing *Allegories of Reading* for the *New York Review of Books* in 1980, Denis Donoghue dwelled on this crucial chapter. De Man discussed the incident, Donoghue pointed out, as though both Rousseau's lie and his later confession were the work of a "text-machine" rather than of an individual bearing some responsibility for his words and deeds. The key sentences in *Allegories of Reading*—they would be quoted often in accounts of the de Man case—addressed the question of guilt. "It is always possible," de Man wrote, "to face up to any experience (to excuse any guilt), because the experience always exists simultaneously as fictional discourse and as empirical event and it is never possible to decide which one of the two possibilities is the right one. The indecision makes it possible to excuse the bleakest of crimes because, as a fiction, it escapes from the constraints of guilt and innocence." Donoghue's comment was precise: "If you've ever felt guilty, the decision has been painfully easy. To remain suspended between de Man's two possibilities is a clear instance of self-mystification." And further:

> Readers of the *Confessions* think they hear someone talking
> about his own experience, accusing himself, justifying him-
> self, and so forth. De Man can't bear to hear that voice,

because he doesn't want to hear any voice: he wants to see a machine working without human intervention. His application of a linguistic model to all situations is pedantic. If it were enforced in practice as rigorously as he proposes, it would dismiss the questions commonly considered in morality, ethics, politics, and psychology, and treat them as purely linguistic functions.

There, in a nutshell, was the problem. Given what we now know of de Man's past, doesn't his theory of language seem not simply "pedantic" but remarkably self-serving? Doesn't his reading of Rousseau seem to exalt evasiveness into a philosophical ideal? A former de Man student recalled the professor's amusement at the magazine title *True Confessions,* a phrase he regarded as oxymoronic. If "true confessions" is a contradiction in terms, why trouble yourself to confess? If it is possible "to excuse the bleakest of crimes because, as a fiction, it escapes from the constraints of guilt and innocence," why draw attention to the guilty thing you once did? You have already reduced empirical events to the status of fictional discourse—and thus your theory spares you from the obligation to confront your guilt. *You didn't confess because it would have been too easy to do so!* If you have secrets you'd rather keep, this is an extremely convenient view to hold. Instead of taking the blame for the indefensible things you said, you put the blame on language. Instead of stepping into an unwelcome spotlight, you slip off into a linguistic night in which all cats are gray.

In an essay published in 1966, de Man discussed "The Literature of Nihilism"—specifically the nihilistic impulse in the German literary tradition—and brought up the question of its relation to Nazism. De Man used the occasion to advance a thesis diametrically opposite to the one that steered his pen in 1941 and 1942. "No one could claim," de Man now wrote, "that the Nazi movement somehow rooted itself in a venerable and mature tradition. It was, if anything, notable for its profound anti-intellectualism and the crude but effective manner in which it played on the most primitive mass instincts, as well as on the shortsighted economic interests of social classes that considered themselves underprivileged. The Nazis received little support from German writers and intellectuals and were not eager to enlist them in their ranks." With what cool confidence de Man makes his case—though his own experience at *Le Soir,* publicizing the cultural pretensions of

Nazi Germany and reviewing German writers who supported the regime, is evidence to the contrary. In "The Literature of Nihilism," De Man goes on to argue that Hitler triumphed in Germany "in spite of the intellectual tradition of the country, rather than because of it. There was *trahison des clercs* [betrayal by the intellectuals] to the precise extent that literary thought and political action had lost contact with each other. The problem is not that a philosophical tradition could be so wrong but that it could have counted for so little when it was most needed. The responsibility rests not with the tradition but with the manner in which it was used or neglected, and this is primarily a sociological problem." De Man's comments on the moral responsibility of intellectuals seem disingenuous to an extreme. What about the *trahison des clercs* of those who sought—as de Man did—to locate a cultural basis for Nazism in the German literary and philosophical tradition? If what they perpetrated was a misrepresentation of that tradition, was the responsibility for this distortion "primarily a sociological problem"? Precisely what was one to think of writers who took pains to palm off the view that Nazism and culture could go hand in hand? Did only "sociology" bear responsibility for their words and deeds? The knowledge we now have of de Man's early career does more than cast doubt on such passages as these from de Man's later writing. They reveal him to be the opposite of disinterested and impersonal—the very values for which de Man was most esteemed. In a deeply personal sense, such writing seems dishonest.

De Man published "The Literature of Nihilism" just before he entered his deconstructionist phase. The damage done by the *Le Soir* disclosures to his subsequent writings was far more damaging. The view that substitutes a "text-machine" for humanity and identifies wars and revolutions as "texts" would minimize—or even eliminate— the notion that people exercise free will and bear some responsibility for their actions. In theory a man can escape "from the constraints of guilt and innocence." Moral judgments give way to the exigencies of a superior skepticism. "Empirical events" are merely linguistic predicaments. History itself is only a text to be reduced, in the deconstructive analysis, to a self-contradictory impasse. These propositions, debatable to begin with, are weakened considerably by our awareness of the writer's duplicity—the fact that he knew more than he ever let on, and that he himself had everything to gain by applying a wet sponge to the blackboard of history.

. . .

As the de Man scandal developed in 1988, Jeffrey Mehlman found himself quoted frequently by journalists. Mehlman's credentials as a critical theorist were impeccable; he had himself translated Derrida into English. But by the mid-1980s Mehlman had begun to air his misgivings about the political drift of deconstruction. In 1986 Mehlman—who had previously published a book about anti-Semitism in France—cited an instance in which a Derridean analysis seemed to confer "amnesty" on a writer who had compromised himself politically in the Second World War. In an essay in the journal *Representations,* Mehlman spoke of "the old dilemma—resistance, collaboration, a certain undecidability between the two," as if, by implication, you could deconstruct "Resistance as always already a dream of Collaboration." Mehlman's use of *deconstruct* in the following sentence was deliberately provocative: Ezra Pound, Mehlman noted, "wrote a maddeningly wrong-headed *Jefferson and/or Mussolini,* an attempt to neutralize—if not deconstruct—the opposition between the father of democracy and the fascist leader ('The heritage of Jefferson . . . is HERE, NOW in the Italian peninsula at the beginning of the second fascist decennio, not in Massachusetts or Delaware')." Mehlman reminded his readers that Pound was one of "the tutelary figures" of Jacques Derrida's book *Of Grammatology,* where he is singled out for "a first break with the deepest Western tradition."

When de Man's wartime journalism surfaced, it struck Mehlman with some force that "no fewer than three of the most sterling careers flanking deconstruction (that is, Derrida's own career) were profoundly compromised by an engagement with fascism." Mehlman had in mind, besides de Man, Heidegger in Germany and the critic Maurice Blanchot in France. Focusing on the word *resistance,* Mehlman spun out an ingenious analogy—or point of continuity—between de Man's early journalism and his later writing. Mehlman knew that deconstruction teaches one that, in Geoffrey Hartman's words, "there are no dead metaphors." The word *resistance,* for example, crops up frequently in deconstructive writings. What Mehlman suggested was that the word was not so innocent as it looked—not if you kept in mind the war between collaborators and resistants in France and Belgium during the Second World War. Might the current conflict between the avatars of deconstruction and those who resist it be seen as a redrawing of the old combat lines?

De Man had described "The Resistance to Theory" in his famous essay of that title in 1982. But the phrase had already been introduced by Geoffrey Hartman in his 1980 book *Criticism in the Wilderness,* which advocates the cause of critical theory. "The resistance to theory in Anglo-American criticism," Hartman wrote, "goes together with a resistance to imported ideas, from non-English countries or from other fields of inquiry." Here *resistance* is identified with xenophobia, narrow-mindedness, insularity. There is both a military and a psychological edge to the word, with an emphasis on the latter: the notion, made intellectually popular by Freud, that the subject's "resistance" to analysis, or to a specific conclusion to which the analysis points, confirms the significance and possibly the validity of what is resisted. Resistance confirms the diagnosis—a species of logic that makes for a kind of fail-safe argument. If you agree with the deconstructive position (or the psychoanalyst), fine; and if you disagree, that's fine, too, for it means you're merely trying to dodge an undesirable truth. The British critic Christopher Ricks was one opponent of deconstruction who did not hesitate to pick up the "resistance" metaphor and fling it back at the deconstructionists. Ricks recommended, he wrote in 1985, "resistance to what seem to some of us, or at any rate to me, the inordinate and unspecific claims of theory." What was needed, Ricks argues, went beyond questions of "professional self-esteem" and "territorial imperatives." What was needed was resistance—that is, defiance of an unwanted invader or occupying force.

According to Jeffrey Mehlman, the belated discovery of de Man's wartime journalism put a sinister new spin on this loaded word, fraught with significance as it already was in the debate over "theory" in general and deconstruction in particular. Mehlman suspected that a con game might be going on—that the deconstructive agenda may include the whitewashing of French collaborationism. Wasn't it an odd coincidence—Mehlman calls it "an odd continuity between the earlier and the later writings"—that de Man began and ended his career by writing against a "resistance" movement? "For in both his writings in French on behalf of the Nazi 'revolution' among the Walloons in the 1940's and his writings in English on behalf of 'deconstruction' among the Americans in the 1970's, the idiosyncratic discursive feature binding the two endeavors, each in furtherance of a radical cultural movement from abroad, is a pronounced pessimism regarding the abilities of his broader audience (the French in the 1940's, American academia in the 1970's) to muster the wherewithal needed to respond to the demands each movement was putting on them." For de Man in 1941 and 1942, Mehlman argues, "a deluded resistance to the salutary revolution from abroad was the vice of the French; in 1982, 'resistance' (to theory) was an American shortcoming in the face of a 'revolution' coming *from* France." In 1941 de Man had written of and for a Belgian elite, the French-speaking Walloons, who were (in de Man's words) "more attuned to the desired revolution" than their counterparts in France. Perhaps, wrote Mehlman, "the Yale graduate students were cast in the role of the Walloons of the 1970's."

Of all the attacks on deconstruction occasioned by the de Man affair, surely Mehlman's was the most bitterly resented. In effect, he was proposing an analogy—in Paul de Man's mind, if nowhere else—between Nazism then and deconstruction now: both were "revolutionary," imported "from abroad," proud of their "ruthlessness," and determined to overcome any native "resistance" in their path. Mehlman's was a singular argument. For most of the other plaintiffs in the case of Paul de Man, deconstruction was troublesome enough on its own—it was scarcely necessary to develop parallels between deconstruction and fascism, beyond the broad but important point that deconstruction provides no safeguard against nihilism and no basis for an ethical critique of either fascism or Nazism. This is how Charles L. Griswold of Howard University put the argument:

> Is there anything in Deconstruction that could serve as a basis for repudiating (and so providing an ethical critique of) Nazism? Grant for a moment that the theory does not logically entail Nazism, and that lots of perfectly respectable persons have taken a shine to the theory. Does the theory provide a basis for criticism of that sort of political program? I doubt that it does, and this because it renders theoretically unintelligible basic moral terms such as "good" and "evil" . . . De Man's theory does not permit us to utter the sentence "Nazism is evil" with any theoretical justification; when pressed, we could only say that, given the sensibility of one's empirical state at the moment the

statement was uttered, it is felt that Nazism is evil (or good, as the case may be). Is not an account to that effect morally suspect?

Mehlman's "resistance" theory compelled interest not only because it was, in contrast to Griswold's more measured tone, so sensational; it was, besides, a notable example of deconstructive logic—Mehlman's whole argument hinges on the etymology of a word—only here turned *against* deconstruction. When the de Man disclosures were new, Mehlman told me a version of his theory during a telephone interview. I wanted to test it out on a critic who had always been sympathetic to de Man—though developments may have shaken that sympathy. I asked Geoffrey Hartman, famous for his *jeux de mots,* to comment on the semantic link between the French Resistance in World War II and the "Resistance to Theory" forty years later. It was worth it to hear Hartman say, without a trace of irony, that this was a prime example of the sort of glib wordplay he deplores.

In his own article on the de Man disclosures, Hartman mounted the shrewdest and most nearly persuasive defense of the later de Man. Having presented with unblinkered eye the disagreeable facts about his deceased friend's past, Hartman made the case for a complete rupture between the de Man of the fascist period and the de Man of *Blindness and Insight* and *Allegories of Reading.* Despite his "shock" at learning of de Man's collaborationist activity, Hartman strove to be dispassionate—and to discourage the notion that de Man "avoid[ed] confession . . . and instead work[ed] out his totalitarian temptation in a purely intellectual and impersonal manner." Against this view, Hartman argued that deconstruction as de Man had practiced it was implicitly "a kind of repudiation" of his wartime errors. According to Hartman, de Man's refusal to analyze himself—to write in the mode of the *Confessions* of Rousseau—amounted to a refusal to exonerate himself; he would live with his guilt instead of making excuses and pleading for forgiveness. The biographical facts that had lately come to light do, Hartman conceded, embed themselves in our consciousness—but with the result that de Man's later work "appears more and more as a deepening reflection on the rhetoric of totalitarianism." Indeed, Hartman concluded, de Man's mature work "looks like a belated, but still powerful, act of conscience."

I have described Hartman's line of argument as the most nearly persuasive of all those that were put up in defense of de Man. Where it founders is in relying on the assumption that de Man was writing in his later years in good faith—that his reputation for "intellectual honesty" could somehow survive the tangible evidence of his evasions and equivocations. De Man's later writings can be seen to constitute a belated "act of conscience"—but only if you accept the idea that "deconstruction is neither nihilistic nor cynical," and only if you put the most benign of all possible constructions on de Man's failure to acknowledge his past. You would have to suppose that de Man had been too fastidious to apologize, too skeptical of the rhetoric of confession to confess. And that is to mythologize a figure that the case of Paul de Man has forever demythologized. For those who have a more suspicious view of human nature—those who attribute de Man's wartime journalism to opportunism rather than ideology—simpler explanations for de Man's silence suggest themselves. Fear, for example—the fear of having his name cast in infamy—and cool self-interest. De Man's silence about his past seems to be, above everything else, expedient and self-protective, the characteristic behavior of a man who would sooner jettison a family and a history than forfeit his second chance at success; for his American years presented de Man with the chance to succeed precisely in establishing for himself the Olympian voice of authority to which he had already aspired in his wartime journalism. Richard Klein, a self-described "Derridean" who had mapped out the oedipal relation between de Man and his uncle years before, now weighed in with "a contribution to the future science of DeManology." Klein's piece was charged with exaggeration; it was dedicated to trying out the supposition that de Man was the devil, Klein's point being that the devil's work is "the most interesting, the most difficult and dangerous" for the critic to contend with. But one of Klein's endnotes was sober enough in explaining what de Man had to gain by keeping silent about his past. Had the articles in *Le Soir* come to light in 1948, they might have deterred the United States Immigration Service from granting de Man a visa, Klein noted. He recalled a recent Federal appellate decision to strip another former Yale professor of his American citizenship. Vladimir Sokolov, who had taught Russian literature at Yale from 1959 to 1976, had once written some highly compromising articles. At his 1986 trial he said "that he wrote articles only to oppose Communism and make a living and that anti-Semitic slurs were ordered inserted by his Nazi censors." Not a very convincing defense, it resembled the one that an attorney for de Man might have felt obliged to mount had the facts surfaced when he was still alive.

On the prodeconstruction side of the de Man debate, the smart move was to argue that de Man was not unusual among European intellectuals of the 1930s, that he was young then, that later he implicitly but utterly broke with his fascist past, and that his latest writings were in fact aimed at dismantling the "aesthetic ideology" of fascism. "It is a striking feature of European history between the wars that so many intellectuals were drawn to political and theoretical programs whose actual instantiations—fascism in Germany, Italy and Spain; communism in Russia and elsewhere—proved totalitarian," Jonathan Culler observed. De Man's early journalism, Culler went on, "bears little resemblance to the sort of analytical criticism, focused on imagery, that he was to develop in the 1950s, and still less to the style of rhetorical readings that he was to develop in the 1970s in contact with Jacques Derrida and deconstruction." This contention, however, is highly debatable; if you take into account the form and structure of de Man's arguments, some points of resemblance do emerge. Alice Yaeger Kaplan, who had studied with de Man at Yale in the mid-1970s, "recognized the de Man I had as a teacher when I read the texts in *Le Soir*," she wrote. "It wasn't because of anything he said, it was his strategies, his process—so familiar—that I recognized across the frontier of 1976 and 1940. The signals were the same: the command of literary history, the vast cultural knowledge he was giving away, because that wasn't what was really important. Then a second paragraph, with a quotation and its logical inconsistency revealed. The same emphasis on rigor, the disdain for vulgarity, indulgence. Except for the endings—and it's a big exception—where, instead of the abyss, the deconstructive finale that I am used to, de Man ends with a kind of proto-fascist community building statement, a slogan." Whatever her sense of the continuities, Kaplan remained convinced that de Man "worked against his early work"—though he was "the same man" and at hand were "the same emotional structures in 1942 and 1981."

Like Hartman and Culler, Barbara Johnson argues that deconstruction as de Man practiced it was an implicit repudiation of totalitarianism. "Whatever Paul de Man is doing in these early essays, it is certainly not deconstruction," Johnson writes. "Indeed, deconstruction is precisely the dismantling of these notions of evolutionary continuity, totalization, organicism, and 'proper' traditions." For Johnson, the vilification of deconstruction is based on a severe misconception. "To say that deconstruction is 'hostile to the very principles of Western thought' *(Newsweek)* is like saying that quantum mechanics is hostile to the notion of substances," she writes. It is a telling choice of analogy but an unconvincing one. For deconstruction, unlike quantum mechanics, is not a science; deconstruction's claims to scientific validity are precisely what many of its opponents dispute. Johnson discerns the spirit of analysis, rather than hostility, in the deconstructive project. But what then is one to make of her assertion that "no one could have been a more enthusiastic upholder of the integrity of Western thought than the Paul de Man of 1940–42"? The statement seems to identify "the integrity of Western thought" with a vision of German hegemony in Europe. And that is a bleaker understanding of Western thought than most of us would credit.

But arguably the bleakest of the responses to the de Man revelations were occasioned not by an excess of zeal—for or against deconstruction, or de Man, or what de Man represented at any particular period of his life—but by its absence. There were those who, with a kind of determined neutrality, held that de Man's life and his work were two separate categories and that there was little sense in locating points of either continuity or discontinuity between the young journalist and the middle-aged Yale eminence. The philosopher Richard Rorty, addressing himself to the controversy that had erupted in Paris over Victor Farias's *Heidegger and Nazism,* argued against "the notion that learning about a philosopher's moral character helps one evaluate his philosophy." Yes, wrote Rorty, Heidegger "fought like a tiger to become the official philosopher, the intellectual leader, of the National Socialist movement." Still, Rorty insisted, it is misguided to suppose that a philosopher's moral indecency has any bearing on his importance as a thinker or on the substance of his thought. Here is the heart of Rorty's argument, with its pointed reference to Paul de Man:

> Many people think that there is something intrinsically fascistic about the thought of Nietzsche and Heidegger, and are suspicious of Derrida and Foucault because they owe so much to these earlier figures. On this view, fascism is associated with "irrationalism," and a decent democratic outlook with "confidence in reason." Aristotle's casual accept-

ance of slavery as natural and proper is taken to be central
to his moral outlook; Heidegger's blood-and-soil rhetoric
is taken to be central to his "history of Being"; Nietzsche's
elitist swaggering is taken as central to his ethic of self-
creation; "deconstruction" is condemned on the basis of the
young Paul de Man's opportunistic anti-Semitism.

Such attempts to simplify the thought of original
thinkers by reducing them to moral or political attitudes
should be avoided, just as we should avoid thinking of
Hemingway as simply a bully, of Proust as simply a sissy,
of Pound as simply a lunatic, of Kipling as simply an
imperialist.

This is witty, but the writer's pungent phrasing and reasonable tone
shouldn't blind us to his misrepresentation of the de Man controversy.
For in truth, deconstruction stood accused not "on the basis of the
young Paul de Man's opportunistic anti-Semitism" but by a host of
factors including de Man's embrace of fascism, his subsequent silence,
the problematic relation of that guilty silence to his theories about
guilt and speech, and the denial campaign undertaken in de Man's
defense by his confederates. For its critics, deconstruction had always
seemed, for reasons vague or precise, to be an unwholesome doctrine.
The belated de Man disclosures did not initiate the accusation; they
renewed it. As the case of Paul de Man turned into the case against
deconstruction, the unsavory biographical details played a part but
were never meant to bear the brunt of the charge.

Leave aside the accuracy or fairness of Rorty's summary statements and you find something disturbing in his logic, something that
is only partly camouflaged by his flip characterizations of Hemingway,
Proust, Pound, and Kipling. For while it would certainly be a mistake
to think of Hemingway as "simply a bully," of Proust as "simply a
sissy," of Pound as "simply a lunatic," and so forth, that is largely
because these are caricatures, and caricatures rarely teach us anything.
If, however, you avoid hyperbole and try for something more exact,
you can get to a more plausible set of propositions. Surely it is relevant
to our understanding of Hemingway's literary achievement that he
strove to embody a masculine ideal; you can hardly overlook this
obsession when you read *Men Without Women* or *Death in the Afternoon*. And it can hardly be denied that homosexual aestheticism ac-

counts for some of the distinctive energy of Proust's masterwork. It is at least arguable that Pound's *Cantos* resemble the product of a deranged sensibility—and that their failure to cohere is not purely a literary defect but a reflection of the author's mental confusion. And it is difficult to imagine a serious study of Kipling that would not take into account his relation to British high imperialism, his sense of the "white man's burden." Naturally the writer's life will be seen as irrelevant to his works if you reduce biography to the level of gossip. But if you respect the biographer's art, a better alternative presents itself. Rather than maintain that a philosopher's moral character has no bearing on his thinking, wouldn't it make more sense to suppose that the life and thought of a philosopher, a writer, or a literary theorist must interact in numerous complex and significant ways?

The title of Rorty's piece was "Taking Philosophy Seriously." That, according to Rorty, was a mistake Heidegger made. He took himself too seriously. He had a deluded sense of the power of philosophy: "Heidegger thought that the scientific, cultural, and political life of a society was simply the working-out of a set of ideas that some great philosopher had formulated." What Rorty calls "philosophical fundamentalism"—"the assumption that anybody who disagrees with some given religious or philosophical doctrine is a danger to democratic society"—follows from such overseriousness. This is the "anti-democratic" element that Rorty finds in "Christianity, or Islam, or Platonism, or Marxism, or Heideggerianism, or 'deconstruction.' " But there is a nagging ambiguity in Rorty's injunction against "taking philosophy seriously." In one sense he is warning us against becoming fanatics or cultists, and who can disagree with that? In keeping a philosopher's life and work in separate categories, however, isn't it Rorty who risks diminishing the importance of philosophy? In Rorty's view the thought of an original philosopher is "the result of some neural kink that occurs independently of other kinks." When such an argument is made by a professor of philosophy, it has a peculiarly disconcerting effect. Why should students study philosophy if it has a merely clinical interest and does not address the way people lead their lives? Rorty supposes that a philosopher's moral character is as irrelevant to his philosophy as Einstein's character is irrelevant to his physics. But that is a false analogy. Einstein's moral character has no relation to his physics because physics is not moral philosophy. A philosopher's doctrine, by contrast, may very well touch on politics and morality—and then surely his actual historical behavior becomes admissible evidence. After all, Rorty himself necessarily takes account of Heidegger's Nazi involvement—his strictures on the "anti-democratic" element of Heideggerianism would otherwise lack full force.

The view that sees no relation between a philosopher's work and his life has its counterpart, perhaps, in the deconstructive view that insists that characters in books have no relation to us. And from the dissociation of an author from his works, it is, unhappily, a short but breathtaking leap to disavow the making of any moral judgments whatsoever. Covering the de Man affair for the *New York Times Magazine*, James Atlas documented the moral disasters of de Man's pre-American life. He had been, Atlas demonstrated, a liar, a bigamist, and a dishonest businessman, a man who had bankrupted his father and abandoned his wife and children. But when it came to deconstruction Atlas shrugged his shoulders, and when it came to de Man's wartime writing he took refuge in an overwhelming question: "As for what he did, how can any of us know what we would have done under those same circumstances? De Man was in his early 20's when he wrote for Le Soir, an erratic young man capable of suggesting that Jews were a 'pollutant' and of sheltering them in his own home." The sentiment was disheartening, because it betokened a lack of confidence in our ability to examine history and to summon up the moral imagination needed to judge people and events. To ask who among us would have done otherwise was to endorse a line of reasoning that could be used to justify an eyes-shut attitude toward all manner of wickedness. It seemed less than fair to the many who resisted Hitler rather than succumb to mass hysteria—the many who did not do as Paul de Man had done.

The notion that "there is a Hitler in each of us"—that the fault lies with mankind in the abstract rather than with particular human beings—has long been a fashionable response to the moral disasters of our age. It is a convenient response and an antihistorical one, enabling the timorous to shirk the task of judging any individual instance of what is held to be, after all, a global condition. The ostentatious breast beating that would preclude the passing of judgment is intolerable because it is a sin against memory—it would eradicate the differences, actual and historical, between torturers and victims, courageous citizens and craven ones. The appropriate standard by which to judge the bystanders and witnesses of Nazi Europe is not the antihero of fiction but the authentic heroes of the period, the men and women of the Resistance who risked their own lives to save the lives of others. In Denmark, after Himmler gave the orders for deportations to begin, over sixty-five hundred of that nation's seven thousand Jews were smuggled safely to Sweden, thanks not only to the Danish underground but to hundreds of ordinary citizens. Monica de Wichfeld, the British-born wife of a Danish aristocrat, became a national heroine for her work in the Resistance, saving Jews and sabotaging the occupation—for which the Nazis condemned her to death. The Resistance in Belgium, though far less effective, had its own heroes and heroines. Joseph-Ernst Cardinal van Roey spoke defiantly against the Nazis, lending the authority of his office to the Resistance. People from all classes and professions worked to save Jewish children from the fate of night and fog that awaited them at the other end of the deportation trains. A 1980 documentary entitled *As If It Were Yesterday* presents interviews with Belgians who had, at risk to themselves, given shelter to Jews. One interview is with the Belgian woman who hid the filmmaker's parents. These are some of the people, the places, and the deeds that should be kept in mind when the case of Paul de Man is weighed in the balance.

It sometimes seemed that every last article on the de Man affair provoked at least one counterarticle, along with a satchel of indignant letters to the editor. The reaction to Atlas's *Times* magazine piece was swift. The poet Louis Simpson fired off a letter in protest. "When President John F. Kennedy was assassinated, I remember hearing a woman say, 'We are all guilty,' " Simpson wrote. "It struck me as a fatuous remark, but it was not as despicable as Mr. Atlas's suggestion that we are all potentially cowards and collaborators." At the same time, Walter Kendrick of the *Voice Literary Supplement* took Atlas to task for writing a "worm's-eye biography of de Man that answers all the trivia questions and none of the important ones." Kendrick maintained that the one "reasonable, judicious voice" in the de Man hubbub was his own; he was referring to an earlier article he had written, one that J. Hillis Miller had pronounced to be "full of resentment, malice and undisguised xenophobia." In that earlier article, Kendrick had diagnosed de Man's wartime writing as symptomatic of a cynical opportunism that was also to be found in the academic careers of de Man's American followers. "De Man's work may or may not remain influential," Kendrick wrote. "In either case, the whole teapot tempest will probably amount to nothing more, since the de Manians never attempted to alter the world as they found it, merely to secure well-padded niches for themselves and their protégés. The worst crime they and their guru were guilty of is opportunism, which in America, deconstruction's destined home, hardly counts as a crime at all."

What now stuck in Kendrick's craw was the assault on journalists and "professor-journalists" that Derrida, Miller, and fellow travelers were mounting; to make sure everyone got the point, Kendrick signed his article "Prof. Walter Kendrick." "Derrida *thinks* he's advancing the orthodox, by now rather tiresome thesis that whatever de Man did or dreamed all those years ago (and we'll never really know, will we?), deconstruction soars above such petty matters, and those who practice it should receive merit bonuses," Kendrick argued. "What he *feels*, though, is rather different: He feels besmirched by newspapers, razzed by the wretches who write for them, indignant that such scum should presume to comment on those who publish in *Critical Inquiry*." Kendrick quoted some examples of Derridean vituperation directed at Jon Wiener, the history professor who wrote the article on de Man that ran in the *Nation;* Wiener teaches at the University of California, Irvine, the same university where Derrida and Miller hold appointments. Taking his biggest windup, Kendrick reared back and threw: "Derrida comes perilously close to proposing a standard of professional purity on a quasi-racial model. Professor Wiener's unforgivable sin was to hide under his chaste academic robes the black-and-white star of journalism." With this figure of speech, Kendrick came perilously close to proposing an equivalence between the persecuted Jews of Nazi Europe and American journalists today. So much for the "reasonable, judicious voice" of "Prof. Walter Kendrick." So much for the civility of professorial debate.

"In a profession full of fakeness, he was real," Barbara Johnson said of de Man at the time of his death. Now, however, the former protégée had no trouble bringing herself to condemn de Man's wartime journalism. In her essay on the revelations, Johnson quotes from the conclusion of "The Jews in Contemporary Literature"—where de Man considers "the creation of a Jewish colony far from Europe"— and comments: "How can one avoid feeling rage and disgust at a person who could write such a thing?" Johnson resists efforts to explain away what de Man had done. "The fact that de Man seems not to have been anti-Semitic in his personal life in 1940–42 (and certainly showed no trace of it in later years) only points up a too limited notion of what anti-Semitism is," she writes. "If there had not been people who, without any particular personal anti-Semitism, found the idea of deportation *reasonable,* there could have been no Holocaust." In declaring that there was a categorical break between de Man's Belgian and American careers, Johnson was thus able to defend the latter and excoriate the former; speaking in favor of deconstruction didn't oblige her to mount an apologia for de Man's collaborationist writings. With Johnson one might debate the merits of deconstruction—whether, for example, it is or isn't "hostile" to some crucial tenets of Western thought—but with her sense of the wrong de Man had done in *Le Soir,* it was hard to quarrel.

There was, then, no need for deconstructionists to hitch their wagon to de Man's fallen star—no need to enlist the methods of deconstruction to demonstrate that de Man's wartime words meant something other, something less odious, than what they appeared to say. Such an attempt would run the risk of achieving the very linkage—between de Man then and deconstruction now—that the deconstructionists presumably wanted to avoid. Yet some of de Man's ex-cohorts chose to make the attempt. By putting the strategies of deconstruction at the service of explaining (or explaining away) de Man's early "texts," the deconstructionists lifted the controversy to a new level of debate and aroused the very fears that they ostensibly sought to dispel.

Jacques Derrida took the lead. In the Spring 1988 issue of *Critical Inquiry,* Derrida wrote at length about the meaning of the de Man revelations. Reading this sixty-two-page barrage of words, one feels as if one had stumbled into a marathon est session in which bathroom breaks are forbidden; one's sense of reality begins to dissolve. The essay is entitled "Like the Sound of the Sea Deep within a Shell: Paul de Man's War." Derrida immediately makes it clear that the "war" he has in mind is the one that broke out in American newspapers in 1988— and only secondarily ("in another sense") the Second World War. "Whatever one may think of the ignorance, the simplism, the sensationalist flurry full of hatred which certain American newspapers displayed in this case, we will not engage in any negative evaluation of the press *in general,*" Derrida asserts—as if the overloading of negative terms in the first half of the sentence didn't override the cautious injunction in its second part. But what was most striking about Derrida's essay was not his vilification of deconstruction's critics but his lengthy labors at explicating—or deconstructing—de Man's articles in *Le Soir*. He would show us how to read de Man's *Le Soir* articles; he would demonstrate the deconstructive approach.

With reference to three specific articles in *Le Soir*, Derrida introduces an "on the one hand . . . on the other hand" set of binary oppositions. The longest of these discussions focuses, inevitably, on "The Jews in Contemporary Literature." *On the one hand,* de Man did write in that essay that Jews played an "important role" in "the phoney and disordered existence of Europe since 1920"; he did offer a stereotypical description of the Jewish mind (cold, detached, cerebral); he did aver that Jewish writers "have always remained in the second rank," and he did entertain the idea of "a solution to the Jewish problem" entailing the deportation of the Jews from Europe. It takes Derrida little more than a page and a half to sum up these terrifying elements of de Man's article. "Will I dare to say 'on the other hand' in the face of the *unpardonable* violence and confusion of these sentences?" Derrida asks. The answer is yes, he will—for the next eight pages.

On the other hand . . . And here all manner of extenuating circumstances are cited, and many unjustified inferences made. Derrida makes much of the fact that de Man gave a favorable mention in "The Jews in Contemporary Literature" to a quartet of writers. The writers de Man praised were Gide, Kafka, Lawrence, and Hemingway. To Derrida the choice of names speaks well of de Man—it was, writes Derrida, a "curious and insolent" list, not only because Kafka was Jewish but because these writers "represent everything that Nazism or the right wing revolutions would have liked to extirpate from history and the great tradition." Could this have been, on de Man's part, a covert way of subverting the Nazi doctrine that he was forced to mouth? Subsequent commentators, taking their cue from Derrida, solemnly cited a reference in de Man's later works to "double-talk, the necessary obliqueness of any persecuted speech that cannot, at the risk of survival, openly say what it means to say."

In response to this species of wishful thinking, one must concede that it is romantic to imagine that a piece of propaganda is really a coded message saying something very different. It also fits in nicely with the deconstructive notion that texts tend to sabotage themselves from within. It is also wrong: the available evidence suggests that Derrida and Co. were clutching at straws. For the inclusion of Kafka's name on de Man's list of praiseworthy writers proves little. Princeton professor Stanley Corngold, a onetime student of de Man, was the first to raise the question of the provenance of de Man's list. Corngold pointed out that de Man had, in an article written a year before "The Jews in Contemporary Literature," simply borrowed his list of canonical modern masters from Aldous Huxley's *Music at Night.* It is difficult to attach much significance, subversive or otherwise, to a rote sequence of names reeled off by one who is eager to display his literary mastery. Moreover, as Corngold observed, Huxley's list included a fifth name—that of Marcel Proust. De Man had put Proust's name under erasure. Perhaps de Man's prudent omission of Proust, in an article emphasizing the mediocrity of French Jewish writers, was the really telling gesture.

De Man's favorable mention of Kafka was one thing. Derrida also stresses that "The Jews in Contemporary Literature" begins with a rejection of "vulgar antisemitism." And it is true that de Man criticized the view that, in his words, European culture between the wars became "degenerate and decadent" because of the influence of the Jews. For the author of "The Jews in Contemporary Literature," it was a question of substituting one form of anti-Semitism for another. The Jews were not racial pollutants, pernicious and potent; rather they were properly to be regarded as mediocrities, who habitually exaggerated their own importance. They were of little essential value to European culture, which was healthy enough to withstand their influence. Were they deported to a colony far from Europe, the loss to Western civilization would be negligible. That is what de Man says in the article, and the context in which he says it is the massive, organized persecution of the Jews in Western Europe. But here is Derrida's deconstructive gloss on de Man's treatment of "vulgar antisemitism":

> What does this article say? It is indeed a matter of criticizing vulgar antisemitism. That is the primary, declared, and underscored intention. But to scoff at vulgar antisemitism, is that also to scoff at or mock the vulgarity of antisemitism? This latter syntactic modulation leaves the door open to two interpretations. To condemn vulgar antisemitism may

leave one to understand that there is a distinguished antisemitism in whose name the vulgar variety is put down. De
Man never says such a thing, even though one may condemn his silence. But the phrase can also mean something
else, and this reading can always contaminate the other in
a clandestine fashion: to condemn "vulgar antisemitism,"
especially if one makes no mention of the other kind, is to
condemn antisemitism itself *inasmuch as* it is vulgar, always
and essentially vulgar. De Man does not say that either. If
that is what he thought, a possibility I will never exclude,
he could not say so clearly in this context. One will say at
this point: his fault was to have accepted the context. Certainly, but what is that, to accept a context?

I have quoted this passage at some length for three reasons. First, there
is the speaker's slithering elusiveness—like a clever trial attorney, he
is careful not to commit himself to the various possibilities he holds
out. He doesn't quite say that de Man's notorious article reduces itself
to an undecidable aporia, but he doesn't deny that possibility either,
and in fact he provides its theoretical logic—that the contradictory
impulses in the article "contaminated [each] other in a clandestine
fashion." Second, there is Derrida's blithe departure from his own
doctrines as and where it suits him. Suddenly he invokes context and
personality, categories that deconstruction has supposedly dissolved;
suddenly he considers what de Man "thought" as distinct from what
he wrote—a ploy he would ordinarily never tolerate, for it is nothing
if not logocentric to suppose that a speaker's thought precedes his
words. Third, there is the way that Derrida proceeds to treat his own
frankly speculative suppositions as though they were somehow proven
statements of fact. In the paragraph following the one I've quoted,
Derrida repeats—without qualification this time—that "it is a matter
of condemning antisemitism *inasmuch as it is vulgar*"—as if, by a kind
of rhetorical fiat, de Man's article secretly condemns the prejudice it
openly displays. Indeed, writes Derrida, "if de Man's article is necessarily contaminated by the forms of vulgar antisemitism that frame it,
*these coincide in a literal fashion, in their vocabulary and logic, with the very
thing that de Man accuses,* as if his article were denouncing the neighboring articles."

In short, de Man's presumed opposition to "vulgar antisemitism" sufficed, for Derrida, to establish that de Man's work for *Le Soir* was "ambiguous and sometimes anticonformist." Never mind that the plain "journalistic" sense of the passage leads to the opposite conclusion. Derrida prefers a reading that would have de Man defending the Jews of Europe, by coded message. It is, of course, irrelevant to Derrida that the key to reading such a code would not be invented for a generation. De Man's rejection of "vulgar antisemitism" is more plausibly read as a conventional rhetorical strategy; a columnist frequently begins by considering and rejecting a point of view prior to formulating his own. In "The Jews in Contemporary Literature," de Man comes to his point soon enough: *"A solution to the Jewish problem that would lead to the creation of a Jewish colony isolated from Europe would not have, for the literary life of the West, regrettable consequences."* In superimposing his "on the one hand . . . on the other hand" structure onto an article that reaches such a conclusion, Derrida highlights just what is so perilous about reducing authors to text-machines, and texts to reversible binary oppositions. The *central* thrust of "The Jews in Contemporary Literature" is a defense of European literature and a willingness to throw the Jews to the wolves. The *marginal* element is a rejection of "vulgar antisemitism" in favor of, say, a less philistine variety. Making a deconstructive move you demote the center and elevate the marginal; you repeat yourself, add an emphasis, drop a qualifier, insert a few parenthetical digressions—and in the end you get just what you expected to find: one of those undecidable aporias that not only let de Man off the hook, just a little, but also let you salute de Man's theory of reading in the process. Derrida's reading of "The Jews in Contemporary Literature" thus seemed to confirm the worst fears of deconstruction's critics. It demonstrated what can happen when textual ingenuity is used not at the service of the truth but simply to allow a highly idiosyncratic personality to strut and fret his hour upon the stage. And this was not just another text to be analyzed with a flourish; this touched a traumatic period of history still alive in the nerve endings of the survivors and their children.

Borrowing Derrida's logic, one could deconstruct *Mein Kampf* to reveal that its author was conflicted on the subject of the Jews: "On the one hand, he did regard the Jews as the enemy of everything German. On the other hand, he repudiated religious anti-Semitism." For Hitler adopts in *Mein Kampf* a rhetorical strategy not unlike that of "The Jews in Contemporary Literature." Like de Man, he begins by making a critique of a prevalent form of anti-Semitism; while de Man rejects "vulgar anti-Semitism," Hitler dismisses "sham anti-Semitism." According to Hitler, the Christian Social Party had the right general idea in vilifying the Jews but went about it the wrong way. The party's mistake was to put anti-Semitism on a religious basis—as though the condition of being Jewish could be altered with a mere "splash of baptismal water." Jews, Hitler insisted, were "not Germans of a special religion but a people in themselves"; therefore, the solution to the Jewish problem had to be racial and biological, not social and religious. Hitler's intent in *Mein Kampf* is unambiguous. But a rhetorical reading could dwell on the author's critique of religious anti-Semitism, which he disparaged as "superficial" and as possibly even "an expression of a certain competitive envy." Farfetched? No more so than some of the briefs filed in behalf of Paul de Man.

Derrida's apologia for de Man proceeded by intimation rather than by direct argument; he spun off possibilities without committing himself to them. But there was no denying the effect that Derrida's essay had on de Man's admirers. One after another followed with essays less subtle than Derrida's in ascribing to "The Jews in Contemporary Literature" a mitigating sense of complexity and ambiguity. A close reading could "prove" that de Man was writing in that essay primarily in defense of European literature and only incidentally lobbing grenades at the Jews. But you could go further. S. Heidi Krueger, for example, dwelled on de Man's "irony" in "The Jews in Contemporary Literature." Krueger went so far as to risk a comparison between de Man's anti-Semitic article and Jonathan Swift's "A Modest Proposal," that masterpiece of savage irony. She reached this stunning conclusion:

> Although one can argue that the irony of "The Jews in Contemporary Literature" misfires, it is difficult, reading the article as a whole and in the context of the articles with which it appears, to read it as other than a calculated (and parodistic) fore-grounding of the premises and applications of "vulgar anti-Semitism" evidenced in the other essays on the page. The tone, moreover, is one of detached mockery throughout the sections dealing with the Jews, and the object of the mockery is clearly not the Jews but rather the anti-Semites. Even the attribution of the view that the Jews

have had disproportionate influence on "occidental" literature to the Jews themselves reads, in this context, less as the
all too familiar strategy of blaming the victim, than as
tweaking the noses of the "vulgar anti-Semites," showing
them that their own most vehemently pronounced positions
are those of the scapegoats they wish to expel.

Krueger's verdict:

> I would submit that what is wrong with "The Jews in
> Contemporary Literature" is not that it is, in the first in-
> stance, anti-Semitic, but rather that if we read it in isolation,
> it is almost impossible to tell where it stands with regard
> to the situation of the Jews.

More astounding yet was Richard Rand's attempt to turn the tables
on the charge of anti-Semitism:

> In its ruminations on Paul de Man, *The Nation* has furnished
> this nation—as well as Germany, France, England and
> Switzerland—with a very neat, a very up-to-date piece of
> old-time "anti-Semitism." But the truly instructive thing
> about the exercise lies less in the perennial retail value of
> its bloodlust, than in the undeniable validity of its insight,
> and in the visionary correctness of its charge: for are not,
> indeed, Paul de Man and his deconstruction somehow over-
> whelmingly Jewish—as Jewish as anyone, perhaps, in our
> multi-national 1980s, can be?

One could scarcely believe one's eyes: Paul de Man had "somehow"
become a Jew! "That Paul de Man, biographically speaking, was not
himself Jewish, is nothing to the point," Rand went on. "From the
sixteenth century onward, American anti-Semitism, among other varieties, has been a discourse of bigotry *displaced.*" If Rand's statement
were a move made in a chess game, one would transcribe it with a
question mark and a double exclamation point. *Paul de Man could not
have been anti-Semitic, for in fact de Man was the real Jew in this affair!*
Surely this was the ultimate defense—and the ultimate absurdity. By
reversing the meanings of "Jew" and "anti-Semite," Rand was making

an application of the deconstructive method. What he dramatized is the eerie similarity of that method to Orwellian doublethink. Happy the deconstructor who can prove, or at least get himself to believe, that black is white, that the four raised fingers of a hand make five, and that those who excoriate Paul de Man's anti-Semitism reveal themselves to be anti-Semites.

Christopher Norris, a prominent British explainer of de Man and Derrida, employed a different denial-campaign device: obfuscation. In the *London Review of Books,* Norris speculated about Paul de Man's probable reaction to the discovery of his wartime "texts": "Though their existence remained a secret all those years, de Man would, I think, have acknowledged their discovery with the attitude *scripta manent:* that what is written is written and cannot be tactfully ignored, no matter how far his convictions had changed in the interim." Norris's use of a conditional construction was bizarre considering that what de Man *did* all his life was—precisely—to "tactfully ignore" his guilty past. Norris proffered a benign interpretation of Hendrik de Man's public declarations welcoming the Nazis into Belgium in 1940. "His response to the catastrophe of German occupation," Norris wrote, "was to draw up a last-ditch tactical plan, arguing that Nazism might, after all, evolve into something like a genuine National Socialism, and that therefore the only course open was to pin one's hope to that saving possibility and not hold out against the occupying forces." But for Hendrik de Man, the German occupation of Belgium was most decidedly not "a catastrophe." On the contrary. Look up what Hendrik de Man said in his "manifesto" to the political party he headed, and this is what you find: "The war has led to the debacle of the parliamentary regime and of the capitalist plutocracy in the so-called democracies. For the working classes and for socialism, this collapse of a decrepit world is, far from a disaster, a deliverance." Hendrik de Man called for collaboration with the Germans. To characterize this as "a last-ditch tactical plan" is to make plain the writer's agenda: to put the best possible face on the de Man disclosures, for the sake of saving the prestige of his name and his movement, and not to let history stand in the way. As for Norris's labors to explicate de Man in relation to Martin Heidegger, the no-nonsense British philosopher A. J. Ayer quoted a representative sample of Norris's prose and pronounced it "gibberish."

In the face of all this strategic defensiveness, it was hard to escape the conclusion that the responses to the de Man case had eclipsed in importance the offensive articles themselves. What de Man wrote in *Le Soir* had the effect of exploding the myth of the man and modifying our understanding of his writings. But what was said in his defense broadened the focus considerably. Deconstruction itself, as a method of reading and as an intellectual movement, now stood in the camera's eye. How benign a method could it be if its proponents could so blatantly use it to explain away inconvenient facts and turn an unfortunate truth on its head? The approved deconstructive reading of "The Jews in Contemporary Literature" would reduce it to an arena of contradictory impulses—this was the *reductio ad absurdum* of Paul de Man's theory of rhetoric. What a curious irony that he had himself provided the posthumous text that would, when subjected to close analysis, demonstrate once and for all the danger of a rhetorical method that can be used to deny disagreeable truths—that can be used to deny *what is there*. One might even say that de Man's *Wartime Journalism* deconstructs the companion volume of *Responses*—that what he actually wrote exposes the pretensions and the fallacies of the deconstructive commentary.

And perhaps American journalists had performed a public service after all, for it was their coverage of the case that obliged the deconstructionists to show their true colors. As if in fulfillment of a prophecy made in the language of a newspaper headline—"Deconstructing de Man," say, or "The (de) Man Who Put the Con in Deconstruction"—deconstruction itself had reached a terminal impasse. The deconstructors had proudly proclaimed the elimination of pathos from their critical vocabulary. Yet here was a spectacle that could be accounted for only as the expression of a pure pathos: the veneration of a personality that could survive any number of grim biographical shocks. Over this fallen idol the self-styled iconoclasts revealed themselves to be, after all, a thoroughly idolatrous crew.

A final word must be said about *rhetoric*—the rhetoric on display as the case of Paul de Man got fought out. Again and again one encountered the most extraordinary recklessness with historical facts—the transformation of those facts, by rhetorical sleight of hand, into metaphor, myth, or fictional construct. Indeed, despite their heavy reliance on rhetorical analysis, it appears that the masters of deconstruction have neglected to examine their own rhetoric with sufficient rigor. For here was rhetoric in full flourish, a parade of figures of speech. Facts, the intractable historical facts of the Second World War, were transmuted into metaphor; history was routinely appropriated to serve the ends of rhetorical persuasion. There was, first of all, Derrida's statement that a condemnation of de Man would "reproduce the exterminating gesture." A critic of de Man was, in other words, no better than an exterminating Nazi. J. Hillis Miller followed with his combative assertion that members of the university were guilty of "collaborating" with the mass media in a plot to defame deconstruction. For Walter Kendrick, fighting fire with fire, the journalists on the de Man beat wore "black-and-white stars"—journalists this time the persecuted minority and the deconstructors their empowered tormenters. Most bizarre of all was Richard Rand's argument that de Man and his partisans were the real Jews in the case. It is not enough to scorn such rhetorical attempts at appropriating the roles of victim and persecutor in all their pathos and horror. It is also necessary to remind oneself of the dangers that ensue when metaphors substitute for facts, when words lose their meaning, and when signifiers and signifieds part company, with the deconstructionist's blessing.

CHAPTER 10

SIGNS

OF THE

TIMES

The fact that universal thought, in all its domains, by all its pathways and despite all differences, should be receiving a formidable impulse from an anxiety about language—which can only be an anxiety of language, within language itself—is a strangely concerted development; and it is the nature of this development not to be able to display itself in its entirety as a spectacle for the historian, if, by chance, he were to attempt to recognize in it the sign of an epoch, the fashion of a season, or the symptom of a crisis. Whatever the poverty of our knowledge in this respect, it is certain that the question of the sign is itself more or less, or in any event something other, than a sign of the times. To dream of reducing it to a sign of the times is to dream of violence.

—*Jacques Derrida,*
"Force and Signification" (1963)

In the first week of October 1988, Jacques Derrida visited the Cornell University campus in his capacity as a professor-at-large on its faculty. It was the final year of a six-year appointment that required him to visit the campus periodically, deliver lectures, and hold seminars. His visit would last a week. On Monday and Wednesday, he would lecture on "The Politics of Friendship," and on Friday he would conduct a seminar on the subject. An overflow audience awaited him on Monday. Every available seat in the auditorium was taken with a quarter of an hour still to go before the start of the lecture. The latecomers among the estimated five hundred students and faculty members present sat in the aisles, stood in the entranceway, and otherwise squeezed themselves in. Some were there just to capture a glimpse of the famous French philosopher—"Europe's foremost philosopher and interdisciplinary scholar," as the university newsletter put it. A dapper man in a blue pinstripe suit appeared, greeted a few friends in the audience, then took his place before the lectern, adjusting his reading glasses. The hum of anticipation in the crowd was palpable. The undergraduate sitting behind me whispered excitedly to her companion, "He isn't God," in the tone of one who is trying to persuade herself of something. That, I remembered, is what one hapless National League batsman said about Dwight Gooden of the New York Mets in 1985, the year Doc was virtually unhittable. *He isn't God, man.*

Derrida had asked his audience to do a little advance reading for the occasion. A packet of essays by Aristotle, Montaigne, Kant, Nietzsche, and Maurice Blanchot was available for a nominal charge at a local photocopy center. The "readings" suggested that we were in for a round of deconstructive textual analysis, but the title of Derrida's lecture aroused a different expectation—the general expectation that he would treat, in some way, the case of Paul de Man. This, too, helped to account for the anticipatory hum in Ives Hall that Monday afternoon. "The Politics of Friendship": perhaps, in time-honored deconstructive fashion, the two concepts designated in the title were like the halves of a contradictory whole—and didn't the de Man affair dramatize the conflicting vectors? Derrida was, after all, a friend and intellectual ally of de Man. Now, presumably, the obligations of friendship tugged him in one direction, while the political nature of the de Man disclosures yanked him in the other. That, at any rate, was one plausible construction of "The Politics of Friendship." There were others, but common to most of them was the sense that de Man would be—and couldn't help being—a vital presence in Derrida's discourse.

What Derrida had in mind, however, was something altogether more abstract, something like the deconstruction of friendship as historically conceived in the Western philosophical tradition. Though he made fleeting references to the question of "friendship with the dead," and though the ghost of de Man never did vacate the lecture hall, Derrida was there to call into question the concepts of *politics* and *friendship*—and to invoke the possibility of a politics based not on the paradigm of friends-and-enemies but on the concept of a friendship "that doesn't yet exist," a concept of friendship "based on equality." All this became evident after the second of Derrida's lectures on Wednesday. That Monday, however, he was intent on posing a conundrum, pondering it, repeating it like a leitmotif meant to connect the otherwise disparate parts of his discourse. He commenced his lecture by quoting Montaigne, who was himself citing Aristotle: "O my friends there is no friend." The two parts of the sentence are incompatible, Derrida observed. If there is no friend, to whom am I speaking? Or, with a shift in the tonal emphasis: if I can address you as my friends, how can I say there is no friend?

O my friends there is no friend. The rhetorical structure of the line was that of the apostrophe—that is, a figure of speech in which an absent being is addressed as though it were present. Derrida repeated the line frequently during the course of the day's lecture, leaving it in no doubt that he found it a fruitful aporia. One of his detours was to Carl Schmitt, an antidemocratic political thinker active in Germany in the 1920s and 1930s. Schmitt stood, Derrida said, in a "complex" relation to Nazism. He quoted Schmitt to the effect that politics is based on "a discrimination between friend and enemy," and that "nations group themselves according to the friend-enemy antithesis." In Schmitt's analysis, the difference between entities amounts not to a tolerable "otherness" but to a determined opposition. Remove the sense of opposition and, in Derrida's words, "the political loses its boundaries." Derrida also presented a passage from Nietzsche's *Human, All Too Human:* " 'Friends, there are really no friends!' Thus cried the expiring old sophist. 'Foes, there is really no foe!' Thus shout I, the incarnate fool." Nietzsche had committed a complex rhetorical gesture; Derrida called it a "catapostrophe"—that is, an inversion of Aristotle's apostrophe. In what way, asked Derrida, did Nietzsche "overturn" Greek tradition? Back to Aristotle. Friendships as Aristotle conceived them can be based on virtue, or usefulness, or pleasure. But "perfect friendship," said Derrida, is a contradiction in terms. Why? Because one must wish for the greatest good for one's friend, which is to wish him to become God, but you can't be friends with God— "there'd be no proportional equality between the partners." Besides, you can't want to deify a friend, since friendship has to do with men, not God. And then, too, God has no need of friends. Therefore, if "perfect" or "true" friendship tends toward raising the "other" into a divinity, perfect friendship is a contradiction. Another aporia. *O my friends there is no friend.* There followed an aside to the audience: "You hold me responsible for the fact that I am speaking, and by holding me personally responsible, you are implying some knowledge of what responsibility means." *O my friends there is no friend.* "A strange affirmation. There must be friends or how could I be addressing them this way?" The sentence turns to the future, a vision of a democracy "still to come." It also turns to the past, implying a prior sense of community—if only the minimal community of a common language. But *O my friends there is no friend* leaves out the present. And so, Derrida asked as Monday's lecture drew to a close, "Is friendship ever present?"

I was eager to know what the persons sitting on either side of me thought of the performance. The professor of cinema on my right said, "Have we learned anything about friendship at this point?" The graduate student on my left found it surprisingly easy to follow, unlike a Derrida lecture she had attended as a Harvard undergraduate. She likened *that* experience to a parlor game in which nursery rhymes are recited backward—"you know, phrases and concepts keep getting reversed." The woman sitting behind me ("He isn't God") disappeared before I could ascertain her reaction, but a man who teaches in the English department told me that he had figured out why Derrida leaves you in a state of mystification. "Have you noticed how many of his sentences seem to begin with conditional clauses? You're always waiting for the main clause and it never comes. Derrida is a prisoner of the subjunctive mood." Another literature professor launched a diatribe against deconstruction and opined that it had gained a strong foothold at Cornell because "most people in English are conflict avoiders," who preferred to remain uninformed about critical theory rather than contend with it. Later, I ran into a professor of philosophy who recalled John Searle's famous critique of deconstruction. Searle's essay was entitled "The Word Upside Down," and in it he argued that "deconstruction had found little appeal among professional philosophers." The exceptions to this rule, wrote Searle, "tend to be ambiguous allies." One such "ambiguous ally" had evidently described Derrida as "the sort of philosopher who gives bullshit a bad name." Searle was acerb: "We cannot, of course, exclude the possibility that this may be an expression of praise in the deconstructionist vocabulary." I asked my friend whether he agreed with Searle and he smiled. In the next day's *Cornell Daily Sun* I read that "reactions to Derrida's lecture varied from refusals to comment to enthusiastic appraisals of his ideas."

On Wednesday, perhaps half as many as Monday's five hundred turned out. They witnessed a bravura performance that lasted two hours. It became clear that Derrida's thoughts were on the ideals of the French Revolution, whose bicentenary was fast approaching. *Liberty, equality, fraternity.* Of the three, fraternity is perhaps the least examined, and it was the concept of fraternity that Derrida meant to deconstruct. "Fraternity? *Cela suffit!*" he said. Fraternity—that is, the treatment of friendship in the Western philosophical tradition—was exclusionary, Derrida maintained. True friendship is understood as possible between two men but never between a man and a woman or between two women. "The double exclusion privileges the brother, even above the father," Derrida said—fighting words in a discourse in which *patriarchy* is in as much disrepute as, say, *phallogocentrism.* Derrida waxed eloquent urging an ideal of friendship based not on fraternity but on equality: nonhierarchic, heterogeneous, and "respectful of the asymmetry that is common to everyone." "When will we be ready for an experience of equality that would at last be just, that would measure up to its measurelessness?" he asked. "How can we build a politics on friendship?" In repeating Aristotle's apostrophe—"O my friends, there is no friend"—Derrida was thus making an appeal to the future. True friendship may not yet be possible in society as it is constituted at present; the concept as adumbrated in the Western philosophical heritage may, what's more, be self-contradictory. Under these circumstances, the speaker's invocation of his "friends" becomes a visionary imperative, prophesying their eventual emergence. *O my friends* is hopeful, oriented toward "the democracy to come"; *there is no friend* mournfully looks to the past. The deconstructive aporia, in this case, turns out to be not an impasse but a vaguely utopian hope, a visionary plea.

Derrida had given us a lesson in the deconstructive method. He had proceeded by allusion and quotation, neologism and rhetorical analysis; most strikingly, he had worked over a figure of speech until it seemed to embody a philosophical position. It was, as an approach to philosophy, curiously poetic in its logic—its arabesques and leaps, though incongruous in philosophical discourse, would not be out of place in a poem. True, it remained difficult to say whether, as the cinema professor had asked, we had "learned anything about friendship at this point"—or, at any rate, anything that required the full deconstructive treatment. But to the upholders of the orthodoxy, that question would have been out of order. The point of the performance was, evidently, the performance itself. Derrida had offered us philosophy as a species of text analysis, the exposure of the rhetorical loopholes in the positions espoused by an Aristotle or a Kant.

Following the formal part of his lecture, Derrida entertained a few questions from the audience. The most entertaining of these illustrated the tendency of the disciple to try to go one better than the master. A bearded graduate student brought up Derrida's analysis of Kant on friendship. According to Derrida, Kant understood friendship to combine the feelings of *love* and *respect.* But, said Derrida, the two feelings contradict one another. Love implies attraction; respect implies repulsion, the maintaining of a distance. Thus, friendship in Kant has a contradictory character. The graduate student, knowing Derrida's penchant for binary oppositions that cancel themselves out, asked whether *love* and *respect* couldn't themselves perhaps be further reduced; couldn't they, too, be subdivided into contradictory halves? I thought of the conclusion of *Fear and Trembling,* in which Kierkegaard explores the ancient lineage of the "impulse to go further." Kierkegaard cites the aphorism of Heraclitus, "You can't walk into the same river twice." A disciple of Heraclitus was determined to go further: "You can't even do it once." The disciple had so "improved" the master's thesis that it became a statement denying the principle of movement and flux. "And yet," writes Kierkegaard, "that disciple wanted only to be a disciple of Heraclitus . . . and to go further—not back to the position Heraclitus had abandoned."

The scheduled "seminar" on Friday turned out to be an extended question-and-answer session. Perhaps fifty people attended. As is frequently the case at such gatherings, many of the questions seemed motivated by something other than the desire for an answer—you could tell by the difficulty the questioners had in coming to a point or in framing a question. Some were simply trying to establish an individual relation, however fleeting, with the renowned speaker. A professor of romance studies tossed him a verbal bouquet, or tried to. He observed that a certain passage in Montaigne's essay on friendship is "the most Derrida-like passage in Montaigne." (Derrida disagreed.) Others were intent on displaying their mastery of the deconstructive prose machine. With the air of the star pupil, a literature professor returned to O my friends there is no friend. Was the "asymmetry" in the apostrophe not an example of the "breakdown between performative and constative language?" This afforded Derrida an opportunity he could seize. "The asymmetry of the sentence makes one wonder which half of the equation is subordinate," he said, then launched a monologue that concluded with the observation that "one of the most interesting features of phallogocentrism" is that "you can't have an animal as a friend." Question: "You said that women are excluded [from traditional concepts of friendship], yet Aristotle likens friendship to the mother's desire to know her child." Answer: "Mothers are not necessarily women."

Among all the questions, two seemed to linger in the air after the performance had ended. A philosophy student took the floor and spoke of wanting "to hold people responsible or blameworthy for their phallogocentrism." Nervously, tentatively, he broached "the name of the friend who can't be named, the person of whom you do not want to speak." "Who would that be?" Derrida asked. "Paul de Man," the student said. There erupted the sort of crowd ripple you get when propriety gives way to curiosity and somebody summons up the nerve to ask the question on everyone's mind. Derrida would have none of it. Reiterating the point he made in his Critical Inquiry essay, he cautioned the group from passing judgment on de Man. "The concept of making a charge itself belongs to the structure of phallogocentrism," he said. "But," the questioner persisted, "aren't you yourself passing judgment on phallogocentrism?" No, replied Derrida. His aim was not to put phallogocentrism on trial. In fact, he added, "I have a deep respect for the phallogocentric tradition." Derrida remained straight-faced, but the laughter in the room was general. Perhaps some in the audience recalled that in the previous day's lecture Derrida had identified "respect" with "repulsion."

The final question of the day was posed by a young woman,

blushing with earnestness, who quoted a line from the psychoanalytical theorist Jacques Lacan: *il n'y a pas des relations sexuelles*—there are no sexual relations. Could there be, she asked, some parallel between this statement and *O my friends there is no friend?* Could Derrida, at any rate, comment on Lacan's line? She was having a hard time formulating her question, and when she did so, Derrida asked her to clarify the point. The young man sitting in front of me turned to the young woman next to him and said, "That was a stupid question." "I think it was a very good question," the young woman answered. For my part, I thought I understood the questioner's logic. There is no friend, yet our vocabulary of friendship implies that there can be; mightn't the same be true of spouses? Only then did the humor of the situation occur to me. If you could separate yourself from this voluble discourse, viewing it as if you were a spy from ordinary life, wasn't there something altogether precious in the spectacle? A young woman in the world's most permissive society asks the visiting celebrity whether there is such a thing as sexual relations, and the audience ponders the profundity of the moment.

Derrida was speaking. In so many words he said that he would have to think about it.

Ten months after Derrida spoke at Cornell on "The Politics of Friendship," a new controversy erupted over "the name of the friend who cannot be named." The editors of *Critical Inquiry* had received "a great many unsolicited responses" to Derrida's "Like the Sound of the Sea Deep within a Shell: Paul de Man's War." Electing to devote the better part of their Summer 1989 issue to the continuing flap, the editors offered six such critical responses along with Derrida's foaming-at-the-mouth reply to his critics. Perhaps it was predictable that Derrida, given the last word, would write at greater length (sixty-one pages) than the others combined (forty-seven pages); Derrida is notoriously garrulous. Whether predictable or not, it was appropriate that Derrida's textual analysis of de Man's wartime journalism would come in for careful scrutiny. It was as if, in the conflict between the deconstructionists and their critics, one area of battle—whether announced or not—was over reading, how to read, how to interpret texts. Derrida's reading of de Man had willy-nilly become a test case of deconstructive criticism. The irony was that Derrida had insisted all along that what de Man wrote during the war had no bearing on the theories he espoused many years later. Yet Derrida's own deconstructive labors to elucidate the complexities of de Man's *Le Soir* articles had hastened the very development he had wanted to avert. Hadn't Derrida encouraged a link between the terms *response* and *responsibility*—so that "responding" to the de Man disclosures, as he was doing, would constitute an act of "responsibility"? Wasn't he thereby inviting readers to examine his essay and arrive at some conclusions about deconstruction's claims to critical "responsibility"?

To the extent that Derrida's essay resembled an apologia for his late friend—to the extent that the deconstruction of de Man's articles entailed an inventory of extenuating circumstances—it was possible that Derrida had managed to hoist deconstruction on its own petard. That was the argument made by John Brenkman and Jules David Law, the co-authors of one of the six responses to Derrida that *Critical Inquiry* published. Brenkman and Law cited Derrida's claim that deconstruction is an intellectual weapon against totalitarianism. With such claims, wrote Brenkman and Law, "Derrida puts the prestige of deconstruction on the line: its political significance, its power to explain political and cultural conjunctures, and its capacity for self-understanding. If these remain staked on the procedures and outcomes of his account of 'Paul de Man's War,' the wager will be lost."

Of the six responses to Derrida in that issue of *Critical Inquiry,* one—Jonathan Culler's—took exception to "Derrida's exceedingly severe" judgment on de Man's wartime writings in *Le Soir* and *Het Vlaamsche Land.* Culler objected in particular to Derrida's "on the one hand" statement that "the *massive, immediate, and dominant* effect of all these texts is that of a *relatively* coherent ideological ensemble which, *most often and in a preponderant fashion,* conforms to an official rhetoric, that of the occupation forces." It will be remembered that Culler is the critical theorist who endorsed, in his book *On Deconstruction,* the procedure of sawing off the branch on which one is sitting. In his response to Derrida, however, Culler more closely resembled the disciple determined to go further than the master. "The important question is what value [de Man's] critical and theoretical writings have for us," Culler wrote. And his answer was that "the wartime writings give a new dimension to much of de Man's work in America, helping one to understand more plainly what is implied by his critique of the aesthetic ideology." By such logic one might feel positively grateful to de Man for the work he did in *Le Soir*. Far from disturbing our presupposed admiration for de Man, these articles will help us, diligent students that we are, in our continuing devotion to his work. The historical significance of the writings is waved away, along with all ethical questions. If the "important question" has to do with de Man's later "theoretical" writings, the articles in *Le Soir* and *Het Vlaamsche Land* have been leveled to the status of annotative footnotes. "De Man's critique of the aesthetic ideology now resonates also as a critique of the fascist tendencies he had known." Well, that was one very charitable way of looking at it.

Culler characterized as "exceedingly severe" Derrida's judgment of what de Man had done. All the other respondents contended that Derrida had not been severe enough. Jean-Marie Apostolides, a Stanford University professor of French, interpreted Derrida's essay as "an argument to exculpate de Man." For Apostolides this was evidence that deconstruction "escapes confrontation with historical development," and for this reason: "Because history reveals the 'decidable,' which sometimes means guilt," whereas deconstruction is committed to the view that all texts are undecidable at the core. Marjorie Perloff, of Stanford's English faculty, faulted Derrida for ignoring the particular history of *Le Soir*. She noted Derrida's ire at the loose and inexact definition of deconstruction that the present-day *Le Soir* provided in its coverage of the de Man disclosures in December 1987: "Whether, in other words, *Le Soir* did or did not collaborate with the Nazis seems to matter less to him than whether today's *Le Soir* can give its readership an accurate picture of deconstruction." Perloff was troubled, too, by Derrida's "assumption that the writer who helps fellow writers and artists is somehow exempt from ordinary moral obligations." As for Wolfgang Holdheim, Derrida's "mystificatory" essay was self-evidently an apology for de Man. The "on the one hand, on the other hand" structure that Derrida had placed on "The Jews in Contemporary Literature" amounted to a determined effort at "making the text say something other than what it says." Holdheim was anxious to dispel the supposition that de Man's guilt was primarily a function of superior hindsight: "Once and for all: the act [of propagandizing in collaborationist journals] was considered even more unacceptable at that time than it may seem today, and pointing this out is not a judgment but the reminder of *a historical fact.*" Holdheim was suspicious of Derrida's exhortations that we now must "reread de Man from A to Z." It is, wrote Holdheim, "almost as if certain circles tried to make the best of a bad situation, turning the very scandal into a further demonstration of their hero's overriding significance. What underlies those exhortations is still another axiom: the unquestioned assumption that de Man's late work is beyond critique and demystifying throughout. But what if this dogmatic assumption is questioned?"

Jon Wiener, who had reported on the de Man disclosures for the *Nation,* attended to Derrida's vilification of the press. Derrida had denounced "the sensationalist flurry full of hatred" in the first journalistic accounts of the de Man case. Derrida had in mind the article with which the *New York Times* broke the story in December 1987. But this, Wiener observed, was how that article began: "In a finding that has stunned scholars, a Yale professor revered as one of the most brilliant intellectuals of his generation wrote for an anti-Semitic, pro-Nazi newspaper in Belgium during World War II." Hardly a voice "full of hatred." Wiener took umbrage, too, at Derrida's assertion that to judge and condemn de Man is tantamount to reproducing "the exterminating gesture which one accuses de Man of not having armed himself against sooner." Wiener's comment: "Derrida thus draws a rhetorical connection between criticism of de Man and extermination of the Jews—an offensive argument that hardly helps de Man's case." Finally, John Brenkman and Jules David Law of Northwestern University concentrated on de Man's "ideological commitment to fascism," which they felt Derrida had obscured. They argued that Derrida, in his quest for the saving ambiguities in de Man's wartime writing, had overlooked "the most obvious tension animating de Man's complex, evolving project: on the one hand, de Man was a Nazi collaborator; on the other hand, he was a Belgian fascist."

Derrida's critics were anything but friendly. Without exception, however, they observed the rules of civility. Several went out of their way to pay their respect. Perloff began her essay with an old-fashioned courtly gesture, a reference to Derrida's "eloquence." Brenkman and Law complimented Derrida on the "often moving testimony of his personal and intellectual ties to de Man," even while maintaining that he had let friendship stand in the way of lucid analysis. Certainly none of the respondents was as playfully irreverent as Walter Kendrick had been in the *Voice Literary Supplement.* Analyzing Derrida's prose in "Like the Sound of a Sea Deep within a Shell: Paul de Man's War," Kendrick thought he could discern five propositions "looming in the murk." The five: "(1) World War II did not take place; (2) World War II took place in Paul de Man's left ear; (3) World War II took place, but only in newspapers; (4) Paul de Man's left ear was made of newspapers; (5) deconstruction is an unfortunate byproduct of the French conditional." In contrast to such high-spirited mockery, the professors who dissented with Derrida in *Critical Inquiry* took care to present their views in sober accents with a minimum of emotional display.

Not so Derrida. In his amazing response to his critics, "Biodegradables: Seven Diary Fragments," Derrida came out swinging. Not the substance of his reply but its hyperbole and belligerence made this an unforgettable performance. It was a sustained rant, proceeding not by argumentation but by invective. Rather than refute his critics, Derrida ridiculed them, heaped contempt on their heads, spewed out vitriol. A brief concordance of the adjectives with which Derrida conducted his rhetorical warfare turns up the following, all directed at those who had the temerity to criticize him: "abusive," "arrogant," "crude," "degraded," "dishonest," "grossly wrong," "ignorant and aberrant," "indecent," "murderous," "naive," "obscene," "obtuse," "outright laughable," "venomous," and "violent." Derrida was, he said, writing in the teeth of a "crusade against de Man and against 'Deconstruction.' " He did not shrink from attributing malign motives to his critics. Other than Culler, the respondents had all expressed their "frightened, painful, and truly excessive hatred." They wrote *"dishonestly and in bad faith* (I am weighing my words carefully)." Moreover, their statements on deconstruction were "uninformed, uneducated and grotesque descriptions (I am weighing my words carefully)." For their elementary refusal—or was it their inability—to read the documents in question, Derrida coined one of his patented neologisms. Combining the French infinitives *pouvoir* and *vouloir,* he declared that his opponents *ne pveulent pas lire*—they "can't/won't" read.

Derrida fancied himself a besieged Napoleon. "An army has been mobilized against an article," he railed. "What effrontery! What a number of fronts I must confront!" Very well: he would divide and conquer. On the one hand, there was Culler's insistence that Derrida had been "exceedingly severe" on de Man; on the other hand, the five other respondents said the opposite. An absolute contradiction! Derrida was ecstatic. "Well," he said, "they can't all be right at the same time." As a debating tactic this was extraordinary—it ascribed to

Culler's highly idiosyncratic position a weight equal to that of the combined force of the other dissenters. But for Derrida extraordinary measures are routine. He was not to be deterred by "anyone who might regret the harshness or the high-handedness of certain of my remarks." Given the "violence" and the "mediocrity" of his opponents, it was positively his duty to respond in "a high-handed tone." Derrida must relish the rhetorical impact of three insults in a series. His critics offered "murderous caricatures, abusive simplifications, unjustified acts of violence." Destined for the oblivion of the compost heap—hence the title "Biodegradables"—were the "confused, hurried, and rancorous professor-journalists." Derrida contrasted the "ignorance, confusion, and bad faith" of one of his detractors with his own penchant for "nuanced, complicated, and meticulous" analysis. In short, his critics were "venomous," or they were "sleepyheads," guilty of "juvenile hysteria," or they radiated "arrogant bad faith," or "dishonesty," or "ignorance," or all of the above, and some had perpetrated "violent journalistic acts." In any case, they weren't merely his detractors. They were, wrote Derrida, his "censors."

Reading "Biodegradables" was a disconcerting experience. And here I am prompted to adopt Derrida's "on the one hand, on the other hand" strategy. On the one hand, Derrida can badger a reader into submission. He overwhelms with the sheer rhetorical force of his writing—his emphatic repetitions, his savage scorn, his elliptical asides, his inveterate wordplay, his admitted "high-handedness." To read Derrida at length, which is how he asks to be read, is to expose oneself to a mesmerist's power. Immersed in "Biodegradables," one feels the full force of his fury—and one understands the seductive attractions of submitting to his rhetoric. On the other hand, one can't ignore Derrida's reliance on insult and assertion to do the work of reasoned argumentation. It is as though he operates by dictatorial fiat: he is right because he says he is right. But isn't this—one hesitates before using the word—strikingly logocentric? For "Biodegradables" depends on the presumed authority of the speaker, the metaphysical "presence" that deconstruction has supposedly debunked. The unexamined assumption is that Derrida, as the author, is in a privileged position with regard to his earlier essay on de Man. He would tell us what he meant to say and ridicule those who revealed their ignorance or ineptness by disagreeing. He thus illustrates the deconstructive double standard: the theorist feels free to exempt himself from his own strictures. It is all very well to argue that all readings are misreadings and that the author doesn't know best. But see what happens when you give the author of that argument a taste of his own medicine. Criticize the deconstructionist, and this advocate of multiple interpretations and indeterminate texts suddenly behaves as though there is one right interpretation and that the author—that allegedly deceased and discredited entity—is entitled to the last word after all: "That is not what I meant at all."

It was a shock to come across Derrida's harangue so shortly after hearing his eloquent peroration on the possibilities of friendship in a society of equals. Where, now, was the visionary who foresaw the dissolving of politics, the end of the friend-enemy antithesis, and a new politics based on true friendship? He was nowhere in sight. Who was this thin-skinned, blustering, abusive fellow? How did this wounded, angry Caliban smuggle his way into Ariel's domain? The quality of rant in "Biodegradables" reminded one reader of the trial scene in *The Caine Mutiny*—the moment when Captain Queeg rolls his marbles in his hand as he loses his self-control. Perhaps, as the philosopher Richard Rorty has argued, the claim that deconstruction proceeds by "rigorous argument" was always so much bosh. For Rorty, "Derridadaism" comes closer to describing deconstruction in action. Rorty admires what he calls "the playful, distancing, oblique way in which Derrida handles traditional philosophical figures and tropes." Well, "rigorous argument" may be absent from "Biodegradables," but it is hard to admire the dance of intellect that permits a writer to confuse his critics with his "censors."

A change in the public perception of deconstruction may be inferred from the title piece of a much-acclaimed collection of stories published in 1990, *In a Father's Place* by Christopher Tilghman. The story's protagonist is Dan, a widower and the scion of a landed estate, whose children gather in the family seat for a summer weekend. Dan, a sympathetic fellow, feels estranged from his son Nick, an aspiring novelist. Nick has brought his friend Patty with him, and she is the villain of the piece. Contemptuous of Dan and his ancestral house, Patty spends most of the weekend in an antisocial posture: reading a book Tilghman identifies not by its title but by its author, Jacques Derrida. What does Nick see in Patty? She "tore the English Department at Columbia *apart*," Nick says. "I've never known anyone who takes less shit in her life." Patty wouldn't mind driving a wedge between Nick and his family. Nick, she says, is "trying to deconstruct this family" in his novel. "Deconstruct? You mean destroy?" Dan replies. The story reaches its climax when Dan throws Patty out of the house. "Oh, cut the crap about his work," he says. "You want his soul, you little Nazi, you want any soul you can get your hands on."

Has deconstruction, so long in the ascendant, begun to lose its momentum in academe? Yes and no. Define it narrowly with reference to the doctrines of Derrida and de Man, and the answer is a qualified yes. It is probable that deconstruction will never again enjoy the cachet that it had before history debunked de Man. The bad news is that nothing has arisen to take deconstruction's place, or rather that the theories now in vogue are in large and vital ways derivative of deconstruction. Unlike love, moreover, tenure is forever, and the tenure system will see to it that deconstructors remain in high institutional place for many years to come, proffering such hybrids as "deconstructive psychoanalysis," "deconstructive feminism," and "poststructuralist Marxism."

Paul de Man wrote "The Resistance to Theory" in 1981. A year later, two Berkeley professors, Steven Knapp and Walter Benn Michaels, took arms "Against Theory" in the pages of *Critical Inquiry;* the article, together with the responses and counterresponses it spawned, was published as a book in 1985. By decade's end, Frank Kermode chose to call his overview of the critical scene "The Limits of Theory." The progression in titles strongly suggests a downturn in the fortunes of critical theory in the academic marketplace. In ten years we have gone from the image of a military phalanx crushing the resistance in its path to that of an overextended army whose supply lines are in trouble. In reality, however, theorists remain the profession's dominant players—it's just that different theories are trying to crowd deconstruction off the stage. In an essay written before the de Man scandal broke, J. Hillis Miller identified deconstruction's main competition as coming from the political Left—from "young Marxists and Foucauldians" eager to restore to literary studies a concern for history and politics. "It is as if a great sigh of relief were rising up from all across the land," Miller writes. "The era of 'deconstruction' is over. It has had its day, and we can return with a clear conscience to the warmer, more human work of writing about power, history, ideology, the 'institution' of the study of literature, the class struggle, the oppression of women, and the real lives of men and women in society as they exist in themselves and as they are 'reflected' in literature."

Miller doesn't much like "the shift away from the rhetorical study of literature." But he is right in observing what the glamour theorists of the profession are up to. One recent development is known as the New Historicism; a related approach to literature goes by the name of "cultural materialism." What these approaches have in common is an interest in literature not in its own right, and not for moral instruction or aesthetic enjoyment, but for the light it may—inadvertently—shed upon the power relations in force at the time of a work's composition. Culture is conceived to be the result of economic and social power struggles, and a literary work—whatever its author's intentions—reflects the dominant ideology of the day. It becomes possible to study Shakespeare as the invention of different audiences from the seventeenth century to the present. Mark Twain may be rendered as a product of the social conventions of his time. George Orwell's books are shunted aside in favor of an investigation into his reputation—as if Orwell's claims on our attention had less to do with what he wrote than with an alleged conspiracy among professors and critics to foist Orwell on us. While studies of this nature vary widely in the quality of mind brought to them, and while they differ implicitly from the "rhetorical readings" championed by de Man and Miller, many of their tactics and their assumptions derive from the deconstructive enterprise: the notion that the "I" is not an autonomous individual but a social construct, that the "margins of the text" hold the interpretive key, that hierarchies cry out to be dismantled. After the deconstructive assault on meaning—the reduction of wars and revolutions to purely linguistic predicaments—it is easy to summon up two cheers for the return to history evinced by such critical theorists. It should also be noted that leftist literary critics were among the most conscientious and toughest-minded of those who wrote about the de Man disclosures. At the same time the ironies of the situation are too pointed to be ignored: the chief ideological drive behind the trendy theories of "social constructionism" and "cultural materialism" is a Marxist analysis of power and society. Who could have predicted that the nations of Eastern Europe would renounce Marxism before American literature professors did?

As a result of the de Man affair, the conflict between hard-core deconstructors and literary leftists—factions in whose mutual interest it may once have been to join forces—has progressed past the point of no return. Sooner or later, this was bound to happen; there was never any legitimate way of reconciling the antimetaphysical metaphysics of the one with the emphatic materialism of the other. There is evidence, too, of concerted new efforts to refute deconstruction on philosophical grounds. Several scholars are making the case that *Speech and Phenomena,* one of Derrida's seminal works, is based on a misreading of the philosopher Edmund Husserl. The charge is potentially quite damaging to Derrida, since *Speech and Phenomena* is one of the early books on which his reputation largely rests.

No, deconstruction is not quite the growth industry that it was a few years ago. But though the local reputations of the "boa-deconstructors" may show some slippage, the larger problem has not fundamentally changed. Pure deconstruction is no longer the height of fashion, but the impulse continues in alloyed form, and it is as ubiquitous as ever. The language, the categories, and the "war is peace" logic of deconstruction keep cropping up. The edicts of deconstruction—merged, to whatever extent, with the ideologies of Marxism, psychoanalytic theory, and feminism—remain the prevailing suppositions of the lit-crit establishment. One can discern a fundamental deconstructive procedure at work in the meteoric rise of "gender" and "ethnic" studies, at present the hottest areas in the lit-crit profession. It is an example of the marginal supplanting the central—and a clear-cut case of the way a theoretical maneuver can translate itself into a professional practice. The profession's latest hotshots are still asking the question de Man lifted from Archie Bunker: "What's the difference?" In 1992 the incoming president of the Modern Language Association will be Houston A. Baker of the University of Pennsylvania, whose most famous pronouncement is that there is no difference. Choosing between Virginia Woolf and Pearl Buck—between high literature and the middlebrow sort—is "no different from choosing between a hoagy and a pizza," Baker told a *New York Times* reporter. "I am one whose career is dedicated to the day when we have a disappearance of those standards."

Writing in the *New Republic,* Professor Lawrence Lipking of Northwestern University tries to acquaint the general reader with the distinguishing features of the current academic "episteme." Once upon a time, he writes, reading was simple: "the author put a meaning into a text, the reader took it out again." Today, however, reading has become "a knotty and treacherous business." The professional reader's rites of passage include a repudiation of much that used to be "common wisdom." One former article of faith held that literary criticism begins in reverence, "a feeling of awe in the presence of art." This assumption, Lipking writes, is not only "outmoded" but positively "embarrassing"; only a retrograde critic has a "reverence problem" or believes it to be the critic's function to illuminate poems or derive inspiration from them. To dramatize just how outmoded such assumptions are today, Lipking reaches for a telltale simile: "Even to say them out loud is embarrassing, like admitting to having voted for Nixon or smoking in public." The simile makes its elegant point about academic conformism—about the assumption, anything but outmoded, that the with-it professor will hold certifiably "correct" positions, political and otherwise. Substitute the words *party line* for Lipking's ponderous *episteme,* and see what you get.

And perhaps this expectation of conformism—this assumption that professionalism entails a party line—helps explain the ease with which professors, universalizing from their own social habits, are able to reject the "genius" of a Dickens or a Mark Twain and fasten instead on the ways in which his age spoke through him. The purveyors of such analyses reveal their provincialism, their inability to distance themselves—as scholars and critics should—from the reigning ideological orthodoxies of their own time. The right-minded assistant professor in the post-Vietnam era imposes his or her own politically correct attitudes upon the literature of the past—at the cost of eliminating the sense of the past. In a fit of historical superiority, the critic proves himself or herself guiltless of the sexism, racism, and assorted other isms that damn the benighted denizens of earlier eras. The imperative has more to do with political correctness—establishing what it is and anxiously proclaiming one's loyalty to the line—than with the nominal subject under study, be it literature or history.

Down, then, with "reverence," with "tradition," with anything that smacks of the "canonical," and up with "a hermeneutics of suspicion" that extols the critic over the artist. Jonathan Culler makes a startling claim in his recent book *Framing the Sign*—at any rate it *would* be startling if we hadn't heard it so often before. In the past, Culler writes, criticism was an adjunct of literature, and the history of criticism was therefore part of the history of literature. Now, however, it's the other way around: "now the history of literature is part of the history of criticism."

Culler's prose style is poker-faced, humorless; there's no evidence of irony, and that is why such pronouncements sound as if they were made to order for an unself-conscious figure of fun in an Evelyn Waugh satire. Why should criticism take precedence over literature? Culler gives several reasons, beyond the unspoken one that binary reversals are good for the patient—the deconstructive doctor routinely prescribes them. A more important reason is that "the critical communities in universities" are where the power is. The public man of letters, the eclectic amateur, and the free-lance intellectual have disappeared; the clerks and bureaucrats of academe have taken their place. It is they who wield the power—they who determine, in Culler's words, "what is canonized, what is explicated, what is articulated as a major problem for literature." In the academic order of priority, therefore, criticism may be said to precede literature.

In a practical sense, Culler's analysis is right on target; academic literary critics fix the canon by deciding what books get on the mandatory reading lists of college courses. But what most distinguishes the critics of today from those of earlier generations is not their frank interest in demystifying the process of canon making, but their insistence that power is the whole of the game—that power is what criticism is all about. No canon is or should be sacred, fixed once forever, beyond revision, but the canon revisionists now at work are perhaps unique in their readiness to subordinate literary and aesthetic values to a political standard. Acquiescing in the notion that disinterested inquiry is an impossibility and that every value judgment is necessarily a power play before it is anything else, they make their decisions by applying ideological litmus tests and determining the sexist and racist quotient in any piece of writing, from Plato to the present. This is, at bottom, a conception of the literary critic as an agent of the thought police, single-minded, obsessively concerned to enforce the party line, willing to subject chosen works to a violent form of interrogation, and more than happy to eliminate literature altogether in favor of pure theory.

For Culler, literary criticism can itself perform the function of avant-garde literature, thus making the latter superfluous and expendable. In this respect, criticism as Culler conceives it need no longer be dependent on literature. The paradox is that the critic demoting literature—presumably for the sake of elevating his own role—risks the drastic diminution of that role. For all its vaunted ambition, academic literary criticism as it is currently practiced occurs at the furthest marginal remove from the texts of our lives, without an audience other than the captive one of colleagues and paying students, without a subject, without even a compelling raison d'être that may be articulated to parents, alumni, and the general public. Since literature is the reason that criticism exists, the deconstructive notion that literature is part of a larger entity called criticism, to be discarded if the critic so chooses, seems a perfect instance of a man sawing off the branch on which he's sitting. Yet Culler, who disparages the view that identifies deconstruction with "Derridadaism," would be the first to deny that his vision of criticism's hegemony is a prankish antic. No, the claims of the deconstructive episteme are put forth in stubborn earnestness, as if they were self-evident axioms from which only the naive would dissent.

The real value of *Framing the Sign* is as a guide to acceptable opinions. In colorless, self-effacing prose, the author lets you know what they're thinking about in deconstruction headquarters. Concerns about the state of the humanities are patronizingly written off as the product of "apocalyptic visions, crisis narratives." Academics who emphasize teaching rather than research are presumptively found guilty of "a conservative, even reactionary gesture." Not teaching, not the "reproduction of culture," but "advanced or innovative critical speculation" is the professor's proper role. Deconstruction "has been the greatest source of energy in criticism," and Critical Legal Studies is the cutting-edge development that Culler can endorse; the law and deconstruction "seem in some sense made for each other," he writes. And he repeats the by now tiresome, dubiously feminist argument that "rationality" itself is to some extent "complicitous with male privilege," a variant on the line, also quite prevalent, that the prose virtues of clarity, concision, and directness are masculine strategies and replicate male sexual behavior, that paradigm of oppression. Though some feminists do mouth this shibboleth, it is actually a terrible slander on women, implying that they cannot write clearly or think straight.

Culler is at his most animated when the subject is religion. "Down with the priests!" he cries, mounting an attack on "the Fryes, Hartmans, Girards, Booths, and Kenners—our most famous critics" for being "promoters of religion." So far as Culler can see, "religious discourse" and "theistic beliefs"—God and religion, in other words—do not "deserve respect, any more than we would assume that sexist or racist beliefs deserve respect." Indeed, Culler recommends reading the Bible "not as poetry or as narrative but as a powerfully influential racist and sexist text." On this rock the deconstructionist builds his antichurch. How partial, prejudicial, and reductive is his view of the Bible, and yet how absolute is his claim for that view. This is, in brief, the creed of atheistic fundamentalism, as extreme in its way as the other kind of fundamentalism, as intolerant, and as hostile to the spirit of secular humanism.

There may be some consolation in the knowledge that the contemporary critic's dogmatic self-celebration is not unprecedented. A cogent comment on the abuses of criticism was formulated by Henry Fielding in his comic masterpiece *Tom Jones*. Fielding's words are nearly as apt today as when he published them in 1749:

> Now, in reality, the world have paid too great a compliment to critics, and have imagined them men of much greater profundity than they really are. From this complaisance the critics have been emboldened to assume a dictatorial power, and have so far succeeded that they are now become the masters, and have the assurance to give laws to those authors from whose predecessors they originally received them.

> The critic, rightly considered, is no more than the clerk, whose office it is to transcribe the rules and laws laid down by those great judges whose vast strength of genius hath placed them in the light of legislators, in the several sciences over which they presided. This office was all which the critics of old aspired to; nor did they ever dare to advance a sentence without supporting it by the authority of the judge from whence it was borrowed.

> But in process of time, and in ages of ignorance, the clerk began to invade the power and assume the dignity of his master. The laws of writing were no longer founded on the practice of the author, but on the dictates of the critic. The clerk became the legislator, and those very peremp-

torily gave laws whose business it was, at first, only to transcribe them.

Hence arose an obvious, and perhaps an unavoidable error; for these critics being men of shallow capacities, very easily mistook mere form for substance. They acted as a judge would, who should adhere to the lifeless letter of law and reject the spirit. Little circumstances, which were perhaps accidental in a great author, were by these critics considered to constitute his chief merit, and transmitted as essentials to be observed by all his successors. To these encroachments, time and ignorance, the two great supporters of imposture, gave authority; and thus many rules for good writing have been established which have not the least foundation in truth or nature, and which commonly serve for no other purpose than to curb and restrain genius, in the same manner as it would have restrained the dancing-master, had the many excellent treatises on that art laid it down as an essential rule that every man must dance in chains.

A generation from now, literary historians are bound to regard our period with some wonderment. It was a time, they will note, when professors of literature solemnly subscribed to the doctrine that literature, while full of sound and fury, signifies nothing. It was a period when language turned in on itself—when the meaning or content of a piece of writing was deferred, or rendered "undecidable," or "reproblematized," while the scholar's energy went into close rhetorical readings of devious linguistic structures. You couldn't get around to the substance of a work of writing because you would necessarily get hung up on the way the language worked. A new vocabulary (or "metalanguage") had to be devised to conduct these forays to the edge of a linguistic abyss. Words were signs, and language was a complex and contradictory system of signs, and the signs themselves were arbitrary and terminally ambiguous—like the sign in an otherwise denuded shop window announcing that the shop has been closed and that "this will help us serve you better."

In an early essay, Jacques Derrida wrote of "an anxiety about language"—which was also "an anxiety of language, within language itself"—and which he discerned across the full spectrum of intellectual activity. This was, wrote Derrida, "a strangely concerted development," yet it should not be seen as merely "the sign of an epoch, the fashion of a season, or the symptom of a crisis." What Derrida called "the question of the sign" was not to be confused with "a sign of the times." Indeed he wrote, with characteristic hyperbole, that "to dream of reducing it to a sign of the times is to dream of violence."

In the shop windows of academe, deconstructionists have posted their enigmatic question-mark sign so persistently over the last twenty years that it's no wonder so many dissastisfied customers have turned away, empty-handed and alienated. Now more than ever deconstruction seems aptly described as "the sign of an epoch" and "the symptom of a crisis"—a moral and cognitive crisis that shows few signs of letting up, though more voices are raised in protest each year.

In the past, the deconstructionists had capitalized on the crisis atmosphere in the humanities. It worked to their advantage. The notoriety of deconstruction brought the benefits of publicity, and the resistance to deconstruction was proof of its vitality; it was radical, it was threatening. In the de Man affair, the deconstructionists tried again to exploit this sense of crisis. They strove to interpret the whole episode as an injunction to reread the misunderstood guru, and their strategy was to turn the tables on the journalists and "journalist-professors" who reported or commented on what de Man had done. This time, however, de Man's defenders played a losing hand. Setting out to expose the conspiracy against deconstruction, they succeeded instead in exposing their own conspiratorial view of the world—and their worshipfulness of de Man. They were so much under the sway of the man that it would take more than mere facts to discourage them. The lesson of the de Man affair has less to do with the unmasking of a scoundrel than with the stubborn refusal of his followers to read the writing on the wall, to read it as it was written, and to understand its import. The de Man revelations brought his disciples to the edge of the abyss that they claim to seek—and they flinched, retreating to the safety of their illusions. In their briefs for de Man, they have provided a dossier of proof that deconstruction is not a value-free science but a program that promotes a reckless disregard of the truth and a propensity for hero-worship. And that is the final paradox of deconstruction: it *is* the crisis that it pretends to expose.

In "Politics and the English Language," George Orwell disputed the assumption that "we cannot by conscious action do anything about" the decline of our language. "Underneath this," Orwell wrote, "lies the half-conscious belief that language is a natural growth and not an instrument which we shape for our own purposes." One dubious achievement of deconstruction has been to take that "half-conscious belief" and turn it into an unwavering maxim. Language, by deconstructive decree, is alien from human purposes, a stranger to human wishes and will. As a doctrine this is pernicious to the precise extent that it acquiesces in the curtailment of human freedom, for that is what is at stake in our ability to shape our words for our own purposes.

A survey of contemporary trends in academic criticism will find a suitable summary statement in an essay that Thomas Carlyle published in 1829. "We have our little *theory* on all human and divine things," Carlyle wrote. "Poetry, the workings of genius itself, which in all times, with one or another meaning, has been called Inspiration, and held to be mysterious and inscrutable, is no longer without its scientific exposition. The building of the lofty rhyme is like any other masonry or brick-laying: we have theories of its rise, height, decline and fall,—which latter, it would seem, is now near, among all people." A casualty of his age, Carlyle wrote, was "the moral, religious, spiritual condition of the people"; in its stead was "their physical, practical, economical condition"—the "Body-politic" worshipped, the "Soul-politic" ignored. Art, treated as if it were a species of masonry, could be reduced to rubble; history was being demystified, "wonder" was dying out (since "it is the sign of uncultivation to wonder"), and individuals were universally seen to be the products of forces beyond their control.

Carlyle entitled his essay "Signs of the Times." The signs are all around us, including some that Carlyle couldn't foresee. Many are ambiguous, some are confusing, but they can all be interpreted, and interpreted correctly. It would be a mistake to think that we cannot by conscious action do anything about them.

APPENDIX

Text of Paul de Man's "The Jews in Contemporary Literature," in *Le Soir*, March 4, 1941 (translated by David Lehman):

Vulgar anti-Semitism readily considers postwar cultural phenomena (after the war of 1914–1918) as degenerate and decadent because Judaized [*enjuivé*]. Literature hasn't escaped this lapidary judgment: it is enough to have discovered several Jewish writers under Latinized pseudonyms for all contemporary production to be considered polluted and harmful. This conception entails some rather dangerous consequences. In the first place, it condemns à priori an entire literature that in no way deserves this fate. Moreover, from the moment one agrees to assign some merit to the literature of our day, it would be an unflattering estimation of Western writers to reduce them to being mere imitators of a Jewish culture that is foreign to them.

The Jews themselves have contributed to this myth. Often, they have glorified themselves as the leaders of the literary movements that characterize our era. But the mistake has, in reality, a deeper cause. The very prevalent opinion, according to which modern poetry and the modern novel were only monstrous outgrowths of the world war, is at the root of the thesis of a Jewish takeover. Since the Jews have, in fact, played an important role in the phoney and disordered existence of Europe since 1920, a novel born in that atmosphere would deserve, up to a certain point, the description *enjuivé*.

But the reality is different. It seems that aesthetic evolutions obey very powerful laws that continue on their course even while humanity is shaken by important events. The world war provoked a profound upheaval in the political and economic world. But artistic life has been affected relatively little, and the forms that we know at present follow in a logical and normal fashion those that came before.

This is particularly clear with regard to the novel. Stendhal's definition, according to which "the novel is a mirror strolling down an open road," contains the law that still rules this literary genre today. What was seen as coming first is the obligation to pay scrupulous respect to external reality. But by digging deeper, the novel has also managed to exploit psychological reality. Stendhal's mirror no longer remains immobile on the road; rather it undertakes to investigate the most secret corners of the souls of characters. And this domain has been so rich and so fruitful in surprises that it still constitutes the novelist's one and only terrain of investigation.

Gide, Kafka, Hemingway, Lawrence—the list could be extended indefinitely—do nothing but attempt, through methods appropriate to their own personalities, to penetrate the secrets of the interior life. By this shared trait, they show themselves to be not innovators breaking with all past traditions, but mere continuators who are pursuing further the realist aesthetic that is more than a century old.

A similar demonstration can be made in the domain of poetry. The forms that seem most revolutionary to us, such as surrealism and futurism, have, in reality, orthodox ancestors from which they cannot be detached.

One realizes, therefore, that to consider contemporary literature as an isolated phenomenon, created by the particular mentality of the 1920s, is absurd. Likewise, the Jews cannot pretend to be its creators, nor even to have exercised a preponderant influence over its evolution. On any close examination, their influence would appear to have extraordinarily little importance, since one might have expected that—given the specific characteristics of the Jewish mind [esprit]—the latter would have played a more brilliant role in such artistic production. Their cerebralness, their capacity to assimilate doctrines while maintaining a cold detachment from them, would seem to be very precious qualities for the work of lucid analysis that the novel requires. But in spite of that, Jewish writers have always remained in the second rank and, to speak only of France, writers on the order of André Maurois, Francis de Croisset, Henri Duvernois, Henri Bernstein, Tristan Bernard, Julien Benda, and so on, are not among the most important figures, and especially not among those who have had some directive influence on literary genres. The statement is, moreover, comforting for Western intellectuals. That they have been able to safeguard themselves from Jewish influence in a domain as culturally representative as literature proves their vitality. We could not have much hope for the future of our civilization if it had let itself be invaded, without resistance, by a foreign force. In keeping its originality and its character intact, despite Semitic interference in all aspects of European life, our civilization has shown that its fundamental nature is healthy. What's more, one can thus see that a solution to the Jewish problem that would lead to the creation of a Jewish colony isolated from Europe would not have, for the literary life of the West, regrettable consequences. It would lose, in all, some personalities of mediocre worth and would continue, as in the past, to develop according to its higher laws of evolution.

NOTES

CHAPTER 1: THE END OF THE WORD

17 "A classic's content": Allan Bloom, in the *New York Times Book Review,* December 4, 1988.

17 "One need not deconstruct the penny": David Van Leer, "Trust and Trade," in *Critical Inquiry* 15, no. 4 (Summer 1989): 762.

18 "Whatever anthropologists may think": Clifford Geertz, *Works and Lives: The Anthropologist as Author* (Stanford: Stanford University Press, 1988), 21.

18 "Flaunted the aestheticism": Richard Ellmann, *Oscar Wilde* (New York: Knopf, 1988), 315.

18 "It was whacked": Roger Angell, "Hard Times (The Movie)," in the *New Yorker,* December 5, 1988.

18 "Should forget about his narrative cliché": Robert J. Wilson, "Giamatti is Baseball's Pedant," in the *New York Times,* Sunday, April 16, 1989. Giamatti's article, "The Story of Baseball: You Can Go Home Again," appeared in the *Times* on April 2, 1989.

20 "Guardians of the Revolution": Charles Peter Freund, "Petracide," in the *New Republic,* March 27, 1989.

20 "We had no idea": Advertisement for *National Review,* in the *New Republic,* March 27, 1989.

21 "Is deconstructed by Hughes's friends": Frances McCullough, "Sylvia Plath's Journals" (letter to the editor), in the *New York Review of Books,* January 18, 1990.

21 "The disease of the age": Jacques Barzun, "Introductory," in *A Catalogue of Crime,* ed. Jacques Barzun and Wendell Hertig Taylor, revised ed. (New York: Harper and Row, 1989), xxii.

21 "In the emphasis on diversity": Richard Bernstein, "Age of Golden Clarity Bows to Hegemonicists," in the *New York Times,* August 27, 1988.

21 "An intellectual fashion": "The Stanford Mind" (editorial), in the *Wall Street Journal,* December 22, 1988.

21 "An intentional subversion": Christopher Lehmann-Haupt, " 'Vineland,' Pynchon's First Novel in 17 Years," in the *New York Times,* December 26, 1989.

21 "As Balkanizing": Michael O'Brien, "A Paradox of Intellectual Life Since the 60's: We Are Cosmopolitan; Our Scholarship Is Not," in *Chronicle of Higher Education,* November 30, 1988.

22 "We sent them Jerry Lewis": Quoted in Alessandra Stanley, "Can 50 Million Frenchmen Be Wrong?" in the *New York Times Magazine,* October 21, 1990.

22 "The episode where rocker": Stephanie Brush, "Three TV Shows That Captured a Decade," in the *New York Times,* June 4, 1989.

23 "The very word": Michael Wood, "Deconstructing Derrida," in the *New York Review of Books,* March 3, 1977.

25 "Since there are no functions": Barbara Herrnstein Smith, *Contingencies of Value: Alternative Perspectives for Critical Theory* (Cambridge: Harvard University Press, 1988), 34.

25 "Bentham said it faster": David Bromwich, "Sure," in the *New Republic,* December 12, 1988.

25 "The experience of pain": Jonathan Culler, *On Deconstruction: Theory and Criticism After Structuralism* (Ithaca: Cornell University Press, 1982), 87–88.

26 "Tissue of confusions": John R. Searle, "The Word Turned Upside Down," in the *New York Review of Books,* October 27, 1983.

26 "A philosopher of science": James Trefil, "The Survival of the Luckiest," in the *Washington Post National Weekly Edition,* October 30–November 5, 1989.

27 "School of Resentment": Harold Bloom, "Literature as the Bible," in the *New York Review of Books,* March 31, 1988.

28 "I cannot find it": Geoffrey Hartman, quoted by Frederick Crews, in *Skeptical Engagements* (New York: Oxford University Press, 1986), 132.

29 "An exercise": Elizabeth Connell Fentress, "Why I Left Graduate School," in the *New Criterion* (June 1989): 77–82.

29 "Students electing to major in literature": Between 1963 and 1970, more than seven percent of all bachelor's degrees were awarded to students majoring in English; between 1979 and 1986, the figure had dropped to below three percent. See the *MLA Newsletter* (Winter 1988): 3; see also Gene I. Maeroff, "Shifting Away from the Liberal Arts," in the *New York Times,* March 26, 1985.

30 "Boa-deconstructors": Geoffrey Hartman, "Preface," *Deconstruction and Criticism* (New York: The Seabury Press, 1979), ix.

30 "A journey to the moon": Frederick Crews, *Skeptical Engagements,* 116. Crews made the observation in the course of a talk he gave at the MLA convention in December 1979.

30 "Clowns or jongleurs": Geoffrey Hartman, "The State of the Art of Criticism," in *The Future of Literary Theory,* ed. Ralph Cohen (New York: Routledge, 1989), 100.

30 "The serious philosophy": M. H. Abrams, "How to Do Things with Texts," in *Partisan Review* 46, no. 4 (1979): 574.

31 "By J. S. Mill's maxim": M. H. Abrams, "Construing and Deconstructing," in *Romanticism and Contemporary Criticism,* ed. Morris Eaves and Michael Fischer (Ithaca: Cornell University Press, 1986), 128.

31 "A palimpsest": Anna C. Chave, *Mark Rothko: Subjects in Abstraction,* quoted in Hilton Kramer, "Was Rothko an Abstract Painter?" in the *New Criterion* (March 1989): 4.

32 "Genres are not to be mixed": Derrida's essay "The Law of Genre," trans. Avital Ronell, appears in *On Narrative,* ed. W.J.T. Mitchell (Chicago: University of Chicago Press, 1980). See Rod Smith's review of Carla Harryman's *Vice* in *Paper Air* 4, no. 2 (1989): 124–26. *Paper Air* is published by Singing Horse Press in Philadelphia.

33 "An assistant professor": Tom Clark, "Stalin as Linguist," *Partisan Review* 54, no. 2 (Spring 1987): 300.

33 "Derrida's summer home": Bob Perelman, *Captive Audience* (Great Barrington, Mass.: The Figures, 1988), 51.

33 "Pastoral for Derrida": Rodney Jones, *Transparent Gestures* (New York: Houghton Mifflin, 1989), 55–56.

33 "The Apocrypha of Jacques Derrida": Norman Dubie, *Groom Falconer* (New York: Norton, 1989), 25–26.

33 "The new thinking": Robert Hass, "Meditation at Lagunitas," in *The Antaeus Anthology,* ed. Daniel Halpern (New York: Bantam, 1986), 183.

33 "The Professor": Louis Simpson, letter to David Lehman, October 13, 1988.

34 "A biblical scholar": Stephen D. Moore, *Literary Criticism and the Gospels: The Theoretical Challenge* (New Haven: Yale University Press, 1989), 130–31, 145, 176–77.

34 "Rabblement of lemmings": Harold Bloom, "Literature as the Bible."

34 "In the act": Paul de Man, *Blindness and Insight: Essays in the Rhetoric of Contemporary Criticism,* rev. ed. (Minneapolis: University of Minnesota Press, 1983), 11.

35 "The true historical significance": Stephen A. Tyler, "Post-Modern Ethnography: From Document of the Occult to Occult Document," in *Writing Culture: The Poetics and Politics of Ethnography,* ed. James Clifford and George E. Marcus (Berkeley and Los Angeles: University of California Press, 1986), 131, 136. See also Geertz, *Works and Lives,* 131–38.

36 "Deconstructivist Architecture": Mark Wigley, quoted in Brendan Gill, "Deconstructivism," in the *New Yorker,* September 5, 1988.

36 "Deconstructive financier": Richard Rand, "Poetic Justice: Milken Decon-structed," in the *Wall Street Journal,* May 1, 1989.

37 "The significance of the deconstructive practice": Gary Peller, "Reason and the Mob: The Politics of Representation," in *Tikkun* 2, no. 3 (1987): 95.

39 "CLS critique of law": Owen M. Fiss, "The Death of the Law?" in the *Cornell Law Review* 72, no. 1 (1986): 10–12.

40 "There is no deconstruction": J. Hillis Miller, "The Critic as Host," in *Deconstruction and Criticism* (New York: The Seabury Press, 1979), 251.

41 "The abyss": J. Hillis Miller, "The Critic as Host," 245.

CHAPTER 2: CRAZY ABOUT DECONSTRUCTION

45 "Apocalyptic hype": Robert Hughes, "The Patron Saint of Neo-Pop," in the *New York Review of Books,* June 1, 1989.

45 "There is an ever-increasing supply": Frank Kermode, "The Limits of The-ory," in *Scripsi* 5, no. 2 (1989): 40.

45 "The common reader": Irving Howe, "The Treason of the Critics," in the *New Republic,* June 12, 1989.

45 "An intellectual heresy": Clara Claiborne Park, "Talking Back to the Speaker," in the *Hudson Review* (Spring 1989): 43.

45 "Dogmatic skepticism": Tzvetan Todorov, "Crimes Against Humanities," in the *New Republic,* July 3, 1989.

46 "Our students can't read": Denis Donoghue, "The Joy of Texts," in the *New Republic,* June 26, 1989.

46 "The Age of Criticism": Randall Jarrell, *Poetry and the Age* (New York: Vintage, 1955), 63–86.

47 "Three of his most formidable theoretical studies": Jacques Derrida, *Writing and Difference,* trans. Alan Bass (Chicago: University of Chicago Press, 1978); *Of Grammatology,* trans. Gayatri Chakravorty Spivak (Baltimore: Johns Hop-kins University Press, 1976); and *Speech and Phenomena,* trans. David B. Allison (Evanston: Northwestern University Press, 1973).

48 "At the Americana Hotel": Richard Ohmann, *English in America: A Radical View of the Profession* (New York: Oxford University Press, 1976), 27–29.

49 "1948": Gerald Graff, *Professing Literature: An Institutional History* (Chicago: University of Chicago Press, 1987), 185–86.

50 "To urge us" and "the classic defense": Lionel Trilling, *Beyond Culture* (New York: Harcourt Brace Jovanovich, 1979), 11, 184.

51 "The reader-critic's claim": Geoffrey Hartman, *Criticism in the Wilderness: The Study of Literature Today* (New Haven: Yale University Press, 1980), 20, 201.

51 "An overgoer": Geoffrey Hartman, *The Fate of Reading* (Chicago: University of Chicago Press, 1975), 3.

53 "The sign": Jacques Derrida, *Of Grammatology,* 19.

54 "Indeterminacy": See Gerald Graff, "Determinacy/Indeterminacy," in *Criti-*

cal Terms for Literary Study, ed. Frank Lentricchia and Thomas McLaughlin (Chicago: University of Chicago Press, 1990), 165.

54 "Great works": J. Hillis Miller, "Deconstructing the Deconstructors," in *Diacritics* 5, no. 2 (Summer 1975): 30–31.

56 "The most dogmatic French deconstructionists": Edith Kurzweil, "An Interview with Julia Kristeva," in *Partisan Review* 53, no. 2 (1986): 217–18.

56 "America *is* deconstruction": Jacques Derrida, *Mémoires: for Paul de Man,* rev. ed. (New York: Columbia University Press, 1989), 18.

56 "On the Teaching of Modern Literature": Lionel Trilling, *Beyond Culture* (New York: Harcourt Brace Jovanovich, 1979), 10, 23–24.

59 "The doctrine of madness": Lionel Trilling, *Sincerity and Authenticity* (Cambridge: Harvard University Press, 1973), 171. If we are determined to find honorable uses of the word *deconstruction,* I think it could be said that Trilling deconstructed "the doctrine that madness is health."

60 "America is crazy": David Lodge, *Small World* (New York: Macmillan, 1985), 118.

60 "The view of deconstruction": Howard Felperin, *Beyond Deconstruction: The Uses and Abuses of Literary Theory* (Oxford: Clarendon Press, 1985), 114–15.

61 "Deconstruction's procedure": Jonathan Culler, *On Deconstruction,* 149.

63 "The poet's way": Examples from Wallace Stevens's "Study of Two Pears" and "Someone Puts a Pineapple Together," in *The Palm at the End of the Mind: Selected Poems and a Play,* ed. Holly Stevens (New York: Vintage, 1972), 159, 298.

64 "Ethicity": J. Hillis Miller, *The Ethics of Reading: Kant, de Man, Eliot, Trollope, James, and Benjamin* (New York: Columbia University Press, 1986), 51. See Robert Scholes, *Protocols of Reading* (New Haven: Yale University Press, 1989), 145–55, for an illuminating discussion.

64 "Everything is phoney": "There is an atmosphere of bluff and fakery that pervades much (not all, of course) deconstructive writing," the philosopher John Searle has written. "To put it crudely, they think that since everything is phony anyway, the phoniness of deconstruction is somehow acceptable, indeed commendable, since it lies right on the surface ready for further deconstruction." In the *New York Review of Books,* February 2, 1984.

CHAPTER 3: ARCHIE DEBUNKING

65 "Deconstruction is the practice": Denis Donoghue, "The Strange Case of Paul de Man," in the *New York Review of Books,* June 29, 1989.

65 "The term invented by Derrida": Jonathan Culler, "It's Time to Set the Record Straight About Paul de Man and His Wartime Articles for a Pro-Fascist Newspaper," in *Chronicle of Higher Education,* July 13, 1988.

65 "A form of commentary": Edward Said, quoted in Jon Wiener, "Deconstructing de Man," in the *Nation,* January 9, 1988.

66 "A deconstructive reading is an attempt": Barbara Johnson, *A World of Difference* (Baltimore: Johns Hopkins University Press, 1989), 17–18.

66 "The dismantling": Christopher Norris, *Derrida* (Cambridge: Harvard University Press, 1987), 19.

66 "To deconstruct a discourse": Jonathan Culler, *On Deconstruction*, 86.

66 "A deconstruction always has": Paul de Man, *Allegories of Reading: Figural Language in Rousseau, Nietzsche, Rilke, and Proust* (New Haven: Yale University Press, 1979), 249.

67 "The neoconservative and sexist subtext": Rosellen Brown, "Once Upon a Time: The Real Story," in the *New York Times Book Review,* March 11, 1990.

67 "Favorable reception": Gertrude Himmelfarb, "The Art of History Was His Credo," in the *New York Times Book Review,* March 11, 1990.

68 "Archie Bunker": Paul de Man, *Allegories of Reading,* 9–10.

69 "Rather obvious": John R. Searle, "The Word Turned Upside Down," 78.

69 "Both deconstructive literature": M. H. Abrams, "Construing and Deconstructing," 160.

70 "Ideology": Hannah Arendt, *The Origins of Totalitarianism* (New York: Harcourt Brace Jovanovich, 1973), 159, 468.

71 "Textuality as Striptease": David Lodge, *Small World,* 28.

71 "Suicidal": M. H. Abrams, "How to Do Things with Texts," 568.

71 "Indeterminism": Frederick Crews, "Criticism Without Constraint," in *Commentary* (January 1982): 71.

71 "Nihilistic view": W. Jackson Bate, "The Crisis in English Studies," in *Harvard* magazine (September–October 1982): 52.

71 "Recent varieties": Rene Wellek, *A History of Modern Criticism, 1750–1950* vol. 6 (New Haven: Yale University Press, 1986), 299.

72 "Martial implications": Robert Alter, "Deconstruction in America," in the *New Republic,* April 25, 1983.

73 "The sense": Frederick Crews, *Skeptical Engagements,* 129.

73 "The real impetus": Robert Alter, "Deconstruction in America," 30.

73 "Post-structuralism": TerryEagleton, *Literary Theory: An Introduction* (Minneapolis: University of Minnesota Press, 1983), 142.

73 "As everyone knows": Morris Dickstein, "School's Out," in the *Voice Literary Supplement* (October 1988): 19.

74 "That what is happening": David Bromwich, "The Future of Tradition," in *Dissent* (Fall 1989): 550–51.

74 "Mischievously radical": Eagleton, *Literary Theory,* 145.

74 "The youth culture": W. Wolfgang Holdheim, *"Idola Fori Academici,"* in the *Stanford Literature Review* (Spring 1987): 19.

75 "Liberation": Wayne Booth, " 'Preserving the Exemplar': or, How Not to Dig Our Own Graves," in *Critical Inquiry* 3, no. 3 (Spring 1977): 416.

76 "Is revolutionary": John M. Ellis, *Against Deconstruction* (Princeton: Prince-

ton University Press, 1989), 87. See also 88, 142–43, 157. "Advocates of deconstruction are dreaming if they really believe that [its] thrust runs radically counter to, and disturbs, the entrenched attitudes of American criticism. Deconstruction's success in America is, in fact, explained by just the reverse—by its playing to the prevailing climate and giving that climate a new air of legitimacy" (157).

76 "Duncan Kennedy": Ken Emerson, "When Legal Titans Clash," in the *New York Times Magazine,* April 22, 1990.

77 "Obscurantist terrorism": Quoted in John R. Searle, "The Word Turned Upside Down," 77.

78 "The *de-* prefix": Robert Alter, *The Pleasures of Reading: Thinking About Literature in an Ideological Age* (New York: Simon and Schuster, 1989), 19–20.

78 "Deconstruction's thrust": Sven Birkerts, in *Sulfur* 19 (1987): 143.

78 "The deconstructive will": Luc Ferry and Alain Renaut, "The Philosophies of '68," trans. Mark Lilla, in *Partisan Review* 56, no. 3 (Summer 1989): 349, 354–55.

79 "Hermeneutical mafia": Frank Lentricchia, *After the New Criticism* (Chicago: University of Chicago Press, 1980), 283. See also Howard Felperin, *Beyond Deconstruction,* 111–12.

79 "The rage": Daniel Hoffman, "The Last of the Chicksaws," in *Shenandoah* 39, no. 1, 1989, 51.

79 "Deconstructive attacks": Clifford Geertz, *Works and Lives,* 131.

81 "Conception of 'greatness' ": Jonathan Culler, *Framing the Sign: Criticism and Its Institutions* (Norman, Okla.: University of Oklahoma Press, 1988), 47.

81 "The bases": Paul de Man, *Blindness and Insight,* rev. ed., 165.

81 "It is not possible": Tzvetan Todorov, *Literature and Its Theorists: A Personal View of Twentieth-Century Criticism,* trans. Catherine Porter (Ithaca: Cornell University Press, 1987), 190.

82 "Instead of": Barbara Johnson, *A World of Difference,* 12–13.

82 "The key word": George Orwell, *1984* (New York: New American Library, 1961), 175.

83 "The plagues of Egypt": Randall Jarrell, *Poetry and the Age,* 78–79.

84 "It is not popularity": Alison Lurie, "Notes on the Language of Poststructuralism," in *The State of the Language,* ed. Christopher Ricks and Leonard Michaels (Berkeley and Los Angeles: University of California Press, 1990), 292.

85 "If someone": Interview with Alison Lurie, Ithaca, New York, December 24, 1988.

85 "Attacking the Abyss": "Rambles in Book-Land," in *Exquisite Corpse* 6, nos. 10–12 (Oct.–Dec. 1988): 3. "Cosmo Dewlap" is a pseudonym for Andrei Codrescu, editor of *Exquisite Corpse.*

86 "One has long": Donald Davie, "Poet: Patriot: Interpreter," in *Critical Inquiry* 9, no. 1 (September 1982): 30. The sentence Davie chooses "virtually at random" is from William V. Spanos, Paul A. Bove, and Daniel O'Hara, Introduction to *Boundary 2* (Fall 1979): 3.

87 "Vocation": Donald Davie, "Poet: Patriot: Interpreter," 42–43.

87 "Clarity": Some advocates of Critical Legal Studies manage to write clearly, notes Kenney Hegland. "It appears, however, that to insist upon clarity is politically repressive." Hegland quotes an article in the *Yale Law Journal:* "Such strictures militate against the articulation of certain types of thinking and criticism. By forcing critics to speak in the traditional idiom, they defuse and deradicalize their critical message." Hegland, "Goodbye to Deconstruction," in the *Southern California Law Review* 58 (1985): 1203–4.

87 *"Diacritics":* Interview with David Grossvogel, Ithaca, New York, October 17, 1988.

88 "Struggled to deconstruct": All quotations from Bruce Lincoln, *Discourse and the Construction of Society: Comparative Studies of Myth, Ritual, and Classification* (New York: Oxford University Press, 1989), 26, 167, 169, 106, 127, 98–99.

89 "Special connection": George Orwell, "Politics and the English Language," in *A Collection of Essays* (New York: Harcourt, Brace, 1953), 165.

90 "Colin MacCabe": See Ian Jack, "On the Trail of the Lonesome Don," in the *Sunday Times* (London), January 25, 1981. Ricks was quoted in Dennis A. Williams, "Unquiet Flow the Dons," *Newsweek,* February 16, 1981.

90 "Deconstructionism is": Frank Kermode, *The Art of Telling: Essays on Fiction* (Cambridge: Harvard University Press, 1983), 7.

CHAPTER 4: TO THE LINGUISTIC ABYSS

93 "Death": Paul de Man, *The Rhetoric of Romanticism* (New York: Columbia University Press, 1984), 81.

94 "Contemporary literary theory": Paul de Man, *The Resistance to Theory* (Minneapolis: University of Minnesota Press, 1986), 8.

95 *"Différance":* See Jacques Derrida, *Positions,* trans. Alan Bass (Chicago: University of Chicago Press, 1981), 26–28.

96 "Semiology": Quoted in Robert Scholes, *Structuralism in Literature: An Introduction* (New Haven: Yale University Press, 1974), 16.

97 "This was the moment": Jacques Derrida, "Structure, Sign and Play in the Discourse of the Human Sciences," in *Writing and Difference,* 278–80.

98 "There's no there there": George Steiner, *Real Presences* (Chicago: University of Chicago Press, 1989), 120–21.

98 "The presence": Paul de Man, *Blindness and Insight,* rev. ed., 18.

98 "Nothing": Ibid., 141.

98 "The deconstruction of literature": Paul de Man, *Allegories of Reading,* 17.

99 "The analysis": Jacques Derrida, "Like the Sound of the Sea Deep within a Shell: Paul de Man's War," trans. Peggy Kamuf, in *Critical Inquiry* 14, no. 3 (Spring 1988): 648.

102 "Words, he thought": Philip K. Dick, *Time Out of Joint* (New York: Carroll and Graf, 1987), 59–60.

102 "Vast metaphysical plot": Michael Wood, "Deconstructing Derrida," 27.

103 "It has always seemed": Edward W. Said, "Opponents, Audiences, Constituencies, and Community," in *Critical Inquiry* 9, no. 1 (September 1982): 9.

104 "Writing in general": Jacques Derrida, *Of Grammatology,* 44.

105 "The history": Ibid, 3.

106 "The law that language": J. Hillis Miller, "The Critic as Host," in *Deconstruction and Criticism,* 224.

106 "The author is reputed": Roland Barthes, "From Work to Text" (1971), in *Image, Music, Text,* trans. Stephen Heath (New York: Hill and Wang, 1977), 155–64.

107 "There is nothing": Jacques Derrida, *Of Grammatology,* 163.

107 "Doing ethnography": Clifford Geertz, *The Interpretation of Cultures* (New York: Basic Books, 1973), 5, 10, 15–16.

108 "Popular wisdom": William Gass, *Habitations of the Word* (New York: Simon and Schuster, 1985), 265.

108 "The Death of the Author": Roland Barthes, *Image, Music, Text,* 142–48.

108 "The idea of the death of the author": William Gass, *Habitations of the Word,* 265.

109 "Death of the father": Ibid., 286.

109 "There was a time": Michel Foucault, "What Is an Author?" in *Textual Strategies: Perspectives in Post-Structuralist Criticism,* ed. Josué V. Harari (Ithaca: Cornell University Press, 1979), 149.

109 "It would be frivolous": Derrida, *Of Grammatology,* 99.

109 "D'ya wanna know the creed'a": Peter Mullen, "Deconstruction," in the *Times Literary Supplement* (London), October 18, 1985.

112 "The logical result of Fascism": Walter Benjamin, *Illuminations,* trans. Harry Zohn (New York: Schocken, 1969), 241–42.

112 "Aesthetic ideology": See, for example, Lindsay Waters, "Paul de Man: Life and Works," in de Man, *Critical Writings 1953–1978* (Minneapolis: University of Minnesota Press, 1989), lviii–lix.

112 "Humpty Dumpty": Lewis Carroll, *Alice in Wonderland,* Norton Critical Edition, ed. Donald J. Gray (New York: Norton, 1971), 163.

112 "Greatness and genius": See David Bromwich, "The Future of Tradition," in *Dissent* (Fall 1989): 549. For certain academic theorists, Bromwich notes, "the adjective most commonly paired with "enlightenment" is "totalitarian."

113 "Pizza": Walker Percy, "Letter" (occasioned by "Tom Wolfe's Novel Ideas"), in *Harper's,* February 1990.

CHAPTER 5: A KEY IDEA

115 "It's still pretty early": Jane Bryant Quinn, "Welcome to the 1990s," in *Newsweek,* May 21, 1990.

116 "Dismantling of Reaganist attitudes": Marshall Blonsky as quoted in Ruth La Ferla, "Sincerely Yours," in the *New York Times Magazine,* April 18, 1990.

116 "Hyper-rich": W. Speers, "Newsmakers," in the *Philadelphia Inquirer,* February 3, 1990.

116 "Words in isolation": Jacques Derrida, *Mémoires: for Paul de Man,* rev. ed., 15.

116 "The French sculptors": Anne and Patrick Poirier exhibited their work at the Storm King sculpture park near Newburgh, New York, in the summer of 1989. Kay Larson, reviewing the exhibition in *New York* magazine, wrote: "Transporting their deconstructed temples into sunshine and rain proves to be the definitive test. Sculpture in a gallery can explain itself through contemporary jargon. Outdoors it's forced to compete against the actuality of trees, sky, and architecture, within real time and space. . . . I have always felt the Poiriers were lightweights, but in daylight they positively vaporize." Kay Larson, "Loose Marbles," in *New York,* August 28, 1989.

116 "K.G.B. Chief": The K.G.B. story appeared on the front page of the *New York Times,* June 2, 1989.

117 "Key-idea": Susanne K. Langer, *Philosophy in a New Key* (New York: Mentor, 1948), 18.

117 "We ought scrupulously": R. P. Blackmur, "A Critic's Job of Work," in *Form and Value in Modern Poetry* (Garden City, N.Y.: Doubleday Anchor, 1957), 340–41.

118 "The first work of thoroughgoing": Howard Felperin, *Beyond Deconstruction,* 104, 119–21.

118 "The utterly pitiless": Stephen D. Moore, *Literary Criticism and the Gospels: The Theoretical Challenge,* 136–37.

120 "Charlie Chaplin": Hollander's comment on *City Lights* was made in conversation. For other useful examples of artful "deconstruction," see John Hollander, *Melodious Guile: Fictive Pattern in Poetic Language* (New Haven: Yale University Press, 1988), 50, 67–68, 103, 200–202.

123 "King Louis XVI": Bruce Lincoln, *Discourse and the Construction of Society,* 169.

124 "Fanatic falsification": R. P. Blackmur, "A Critic's Job of Work," in *Form and Value in Modern Poetry,* 347.

126 "Metaphysical assumptions": All quotations are from J. Hillis Miller, "On Edge," in *Romanticism and Contemporary Criticism,* 101–11.

127 "To say that all narratives": J. Hillis Miller, "Narrative," in *Critical Terms for Literary Study,* ed. Frank Lentricchia and Thomas McLaughlin, 76.

128 "MLA convention in 1976": M. H. Abrams, "The Deconstructive Angel," in *Critical Inquiry* 3, no. 3 (Spring 1977): 434; and J. Hillis Miller, "The Critic as Host," ibid., 447.

128 "Shootout": *Partisan Review* 47, no. 3 (1980): 390.

128 "A traditionalist": M. H. Abrams, "Construing and Deconstructing," in *Romanticism and Contemporary Criticism,* 128, 148, 157–58.

129 "Two incompatible, mutually self-destructive": Paul de Man, *Allegories of Reading,* 13.

130 "For it turns out": Ibid., 11–12.

133 "The stakes are enormous": J. Hillis Miller in *The Lesson of Paul de Man* (*Yale French Studies* no. 69 [1985]), 3. See also *Romanticism and Contemporary Criticism,* 126.

134 "Stravinsky": See Richard Taruskin, "The Dark Side of Modern Music," in the *New Republic,* September 5, 1988.

134 *"Historikerstreit":* For an excellent account, see Charles S. Maier, *The Unmasterable Past: History, Holocaust, and German National Identity* (Cambridge: Harvard University Press, 1989).

136 "One Parisian commentator": Alain Finkielkraut, quoted in Luc Ferry and Alain Renaut, *Heidegger and Modernity,* trans. Franklin Philip (Chicago: University of Chicago Press, 1990), 38–39, 42. See also Robert Zaretsky, "Sometimes a Great Commotion: The Heidegger Affair and French Intellectuals," in *Southwest Review,* Summer 1990, 380–92.

137 "Lacoue-Labarthe": Quoted in Luc Ferry and Alain Renaut, *Heidegger and Modernity,* 2, 87, 89.

137 "Beyond the fact": Barbara Johnson, *A World of Difference,* xi.

137 "Considerations of the actual": Paul de Man, *Blindness and Insight,* rev. ed., 35.

137 "Technically correct": Paul de Man, *The Resistance to Theory* (Minneapolis: University of Minnesota Press, 1986), 19.

139 "The reading of despair": Stanley Cavell, *Themes Out of School: Effects and Causes* (Chicago: University of Chicago Press, 1988), 45–47. See also John Hollander, *Melodious Guile,* 37.

CHAPTER 6: THE FALLEN IDOL

143 "The most celebrated member": Frank Kermode, "Paul de Man's Abyss," in the *London Review of Books,* March 16, 1989.

143 "He did not seek leadership": Shoshana Felman and Ellen Burt in *The Lesson of Paul de Man* (*Yale French Studies* no. 69 [1985]), 3–13.

144 "It seemed to me paradoxical": Barbara Johnson, quoted in Imre Salu-sinszky, *Criticism in Society* (New York: Methuen, 1987), 160.

144 "Rigor" and "authority": Ellen Burt, Andrzej Warminsky, Barbara John-son, J. Hillis Miller, and Shoshana Felman, in *The Lesson of Paul de Man* (*Yale French Studies* no. 69 [1985]), 3–13.

144 "The center of theoretical gravity": Interview with Barbara Johnson, in *Criticism in Society,* 156.

145 "There is an impact": Paul de Man, *The Resistance to Theory,* 117.

145 "The accommodation or appropriation of deconstruction": *Criticism in Society,* 222–23.

146 "Derridadaism": Geoffrey Hartman, *Saving the Text: Literature, Derrida, Philosophy* (Baltimore: Johns Hopkins University Press, 1981), 33.

146 "Bloom and Hartman": Geoffrey Hartman, "Preface," in *Deconstruction and Criticism,* ix.

146 "I have no relation to deconstruction": Harold Bloom, *Criticism in Society,* 68.

146 "A displaced version": Paul de Man, *Blindness and Insight,* rev. ed., 273–75.

147 "Jacques Derrida is a close personal friend": Interview with Harold Bloom, New Haven, May 1, 1986.

148 "Personal joke": *Criticism in Society,* 68.

149 "Dirty Harry": Maureen Corrigan in the *Voice Literary Supplement,* March 1984.

149 "In the manner of a don": Frank Lentricchia, *After the New Criticism* (Chicago: University of Chicago Press, 1980), 283–84.

150 "There is absolutely no reason": Paul de Man, *Allegories of Reading,* 16–17.

150 "Deconstruction, as was easily predictable": Ibid., x.

150 "Startled by the vehemence": Barbara Johnson, *A World of Difference,* 6.

151 "Ringing defense": Telephone interview with Geoffrey Hartman, January 16, 1988.

152 "Politics was the lingua franca": Donald Hall, telephone interview on February 6, 1988 and letter to David Lehman, September 20, 1988.

153 "The most photocopied essay": Wlad Godzich, quoting Jonathan Culler, in "Caution! Reader at Work!"—Godzich's introduction to the revised edition of *Blindness and Insight.* In Paul de Man, *Blindness and Insight,* rev. ed., xvi.

153 "A more sober assessment": David Bromwich, *A Choice of Inheritance: Self and Community from Edmund Burke to Robert Frost* (Cambridge: Harvard University Press, 1989), 273.

153 "Mock sensationalism": All quotations from Paul de Man, *Blindness and Insight,* rev. ed., 3, 10, 17, 25, 35, 141, 165, 232.

154 "The Resistance to Theory": Paul de Man, *The Resistance to Theory,* 5, 12, 19–20.

155 "Trilling's students": Frank Kermode, "Paul de Man's Abyss," 7.

156 "Already classic essay": J. Hillis Miller, "Presidential Address 1986. The Triumph of Theory, the Resistance to Reading, and the Question of the Material Base," in *PMLA* 102, no. 3 (May 1987): 281–91.

157 "As we know already": Jacques Derrida, in *The Lesson of Paul de Man* (*Yale French Studies* no. 69 [1985]), 324.

157 "If I may dare to say so": J. Hillis Miller, ibid., 4.

157 "Yale Still Feeling Loss of Revered Professor": Susan Chira, in the *New York Times,* February 25, 1984.

158 "To read de Man, from A to Z": Jacques Derrida, "Like the Sound of the Sea Deep within a Shell: Paul de Man's War," 639.

159 "The Poverty of Philosophy": John Hollander, *Melodious Guile,* 117–19.

161 "The spirit of criticism": Geoffrey Hartman, "Looking Back on Paul de Man," in *Reading De Man Reading,* ed. Lindsay Waters and Wlad Godzich (Minneapolis: University of Minnesota Press, 1989), 11.

CHAPTER 7: THE STOLEN EVENING

163 "Arguably the most challenging writer": Ortwin de Graef, "Aspects of the Context of Paul de Man's Earliest Publications," in *Responses: On Paul de Man's Wartime Journalism,* ed. Werner Hamacher, Neil Hertz, and Thomas Keenan (Lincoln: University of Nebraska Press, 1989), 115.

164 "By choosing Germany": Quoted in E. Ramon Arango, *Leopold III and the Belgian Royal Question* (Baltimore: Johns Hopkins Press, 1961), 169.

165 "Everybody reads quisling papers": Anne Somerhausen, *Written in Darkness: A Belgian Woman's Record of the Occupation, 1940–1945* (New York: Knopf, 1946), 228.

165 "Like a defeated flock": Ibid., 18, 20.

166 "A fascist, an anti-Semite": John Brenkman, "Fascist Commitments," in *Responses,* ed. Werner Hamacher et al., 34.

166 "A classic deconstructive reading": Jonathan Culler, *On Deconstruction,* 283.

168 "He and his brave, efficient army": David Cannadine, ed., *Blood, Toil, Tears and Sweat: The Speeches of Winston Churchill* (Boston: Houghton Mifflin, 1989), 158.

169 "Belgian unity could be restored": David Littlejohn, *The Patriotic Traitors: A History of Collaboration in German-Occupied Europe, 1940–1945* (London: Heinemann, 1972), 184.

170 "More than one": E. Ramon Arango, *Leopold III and the Belgian Royal Question,* 5–6.

171 "If you abandon their cause": Ibid., 63–64; quoting from pages 87–89 of *Recueil de documents établi par le Secrétariat du Roi concernant la période 1936– 1949* (Brussels: Imprimerie et Publicité du Marais), a volume containing official documents of the stated period, including those exchanged between the king and the ministers of the Belgian government.

171 "Later it will turn out": In *Le Soir,* July 21, 1942, in Paul de Man, *Wartime Journalism 1940–1942* (Lincoln: University of Nebraska Press, 1989), 253–54. Cited in John Brenkman, *Responses,* ed. Werner Hamacher et al., 27.

172 "Plugged the Nazi hit-parade": Quoted in Jon Wiener, "Deconstructing de Man," in the *Nation,* January 9, 1988.

173 "More dignified, more just, and more humane": In *Le Soir,* April 12–14, 1941, in Paul de Man, *Wartime Journalism,* 66.

173 "Organizing European society": In *Le Soir,* August 26, 1941, ibid., 137–38.

173 "The will to unify": In *Le Soir,* March 16, 1942, ibid., 207.

173 "A sincere artist": In *Het Vlaamsche Land,* July 26–27, 1942, ibid., 322.

173 "Entering a mystical era": In *Le Soir,* April 28, 1942, ibid., 226–27.

173 "The whole continuity": In *Le Soir,* March 16, 1942, *ibid.,* 207.

173 "Irresistible necessity": In *Le Soir,* July 21, 1942, ibid., 253–54.

173 "In the best interests of Germany": David Littlejohn, *The Patriotic Traitors,* 210–11.

174 "French survivor": John Brenkman, in *Responses,* ed. Werner Hamacher et al., 27.

174 "Hegemony in Europe": In *Le Soir,* October 28, 1941, in Paul de Man, *Wartime Journalism,* 158.

174 "A sort of fascist Rupert Brooke": David Littlejohn, *The Patriotic Traitors,* 200.

174 "Brasillach's accomplishments": In *Le Soir,* August 12, 1941, in Paul de Man, *Wartime Journalism,* 130–131.

175 "Very particular idiosyncrasies": Wolfgang Holdheim, "Fatal Swerve," in the *London Review of Books,* March 17, 1988.

176 "The people who had killed God": Edouard Colinet, "Paul de Man and the Cercle du Libre Examen," in *Responses,* ed. Werner Hamacher et al., 431.

176 "Postwar Belgian justice": Wolfgang Holdheim, Letter to David Lehman, May 22, 1990.

176 "After curfew": Edouard Colinet reports a telephone conversation with Esther Sluszny, who had taken refuge with Anaide and Paul de Man "sometime in 1942 or 1943." In *Responses,* ed. Werner Hamacher et al., 436.

176 "Profound lack of moral conscience": "Paul de Man and the Cercle du Libre Examen," Georges Goriely, quoted in Edouard Colinet, ibid., 436.

177 "The poor little carcass": Edouard Colinet, ibid., 435–36.

178 "The distinction is almost always blurred": William Flesch, "Ancestral Voices: De Man and His Defenders," ibid., 173–74.

178 "The literary critic for a newspaper": Quoted in Edouard Colinet, "Paul de Man and the Cercle du Libre Examen," ibid., 436.

178 "The failure of their Kultur campaign": Anne Somerhausen, *Written in Darkness, 238.*

179 "Any chance of French collaboration": George Orwell, *The War Commentaries,* ed. W. J. West (New York: Schocken, 1989), 181–83.

179 "An extremely useful instrument": Ortwin de Graef, "Aspects," in *Responses,* ed. Werner Hamacher et al., 116–17.

180 "His energetic propaganda": See Edouard Colinet "Paul de Man and the Cercle du Libre Examen," ibid., 436.

181 "The Wannsee conference": The question of who knew what when regarding the proposed annihilation of the Jews is one that continues to vex historians. Though "the Final Solution" was under wraps until Wannsee, there is documentary evidence that the genocide was in the planning stages— in Hitler's mind and in the workings of the SS—long before then. As early as December 10, 1939, the Brigadenführer in charge of Lodz, Poland, declared in a top-secret memorandum that the concentration of the Jews in a ghetto was a "transitional step"—and that he, Friedrich Uebelhoer, reserved for himself "the decision of when and how the city of Lodz will be cleansed of Jews. In any case, the final aim must be to burn out entirely this pestilent abscess." See Alan Adelson, Letter, in the *New York Review of Books,* December 21, 1989.

181 "The Madagascar plan": Arno J. Mayer, *Why Did the Heavens Not Darken?: The "Final Solution" in History* (New York: Pantheon, 1990), 195–97.

182 *"Volksverwering":* Hitler's Ten-Year War on the Jews (New York: Institute of Jewish Affairs of the American Jewish Congress, 1943), 251.

182 "One would have had to live": Telephone interview with Michael Marrus, December 5, 1988.

182 "Aberrant": In *Het Vlaamsche Land,* August 20, 1942, in Paul de Man, *Wartime Journalism,* 325.

182 "Fantastic Tales": Anne Somerhausen's entry for August 8, 1942, in Anne Somerhausen, *Written in Darkness,* 147.

182 "At least 25,000 Belgian Jews": Gerald Reitlinger, *The Final Solution: The Attempt to Exterminate the Jews of Europe* (New York: A. S. Barnes, 1961), 494; Paul Johnson, in *A History of the Jews* (New York: Harper and Row, 1987), cites higher figures. "In Belgium, despite local resistance, [the SS] killed 40,000 out of 65,000 Jews and almost wiped out the famous diamond-trading quarter of Antwerp" (502).

183 "A stranger": Geoffrey Hartman, "The Longest Shadow," in *Testimony,* ed. David Rosenberg (New York: Times Books, 1989), 429, 433.

183 "There is nothing explanatory": Quoted in David Lehman, "Deconstructing de Man's Life," in *Newsweek,* February 15, 1988.

183 "Haimish": Leo Rosten, *The Joys of Yiddish* (New York: Pocket Books, 1970), 149.

183 "We were dismayed": Ted Weiss, Letter to David Lehman, October 22, 1988.

183 "Some of his best friends": Quoted in James Atlas, "The Case of Paul de Man," in the *New York Times Magazine,* August 28, 1988.

CHAPTER 8: LIKE UNCLE, LIKE SON

186 "At least for Europeans": John Updike, "Michel Tournier," in the *New Yorker,* July 10, 1989.

186 "The prosopopeia": Paul de Man, "Autobiography as Defacement," in *The Rhetoric of Romanticism,* 77.

187 "Hermes": Ortwin de Graef, "Aspects," in *Responses,* ed. Werner Hamacher et al., 115.

187 "Charming, humorous": Quoted in James Atlas, "The Case of Paul de Man," 37.

188 "Jules and Jim": Telephone interview with Marc de Man, July 26, 1989.

188 "As many as 2 million": Alistair Horne, *To Lose a Battle: France 1940* (Boston: Little, Brown, 1969), 451.

190 "Only on that particular day": Hannah Arendt, "Walter Benjamin: 1892–1940," in Walter Benjamin, *Illuminations,* ed. Hannah Arendt, trans. Harry Zohn (New York: Schocken, 1969), 17–18.

190 "He was very private": Quoted in James Atlas, "The Case of Paul de Man," 69.

191 "My father": Telephone interview with Marc de Man, July 26, 1989.

191 "Come from the left": Letter from Paul de Man to Harry Levin, June 6, 1955, quoted in Paul de Man, *Critical Writings 1953–1978,* lxv.

192 "As many homelands": Peter Dodge, "Introduction" to *A Documentary Study of Hendrik de Man, Socialist Critic of Marxism,* ed. Peter Dodge (Princeton: Princeton University Press, 1979), 5.

193 "The German form": Quoted in Peter Dodge, *Beyond Marxism: The Faith and Works of Hendrik de Man* (The Hague: Martinus Nijhoff, 1966), 211.

193 "I am not a German nationalist": Quoted in E. Ramon Arango, *Leopold III and the Belgian Royal Question,* 111.

194 "One can no longer": Zeev Sternhell, *Neither Right Nor Left: Fascist Ideology in France,* trans. David Maisel (Berkeley and Los Angeles: University of California Press, 1986), 194.

194 "National revival": David Littlejohn, *The Patriotic Traitors,* 150–51.

194 "Peace with Hitler": Peter Dodge, *Beyond Marxism,* 190.

195 "Manifesto": Ibid., 197–98.

196 "Knowingly and maliciously": Ibid., 208–9, 241–43.

196 "Have a government": Zeev Sternhell, *Neither Right Nor Left,* 144.

196 "Henceforth democracy": Peter Dodge, *Beyond Marxism,* 201.

197 "Surrendered to a maternal aunt": Peter Dodge, *Beyond Marxism,* 1.

198 "He knew Camus": Letter from Donald Hall to David Lehman, September 20, 1988.

199 "My father, Hendrik de Man": Paul de Man's letter of January 26, 1955, is quoted in full in *Responses,* ed. Werner Hamacher et al., 475–77.

201 "What, after all": Richard Klein, "The Blindness of Hyperboles, The Ellipses of Insight," in *Diacritics* (Summer 1973): 33–44.

202 "The Ninth Commandment": Shoshana Felman, "Paul de Man's Silence," in *Critical Inquiry* 15, no. 4 (Summer 1989): 720–22.

203 "Why didn't he": Andrzej Warminski, "Terrible Reading (Preceded by Epigraphs)," in *Responses,* ed. Werner Hamacher et al., 388.

203 "Moby Dick": Shoshana Felman, "Paul de Man's Silence," 717–19.

204 "I am not given": Paul de Man, "Foreword," in *Blindness and Insight,* rev. ed., xii.

205 "Movement of effacing": Paul de Man, "Shelley Disfigured," in *Deconstruction and Criticism,* 44.

206 "Gatsby": Barry Gross, "F. Scott Fitzgerald's 'The Great Gatsby' and Oswald Spengler's 'The Decline of the West,' " quoted in A. E. Elmore, *"The Great Gatsby* as Well-Wrought Urn," in *Modern American Fiction: Form and Function,* ed. Thomas Daniel Young (Baton Rouge: Louisiana State University Press, 1989), 87. The article "Germany's New Prophets" by "Henry de Man" is also identified as the work of Hendrik de Man in Peter Dodge, *Beyond Marxism,* 255. The article appears in the *Yale Review* 13, no. 4 (July 1924): 665–83.

CHAPTER 9: A SCANDAL IN ACADAME

210 "Morris Zapp": David Lodge, *Small World,* 43–44, 64.

211 "A preemptive and highly tendentious defense": Jacques Derrida, "Like the Sound of the Sea Deep within a Shell: Paul de Man's War," 597, 634–37.

212 "Camouflage operation": Ibid., 635.

212 "Students need independence": Jon Wiener, "Deconstructing de Man," in the *Nation,* January 9, 1988.

213 "A vast amnesty project": Quoted in David Lehman, "Deconstructing de Man's Life," in *Newsweek,* February 15, 1988.

213 "They cannot bear to consider": Jon Wiener, "Deconstructing de Man," 24.

214 "I am indignant and worried": Jacques Derrida, "Like the Sound of the Sea Deep within a Shell: Paul de Man's War," 647.

214 "Rife with distortions and insinuations": Cynthia Chase, "In Defense of Kristeva" (letter), in the *Nation,* April 9, 1988.

214 "The necessary vigilance": Jacques Derrida, "Like the Sound of the Sea Deep within a Shell: Paul de Man's War," 651.

215 "De Man's article about the Jews": "The [essay] by David Lehman in *Newsweek* . . . is especially disturbing because its layout, which juxtaposes pictures of de Man and Nazi soldiers on the march, bears a remarkable similarity to the original page of *Le Soir* where de Man's essay first appeared." In Tobin Siebers, "Mourning Becomes Paul de Man," in *Responses,* ed. Werner Hamacher et al., 366.

215 "The rhetorician's didactic effectiveness": Jerome Christensen, "From Rhetoric to Corporate Populism: A Romantic Critique of the Academy in an Age of High Gossip," in *Critical Inquiry* 16, no. 2 (Winter 1990): 455.

216 "Reading over his shoulder": Jacques Derrida, "Like the Sound of the Sea Deep within a Shell: Paul de Man's War," 647.

216 "A new moment": J. Hillis Miller, "NB," in the *Times Literary Supplement* (London), June 17–23, 1988.

216 "Wartime journalism": Jacques Derrida, "Like the Sound of the Sea Deep within a Shell: Paul de Man's War," in *Critical Inquiry* 14, no. 3 (Spring 1988): 594.

217 "The tradition of German Culture": Jonathan Culler, in "It's Time to Set the Record Straight about Paul de Man and His Wartime Articles for a Pro-Fascist Newspaper," *Chronicle of Higher Education,* July 13, 1988.

217 "The rocks of their pathologies": Andrzej Warminski, "Terrible Reading (Preceded by 'Epigraphs')," in *Responses,* ed. Werner Hamacher et al., 388–89.

217 "So he was a Nazi": Jeffrey Mehlman, "Perspectives: On De Man and *Le Soir,"* ibid., 331.

217 "Anti-historical": "Yale Scholar's Articles Found in Nazi Paper," the unsigned article in the *New York Times* that broke the de Man story (December 1, 1987), quotes R. W. B. Lewis of Yale University. "It seems to me deconstruction is anti-historical. . . . It encourages skepticism about almost anything in the realm of human experience. That's one of the things I hold against it." It was possible for a reporter to hear, from professors of comparable stature, instant assessments of deconstruction that were far more scathing.

219 "Political activity": Paul de Man, *Allegories of Reading,* 156–57.

219 "The bleakest of crimes": Ibid., 293.

220 "Linguistic functions": Denis Donoghue, "Deconstructing Deconstruction," in the *New York Review of Books,* June 12, 1980.

220 *"True Confessions"*: Alice Yaeger Kaplan, "Paul de Man, *Le Soir,* and the Francophone Collaboration (1940–1942)," in *Responses,* ed. Werner Hamacher et al., 278.

220 "The Nazis received little support": Paul de Man, *Critical Writings, 1953–1978,* 163.

221 "A sociological problem": Ibid., 163.

222 "The deepest Western tradition": Jeffrey Mehlman, "Writing and Deference: The Politics of Literary Adulation," in *Representations* 15 (Summer 1986): 3, 7, 8–9, 12.

222 "Maurice Blanchot in France": Idem, "Perspectives: On De Man and *Le Soir,*" in *Responses,* ed. Werner Hamacher et al., 329. On Blanchot's "forgotten political writings of the 1930's, activist, fascist, a protracted apology for terrorism," see Jeffrey Mehlman, "Deconstruction, Literature, History: The Case of *L'Arrêt de mort,*" in *Proceedings of the Northeastern University Center for Literary Studies* 2 (1984): 33–52.

222 "No dead metaphors": Geoffrey Hartman, "Blindness and Insight," in the *New Republic,* March 7, 1988.

223 "Narrow-mindedness": Idem, *Criticism in the Wilderness,* 297.

223 "What was needed was resistance": Christopher Ricks, "Theory and Teaching," in *Proceedings of the Northeastern University Center for Literary Studies,* 1985, 4.

224 "The Walloons of the 1970's": Jeffrey Mehlman, "Perspectives," 327–28.

225 "Morally suspect": Charles L. Griswold, "Deconstruction, the Nazis, and Paul de Man" (letter), in the *New York Review of Books,* October 12, 1989.

225 "Act of conscience": Geoffrey Hartman, "Blindness and Insight," 26–31.

226 "Anti-Semitic slurs": Richard Klein, "De Man's Resistances: A Contribution to the Future Science of DeManology," in *Responses,* ed. Werner Hamacher et al., 295.

227 "In contact with Jacques Derrida": Jonathan Culler, "Paul de Man's Contribution to Literary Criticism and Theory," in *The Future of Literary Theory,* ed. Ralph Cohen (New York: Routledge, 1989), 269.

227 "The same emotional structures": Alice Yaeger Kaplan, "Paul de Man, *Le Soir,* and the Francophone Collaboration," in *Responses,* ed. Werner Hamacher et al., 278–79.

228 "The Paul de Man of 1940–42": Barbara Johnson, *A World of Difference,* xvi–xvii.

231 "Heidegger's Nazi involvement": Richard Rorty, "Taking Philosophy Seriously," in the *New Republic,* April 11, 1988.

231 "An erratic young man": James Atlas, "The Case of Paul de Man," in the *New York Times Magazine,* August 28, 1988.

231 "There is a Hitler in each of us": Alfred Kazin reports hearing this line while the Second World War was still in progress: "This unpolitical excuse for the Nazis seemed to gratify ex-radicals by confirming their disappointment with human nature. There was a positive acceptance of some 'universal' guilt whose real purpose was to make the Holocaust *ordinary,* even to sweep it

under the rug." In Alfred Kazin, *New York Jew* (New York: Vintage, 1989), 95.

232 *"As If It Were Yesterday": Comme Si C'Etait Hier,* dir. Myriam Abramowicz and Esther Hoffenberg (1980; ninety minutes).

232 "All potentially cowards": Louis Simpson, letter, in the *New York Times Magazine,* September 25, 1988.

232 "All the trivia questions": Walter Kendrick, "Blindness and Hindsight: Dispatches from the de Man Front," in the *Voice Literary Supplement,* October 1988.

232 "Undisguised xenophobia": J. Hillis Miller, "NB," in the *Times Literary Supplement* (London), June 17–23, 1988.

233 "Deconstruction's destined home": Walter Kendrick, "De Man That Got Away: Deconstructors on the Barricades," in the *Voice Literary Supplement,* April 1988.

233 "His chaste academic robes": Idem, "Blindness and Hindsight," in the *Voice Literary Supplement,* October 1988.

234 "There could have been no Holocaust": Barbara Johnson, *A World of Difference,* xv–xvi.

235 "The cautious injunction": Jacques Derrida, "Like the Sound of the Sea Deep within a Shell: Paul de Man's War," 590–91.

235 "The *unpardonable* violence and confusion": Ibid., 621–23.

235 "The right wing revolutions": Ibid., 628.

235 " 'Double-talk' ": Paul de Man, "Dialogue and Dialogism," in *The Resistance to Theory,* 107; cited in Ian Balfour, " 'Difficult Reading': De Man's Itineraries," in *Responses,* ed. Werner Hamacher et al., 7.

236 *"Music at Night":* Stanley Corngold, "On Paul de Man's Collaborationist Writings," ibid., 84.

237 "To accept a context": Jacques Derrida, "Like the Sound of the Sea Deep within a Shell: Paul de Man's War," in *Critical Inquiry* 14, no. 3 (Spring 1988), 624–25.

237 "The neighboring articles": Ibid., 625–56.

238 *"Mein Kampf":* Adolf Hitler, *Mein Kampf,* trans. Ralph Manheim (Boston: Houghton Mifflin, 1971), 56, 119–21.

240 "The situation of the Jews": S. Heidi Krueger, "Opting to Know: On the Wartime Journalism of Paul de Man," in *Responses,* ed. Werner Hamacher et al., 304–6.

240 "American anti-Semitism": Richard Rand, *"Rigor Vitae,"* ibid., 354.

241 "The occupying forces": Christopher Norris, "Paul de Man's Past," in the *London Review of Books,* February 4, 1988.

241 "This collapse of a decrepit world": Hendrik de Man, "Manifeste aux

membres du parti ouvrier belge," trans. Peter Dodge, in *A Documentary Study of Hendrik de Man, Socialist Critic of Marxism,* 326.

241 "Gibberish": A. J. Ayer, "Fateful Swerve" (letter), in the *London Review of Books,* February 18, 1988.

CHAPTER 10: SIGNS OF THE TIMES

249 "The deconstructionist vocabulary": John R. Searle, "The Word Turned Upside Down," in the *New York Review of Books,* October 27, 1983.

249 "Reactions to Derrida's lecture": Patrick Joyce, "Derrida Discusses Political Friendship," in the *Cornell Daily Sun,* October 4, 1988.

250 "The position Heraclitus had abandoned": See Søren Kierkegaard, *Fear and Trembling,* trans. Walter Lowrie (Princeton: Princeton University Press, 1954), 132.

253 "The terms *response* and *responsibility*": Jacques Derrida, "Like the Sound of the Sea Deep within a Shell: Paul de Man's War," 592–94.

253 "The wager will be lost": John Brenkman and Jules David Law, "Resetting the Agenda," in *Critical Inquiry* 15, no. 4 (Summer 1989): 805.

253 "De Man's wartime writings": Jonathan Culler, " 'Paul de Man's War' and the Aesthetic Ideology," ibid., 777.

253 "An official rhetoric": Jacques Derrida, "Like the Sound of the Sea Deep within a Shell: Paul de Man's War," 607. Derrida's emphasis.

254 "The fascist tendencies": Jonathan Culler, " 'Paul de Man's War' and the Aesthetic Ideology," 780.

254 "All texts are undecidable": Jean-Marie Apostolides, "On Paul de Man's War," in *Critical Inquiry* 15, no. 4 (Summer 1989): 766.

254 "The writer who helps fellow writers": Marjorie Perloff, "Response to Jacques Derrida," ibid., 771–75.

255 "This dogmatic assumption": W. Wolfgang Holdheim, "Jacques Derrida's Apologia," ibid., 789, 793, 796.

255 "An offensive argument": Jon Wiener, "The Responsibilities of Friendship: Jacques Derrida on Paul de Man's Collaboration," ibid., 797–98, 801.

255 "A Belgian fascist": John Brenkman and Jules David Law, "Resetting the Agenda," 806–8.

255 "Derrida's 'eloquence' ": Marjorie Perloff, "Response to Jacques Derrida," 767.

255 "In the way of lucid analysis": John Brenkman and Jules David Law, "Resetting the Agenda," 805.

255 "Five propositions": Walter Kendrick, "Blindness and Hindsight: Dispatches from the de Man Front," in the *Voice Literary Supplement,* October 1988.

256 *"Ne pveulent pas lire":* Jacques Derrida, "Biodegradables: Seven Diary Fragments," trans. Peggy Kamuf, in *Critical Inquiry* 15, no. 4 (Summer 1989): 819, 823, 825, 843.

257 " 'Violent journalistic acts' ": Ibid., 817, 823, 832, 839, 841, 843, 845, 850–51, 859, 872.

258 "Traditional philosophical figures and tropes": Richard Rorty, "Is Derrida a Transcendental Philosopher?" in the *Yale Journal of Criticism* 2, no. 2 (Spring 1989): 207.

259 "You little Nazi": Christopher Tilghman, *In a Father's Place* (New York: Farrar, Straus and Giroux, 1990), 163, 177, 189.

260 "The real lives of men and women": J. Hillis Miller, "The Function of Literary Theory at the Present Time," in Ralph Cohen, ed., *The Future of Literary Theory,* 103.

261 "A disappearance of those standards": Joseph Berger, "U. S. Literature: Canon under Siege," in the *New York Times,* January 6, 1988.

262 *"Party line":* Lawrence Lipking, "Competitive Reading," in the *New Republic,* October 2, 1989.

263 "The other way around": Jonathan Culler, *Framing the Sign,* 40.

266 "The many excellent treatises": Henry Fielding, *Tom Jones* 5.1 (New York: Modern Library, 1950), 160–61.

267 "A sign of the times": Jacques Derrida, "Force and Signification," in *Writing and Difference,* 3.

268 "Forces beyond their control": Thomas Carlyle, "Signs of the Times," in *Sartor Resartus and Selected Prose* (New York: Holt, Rinehart and Winston, 1970), 3–29.

SELECTED BIBLIOGRAPHY

Abrams, M. H. *Doing Things With Texts: Essays in Criticism and Critical Theory.* New York: Norton, 1989.

Alter, Robert. *The Pleasures of Reading: Thinking about Literature in an Ideological Age.* New York: Simon and Schuster, 1989.

Arac, Jonathan, Wlad Godzich, and Wallace Martin, eds. *The Yale Critics: Deconstruction in America.* Minneapolis: University of Minnesota Press, 1983.

Arango, E. Ramon. *Leopold III and the Belgian Royal Question.* Baltimore: Johns Hopkins Press, 1961.

Assouline, Pierre. *Gaston Gallimard: A Half-Century of French Publishing.* Trans. Harold J. Salemson. New York: Harcourt Brace Jovanovich, 1988.

Barthes, Roland. *Image, Music, Text.* Trans. Stephen Heath. New York: Hill and Wang, 1977.

Barzun, Jacques. *The Culture We Deserve.* Middletown, Conn.: Wesleyan University Press, 1989.

Benjamin, Walter. *Iluminations.* Ed. Hannah Arendt. Trans. Harry Zohn. New York: Schocken, 1969.

Berman, Art. *From the New Criticism to Deconstruction: The Reception of Structuralism and Post-Structuralism.* Urbana: University of Illinois Press, 1988.

Blackmur, R. P. *Form and Value in Modern Poetry.* Garden City, N.Y.: Doubleday Anchor, 1957.

Bloom, Allan. *The Closing of the American Mind.* New York: Simon and Schuster, 1987.

Bloom, Harold. *The Anxiety of Influence: A Theory of Poetry.* New York: Oxford University Press, 1973.

———. *A Map of Misreading.* New York: Oxford University Press, 1975.

———, Paul de Man, Jacques Derrida, Geoffrey Hartman, and J. Hillis Miller. *Deconstruction and Criticism.* New York: Seabury, 1979. Essays.

Bromwich, David. *A Choice of Inheritance: Self and Community from Edmund Burke to Robert Frost.* Cambridge: Harvard University Press, 1989.

Brooks, Peter, Shoshana Felman, and J. Hillis Miller, eds. *The Lesson of Paul de Man. Yale French Studies* no. 69 (1985).

Cavell, Stanley. *Themes Out of School: Effects and Causes.* Chicago: University of Chicago Press, 1988.

Clifford, James, and George E. Marcus, eds. *Writing Culture: The Poetics and Politics of Ethnography.* Berkeley and Los Angeles: University of California Press, 1986.

Cohen, Ralph, ed. *The Future of Literary Theory.* New York: Routledge, 1989.

Crews, Frederick. *Skeptical Engagements.* New York: Oxford University Press, 1986.

Culler, Jonathan. *Framing the Sign: Criticism and Its Institutions.* Norman, Okla.: University of Oklahoma Press, 1988.

———. *On Deconstruction: Theory and Criticism After Structuralism.* Ithaca: Cornell University Press, 1982.

De Man, Paul. *Allegories of Reading: Figural Language in Rousseau, Nietzsche, Rilke, and Proust.* New Haven: Yale University Press, 1979.

———. *Blindness and Insight: Essays in the Rhetoric of Contemporary Criticism.* Rev. ed. Minneapolis: University of Minnesota Press, 1983.

———. *Critical Writings, 1953–1978.* Ed. Lindsay Waters. Minneapolis: University of Minnesota Press, 1989.

———. *The Resistance to Theory.* Minneapolis: University of Minnesota Press, 1986.

———. *The Rhetoric of Romanticism.* New York: Columbia University Press, 1984.

———. *Wartime Journalism, 1940–1942.* Ed. Werner Hamacher, Neil Hertz, and Tom Keenan. Lincoln: University of Nebraska Press, 1989.

——— et al. *Deconstruction and Criticism.* New York: Seabury, 1979.

Derrida, Jacques. *Dissemination.* Trans. Barbara Johnson. Chicago: University of Chicago Press, 1983.

———. *Mémoires: for Paul de Man.* Rev. ed. Trans. Cecile Lindsay et al. New York: Columbia University Press, 1989.

———. *Of Grammatology.* Trans. Gayatri Chakravorty Spivak. Baltimore: Johns Hopkins University Press, 1976.

———. *Positions.* Trans. Alan Bass. Chicago: University of Chicago Press, 1981.

———. *Speech and Phenomena.* Trans. David B. Allison. Evanston: Northwestern University Press, 1973.

———. *Writing and Difference.* Trans. Alan Bass. Chicago: University of Chicago Press, 1978.

——— et al. *Deconstruction and Criticism.* New York: Seabury, 1979.

Dodge, Peter. *Beyond Marxism: The Faith and Works of Hendrik de Man.* The Hague: Martinus Nijhoff, 1966.

——, ed. *A Documentary Study of Hendrik de Man, Socialist Critic of Marxism.* Princeton: Princeton University Press, 1979.

Donoghue, Denis. *Ferocious Alphabets.* New York: Columbia University Press, 1984.

Eagleton, Terry. *Literary Theory: An Introduction.* Minneapolis: University of Minnesota Press, 1983.

Eaves, Morris, and Michael Fischer. *Romanticism and Contemporary Criticism.* Ithaca: Cornell University Press, 1986.

Ellis, John M. *Against Deconstruction.* Princeton: Princeton University Press, 1989.

Farias, Victor. *Heidegger and Nazism.* Ed. Joseph Margolis and Tom Rockmore. Trans. Paul Burrell and Gabriel R. Ricci. Philadelphia: Temple University Press, 1989.

Felperin, Howard. *Beyond Deconstruction: The Uses and Abuses of Literary Theory.* Oxford: Clarendon Press, 1985.

Ferry, Luc, and Alain Renaut. *Heidegger and Modernity.* Trans. Franklin Philip. Chicago: University of Chicago Press, 1990.

Gass, William. *Habitations of the Word.* New York: Simon and Schuster, 1985.

Geertz, Clifford. *The Interpretation of Cultures.* New York: Basic Books, 1973.

——. *Works and Lives: The Anthropologist as Author.* Stanford: Stanford University Press, 1988.

Gordon, Bertram M. *Collaborationism in France during the Second World War.* Ithaca: Cornell University Press, 1980.

Graff, Gerald. *Professing Literature: An Institutional History.* Chicago: University of Chicago Press, 1987.

Hamacher, Werner, Neil Hertz, and Thomas Keenan, eds. *Responses: On Paul de Man's Wartime Journalism.* Lincoln: University of Nebraska Press, 1989.

Harari, Josué V., ed. *Textual Strategies: Perspectives in Post-Structuralist Criticism.* Ithaca: Cornell University Press, 1979. Includes pertinent essays by Jacques Derrida, Paul de Man, Michel Foucault, Edward Said, et al.

Hartman, Geoffrey. *Criticism in the Wilderness: The Study of Literature Today.* New Haven: Yale University Press, 1980.

——. *The Fate of Reading.* Chicago: University of Chicago Press, 1975.

——. *Saving the Text: Literature, Derrida, Philosophy.* Baltimore: Johns Hopkins University Press, 1981.

—— et al. *Deconstruction and Criticism.* New York: Seabury, 1979.

Hoffmann, Stanley. *Decline or Renewal? France Since the 1930s.* New York: Viking, 1974.

Hollander, John. *Melodious Guile: Fictive Pattern in Poetic Language.* New Haven: Yale University Press, 1988.

Horne, Alistair. *To Lose a Battle: France 1940.* Boston: Little, Brown, 1969.

Huizinga, James H. *Mr. Europe: A Political Biography of Paul Henri Spaak.* New York: Frederick A. Praeger, 1961.

Jarrell, Randall. *Poetry and the Age.* New York: Vintage, 1955.

Johnson, Barbara. *A World of Difference.* Baltimore: Johns Hopkins University Press, 1989.

Kermode, Frank. *The Art of Telling: Essays on Fiction.* Cambridge: Harvard University Press, 1983.

Kimball, Roger. *Tenured Radicals: How Politics Has Corrupted Our Higher Education.* New York: Harper and Row, 1990.

Lentricchia, Frank. *After the New Criticism.* Chicago: University of Chicago Press, 1980.

————, and Thomas McLaughlin, eds. *Critical Terms for Literary Study.* Chicago: University of Chicago Press, 1990.

Lincoln, Bruce. *Discourse and the Construction of Society: Comparative Studies of Myth, Ritual, and Classification.* New York: Oxford University Press, 1989.

Littlejohn, David. *The Patriotic Traitors: A History of Collaboration in German-Occupied Europe, 1940–1945.* London: Heinemann, 1972.

Lodge, David. *Small World.* New York: Macmillan, 1985.

Marrus, Michael R. *The Holocaust in History.* Hanover, N.H.: University Press of New England, 1987.

Mayer, Arno J. *Why Did the Heavens Not Darken?: The "Final Solution" in History.* New York: Pantheon, 1990.

Miller, J. Hillis. *The Linguistic Moment: From Wordsworth to Stevens.* Princeton: Princeton University Press, 1985.

————. *The Ethics of Reading: Kant, de Man, Eliot, Trollope, James, and Benjamin.* New York: Columbia University Press, 1986.

———— et al. *Deconstruction and Criticism.* New York: Seabury, 1979.

Mitchell, W.J.T., ed. *Against Theory: Literary Studies and the New Pragmatism.* Chicago: University of Chicago Press, 1985.

————, ed. *On Narrative.* Chicago: University of Chicago Press, 1980.

Moore, Stephen D. *Literary Criticism and the Gospels: The Theoretical Challenge.* New Haven: Yale University Press, 1989.

Norris, Christopher. *Derrida.* Cambridge: Harvard University Press, 1987.

————. *Paul de Man: Deconstruction and the Critique of Aesthetic Ideology.* New York: Routledge, 1988.

Ohmann, Richard. *English in America: A Radical View of the Profession.* New York: Oxford University Press, 1976.

Orwell, George. *1984.* New York: Signet, 1961.

————. *The War Commentaries.* Ed. W. J. West. New York: Schocken, 1989.

Paxton, Robert O. *Vichy France: Old Guard and New Order, 1940–1944.* New York: Alfred A. Knopf, 1972.

Poirier, Richard. *The Renewal of Literature: Emersonian Reflections.* New York: Random House, 1987.

Posner, Richard A. *Law and Literature: A Misunderstood Relation.* Cambridge: Harvard University Press, 1988.

Said, Edward. *The World, the Text, and the Critic.* Cambridge: Harvard University Press, 1983.

Salusinszky, Imre. *Criticism in Society.* New York: Methuen. 1987. Interviews with Jacques Derrida, Harold Bloom, Geoffrey Hartman, J. Hillis Miller, Barbara Johnson, et al.

Scholes, Robert. *Protocols of Reading.* New Haven: Yale University Press, 1989.

————. *Structuralism in Literature: An Introduction.* New Haven: Yale University Press, 1974.

Shirer, William L. *The Collapse of the Third Republic: An Inquiry into the Fall of France in 1940.* New York: Simon and Schuster, 1969.

Siebers, Tobin. *The Ethics of Criticism.* Ithaca: Cornell University Press, 1988.

Smith, Barbara Herrnstein. *Contingencies of Value: Alternative Perspectives for Critical Theory.* Cambridge: Harvard University Press, 1988.

Smith, Page. *Killing the Spirit: Higher Education in America.* New York: Viking, 1990.

Somerhausen, Anne. *Written in Darkness: A Belgian Woman's Record of the Occupation, 1940–1945.* New York: Knopf, 1946.

Steiner, George. *Real Presences.* Chicago: University of Chicago Press, 1989.

Sternhell, Zeev. *Neither Right nor Left: Fascist Ideology in France.* Trans. David Maisel. Berkeley and Los Angeles: University of California Press, 1986.

Todorov, Tzvetan. *Literature and Its Theorists: A Personal View of Twentieth-Century Criticism.* Trans. Catherine Porter. Ithaca: Cornell University Press, 1987.

Trilling, Lionel. *Beyond Culture.* New York: Harcourt Brace Jovanovich, 1979.

————. *Sincerity and Authenticity.* Cambridge: Harvard University Press, 1973.

Waters, Lindsay, and Wlad Godzich, eds. *Reading de Man Reading.* Minneapolis: University of Minnesota Press, 1989.

Wellek, Rene. *A History of Modern Criticism, 1750–1950* vol. 6. New Haven: Yale University Press, 1986.

I N D E X

INDEX